Always at War

This book studies strategic narratives from the perspective of ordinary citizens. It examines the stories told by a broad cross section of British society about their country's past, present, and future role in war, using in-depth interviews with 67 diverse citizens. The open-ended and inductive approach brings to the fore the voices of ordinary people in ways typically absent in existing public opinion research. In this respect, it models a bottom-up, narrative methodological approach applicable to a range of countries and foreign policy issues.

Compelling narratives are considered integral to successful foreign policy, military strategy, and international relations. Often narrative is conceived so broadly it represents all discourse, making it hard to identify. Thomas Colley separates narrative from other modes of discourse and examines the way individual events combine to create overall patterns. Research on 'strategic narratives' has focused overwhelmingly on states, while citizens' narratives are rarely examined. The formation of strategic narratives is informed by the stories governments *think* their people tell, rather than those they *actually* tell.

One unexpected finding was that rather than perceiving distinct periods between war and peace, British citizens see their country as so frequently involved in conflict that they consider it to be continuously at war. At present, public opinion appears to be a stronger constraint on Western defence policy than ever. *Always at War* complements a small but significant body of quantitative research into British attitudes to war and presents an alternative case in a field dominated by US public opinion research.

Thomas Colley is a Senior Lecturer in Defense and International Affairs at Royal Military Academy, Sandhurst, and a Visiting Research Fellow in War Studies at King's College London.

Always at War

BRITISH PUBLIC NARRATIVES OF WAR

Thomas Colley

UNIVERSITY OF MICHIGAN PRESS

ANN ARBOR

First paperback edition 2021
Copyright © 2019 by Thomas Colley
All rights reserved

For questions or permissions, please contact um.press.perms@umich.edu

Published in the United States of America by the
University of Michigan Press
Manufactured in the United States of America
Printed on acid-free paper
First published in paperback July 2021

A CIP catalog record for this book is available from the British Library.

Library of Congress Cataloging-in-Publication Data

Names: Colley, Thomas, 1983– author.
Title: Always at war : British public narratives of war / Thomas Colley.
Description: Ann Arbor : University of Michigan Press, 2019. | Includes bibliographical
  references and index.
Identifiers: LCCN 2019005772| ISBN 9780472131440 (hardcover : alk. paper) |
  ISBN 9780472125722 (ebook)
Subjects: LCSH: War and society—Great Britain. | Great Britain—Military policy—
  Public opinion. | War—Public opinion. | Narrative inquiry (Research method)
Classification: LCC HM554 .C638   2019 | DDC 303.6/6—dc23
LC record available at https://lccn.loc.gov/2019005772

ISBN 978-0-472-03869-5 (pbk.)

Cover credit: Richard Budd Design

Contents

Digital materials related to this title can be found on the Fulcrum platform via the following citable URL: https://doi.org/10.3998/mpub.10168682

Preface

Sometimes in life one is struck by the realisation that one's assumptions about the way others think are wrong. I finished high school a few months after 9/11. Like so many others, I remember exactly what I was doing at the time. My adult life as a British citizen was shaped by this tumultuous event. In both the media and academia, 9/11 is routinely portrayed as a day the world changed, where the post-Cold War period ended and the War on Terror began. Not just for American citizens, but across the world, it was an event so horrific as to be unforgettable. Or so I thought. Listening to the stories of everyday people that inspired this book, I began to realise that even knowledgeable, politically engaged British people had begun to forget 9/11, or at least that war in Afghanistan started because of it. People explained to me that they could remember that the First World War began after Franz Ferdinand was shot, that World War Two began when Germany invaded Poland, that the Falklands War began when Argentina invaded the Falkland Islands, and that the Gulf War began when Iraq invaded Kuwait. Yet puzzlingly they could not remember why Afghanistan began, despite it being preceded by one of the most unforgettable events in human history. My assumptions—and those of many policymakers and scholars—appeared to be wrong. People do not always narrate the stories you think they do.

The sense that the way people understand the world might not be the same as the way political elites think they do motivated me to research how ordinary citizens understand war by analysing the stories they tell about it. The result is a groundbreaking, bottom-up investigation of a topic usually studied from the perspectives of presidents, prime ministers, and policymakers. The book presents a radically different viewpoint, based on the frames of reference everyday people use to interpret war rather than those policymakers assume that they use.

The focus is not just on what people say but specifically the stories they narrate. This reflects a desire to provide clarity on the concept of narrative, which now appears so ubiquitous that it has come to mean almost anything anyone says or thinks. It seems to be widely taken for granted that 'strategic narratives' can be so powerful that simply structuring a series of words in the form of a story can achieve anything from guaranteeing business success to persuading people to blow themselves up. And yet there is relatively little clarity on what a narrative is and isn't. Even when people define it clearly, few appear to separate narrative from other ways of communicating when they study it.

The theoretical focus on narrative and the empirical focus on how British citizens understand war give the book relevance to different audiences in different ways. Primarily an academic text, its attempt to clear up theoretical uncertainty about what narratives are and how they persuade will be of interest to researchers engaging with strategic narratives and narrative theory in a range of fields. Its ground-up, inductive methodology is applicable to those investigating social issues from the perspective of ordinary citizens, whatever their specialism. The introduction and chapter 1 will be of particular interest to these readers. The primary topic, however, concerns war, brought to life through the stories of everyday British people. After the introduction, those more interested in this may wish to skim chapter 1 and move forward from chapter 2. These stories have rarely been told and will potentially be of interest to scholars in politics and international relations, military historians, sociologists, foreign policy practitioners, and public opinion researchers. International relations researchers may be particularly interested in the focus on how national identity and ontological security are constructed from the ground up, through the stories individuals narrate about the nation and war.

It is a difficult time to be writing about British politics given the rapidly evolving situation following the 'Brexit' vote to leave the European Union. It is striking how similar the stories we tell today are compared to the past, particularly when it comes to Britain and war, given its military's almost constant engagement for more than three centuries. Still, I hope readers will forgive any moments when the book appears to be held hostage to ongoing events.

Acknowledgments

I am indebted to a number of individuals without whom this book would not have been completed. First, my sincerest thanks must go to Elizabeth Demers, Danielle Coty, and Kevin Rennells at the University of Michigan Press, for their vision and patient guidance throughout the production process. I must also thank Sir Evelyn De Rothschild and the War Studies Department at King's College London for the opportunity to bring the book to fruition. My heartfelt thanks go to Peter Busch in particular. Peter has provided wisdom, frequent reassurance, and a sense of humour that has been invaluable from the outset. My thanks also go to Neville Bolt, Ben O'Loughlin, and Nicholas O'Shaughnessy, who have provided intellectual inspiration and encouragement. Thanks also go to my colleagues and friends Claire Yorke, Joana Cook, Maryyum Mehmood, Nikolai Gourof, David Betz, John Stone, Alister Miskimmon, Nicholas Michelsen, Mark Workman, Simon Bushell, and others who provided moral support, encouragement, and friendship. Working alongside such exceptional people has been a privilege.

I also extend my thanks to the study's participants, and to Sue, Les, Rose, Wayne, and Anthony, among others, for helping to find such a diverse array of participants. Emily Heavey provided indispensable theoretical guidance at a key time. Thanks also to Nicholas Reed for his last-minute advice and friendship throughout the project. There are many others not mentioned here, and to those I also offer my sincerest gratitude. So many have endured my long rambles about the book with forbearance and good humour.

Aspects of the book have previously been published elsewhere. Elements of chapters 4 and 5 can be found in "Britain's Public War Stories: Punching Above

Its Weight or Vanishing Force?" *Defence Strategic Communications*, vol. 2, 2017, pp. 162–90. I would like to thank NATO Strategic Communications, Riga, Latvia, for permission to reproduce this material. Much of chapter 6 can be found in "Is Britain a Force for Good? Investigating British Citizens' Narrative Understanding of War," *Defence Studies* 17, no. 1 (2017): 1–22. I would like to thank Taylor and Francis Ltd. for permission to reprint these elements.

The addition of my children Grace and Dominic to the editorial team provided some initial challenges but also boundless inspiration, along with an invaluable sense of perspective. Thanks must go to reviewers who suffered a notable decline in the quality of my writing as sleep deprivation kicked in during the early months. I will always be grateful to the wholehearted support of Dr. Michielon and Dr. Rowlinson, whose surgical precision kept everything together as the project progressed.

My family have provided more support than they realise. Their quiet faith in me has been comforting at key moments, and their support with Grace and Dominic was essential in keeping the project on track.

Most of all, my unending gratitude goes to my wife, Alice, who has shown immense patience not just with late nights but also in suffering endless monologues about the minutiae of narrative theory. She is, I suspect, far more knowledgeable about the topic than she would ever have wanted to be, and is also my inspiration on every level. The book is dedicated to her.

Introduction

BRIAN (65+, DORSET): In the old days, we were dealing with countries. We don't seem to be doing that now. We're dealing with an idea. That's actually quite difficult.

RESEARCHER: Why do you think that's quite difficult?

BRIAN: Why is it difficult? Oh because countering an idea is always difficult. You can only actually do it with another idea. You can't do it with a rifle. A rifle never changed anybody's ideas about anything.

The power of ideas is nothing new. Ideas have always been powerful in motivating wars and those who fight them. Today however it is recognised across multiple fields that it is not just ideas that matter; they must be presented in a certain way. Be it soldiers, politicians, business people, or charities, it is increasingly taken for granted that clever arguments are not enough to achieve one's objectives; what is needed is a compelling *narrative*, a story. Get the story straight, ideally act in accordance with it, and in theory one may be in a stronger position to counter terrorist propaganda, sustain alliances, defeat insurgencies, and win wars. Such thinking reflects a broader trend across multiple fields in which narrative is seen increasingly as a communication panacea of 'startling power'.[1] Meanwhile, *strategic narratives*—narratives deliberately designed to achieve political objectives—have been heralded as the key to 'soft' power in the twenty-first century, and even the 'foundation of all strategy'.[2] 'Whose story wins' is thought by some to be as important as 'whose army wins'.[3]

Narratives are not just considered vital to winning wars; governments increasingly consider them integral to persuading domestic populations to support them. The power of narrative to persuade is based on the assumption that stories are the most natural form of communication and the main way humans understand the world.[4] Logically therefore, the key to using narratives to persuade is to design them strategically so that they 'resonate' with the narratives people already use to understand the world.[5]

For example, a common way governments across the world try and use narrative to obtain public support for war is to compare the current conflict situation to the run-up to the Second World War. So the story goes, Hitler was the epitome of evil, and the allies had numerous chances to stop him before he got too strong. Instead, they appeased him repeatedly, most notably through the Munich Agreement in 1938, which merely encouraged him to continue his conquests. The supposedly universal lesson offered by this 'Munich' analogy is that, like playground bullies, dictators should never be appeased. In invoking it time and time again, political leaders assume that citizens would narrate the current conflict as a story in which 'there is a dictator who has been in power that threatens us or others, so we must act now because if we don't, this evil will spread in the future'.[6] Comparison with the demonic figure of Hitler is designed to invoke fear and instil support for urgent action by the self-sacrificing hero, typically the West.

The question is, is it this simple to create public support for war? Do citizens understand wars in this way? Are their stories about wars so uniform? Do they repeat the official narratives governments use, or do they tell entirely different stories about contemporary conflicts, with different plots, characters, and endings? The answer is, we don't know. We don't know because despite a fast-growing body of research in foreign policy and International Relations (IR) on how states should use narratives strategically, few studies examine the narratives told by ordinary citizens. As Miskimmon et al. observe, 'nobody analyses the narratives through which audiences interpret international affairs. It is the elephant in the room of international political communication'.[7] It is an elephant this book seeks to address.

When public understandings of international affairs *have* been examined, research has been overwhelmingly quantitative, focusing on aggregating what people think rather than studying in depth the stories they tell. On war for example, researchers have correlated state strategic narratives with public opinion polls and used this to suggest why some attempts to maintain public support are more successful than others.[8] However, such approaches say far less about how people understand a given conflict, where it fits in their plot of their nation's history, how they relate present conflicts to the past and future, or how they construct their national identities. States and nonstate actors are therefore constructing strategic narratives based only on the stories they *think* citizens tell, rather than those they *actually* tell.

As well as a failure to examine the stories ordinary citizens tell, a further factor has limited existing understandings of the significance of narratives in international politics: it is often unclear how narrative researchers and strategic communication practitioners separate what is narrative from what is not. Much ink has been spilled on why narratives are so special, and yet when it comes to analysing language itself, authors often conflate narrative with argument, explanation, or discourse more generally. This matters because the assumption that narratives are uniquely persuasive rests on there being something about them that is identifiably different. While it is always difficult to differentiate modes of communication in everyday speech, failing to differentiate narratives undermines claims that they are particularly persuasive.

I advocate an alternative approach. Narratives are interpretations. If one is genuinely interested in how narratives might be used to persuade citizens to support or oppose political causes, it is insufficient to know *what people think* or *what they say*; one should ask *how they narrate*. This book does this, adopting an interpretive, qualitative approach, designed to provide a fresh and more nuanced perspective than most quantitative studies tend to provide. Moreover, it offers a narrative-specific methodology, so that whatever a researcher or practitioner's topic of study, it is clear what is narrative and what is not. I argue that the key feature that differentiates narrative from other modes of discourse is *plot: a temporally, spatially and causally connected sequence of events*. Plot comprises not just the process of selecting events in a story; it also includes the overall pattern these events create, such as progress, decline, or continuity. This study examines narratives at both of these levels, from the most general patterns of history (genre) to the minutiae of how narrators include and exclude specific events to try and make their stories more persuasive (emplotment).

This novel framework provides a deep and broad analysis applicable to a vast range of cases where analysts are looking to understand not just what people think but how they narrate certain issues, from counterinsurgency to climate change, from terrorism to the rise of Donald Trump. For if researchers or communication professionals are genuinely interested in narrative as a specific form of communication, rather than simply coordinating messaging in any format, then understanding the stories told by target audiences is crucial, whatever the issue.

The case in question is Britain and the way its citizens interpret war. The study of British public interpretations of war is especially timely, because the country is currently experiencing the effects of a number of international political trends. First, Western defence policy appears to be increasingly constrained by public opinion.[9] In Britain this is reflected in the emerging norm where leaders seek parliamentary consent before taking military action—which the executive is not required to do.[10] This makes understanding how target audiences in military interventionist states interpret war especially pressing.

Second, the efficacy of military intervention in achieving foreign policy objectives is arguably more uncertain than ever in the wake of conflicts such as Afghanistan, Iraq, Libya, and Syria. This is particularly challenging for military interventionist states like Britain, which, according to Anthony Forster, is so frequently at war that it has only seen one year since 1660 without a military casualty (1968).[11] It is even more challenging since military strength and competence is long-recognised as playing a significant role in the construction of British national identity.[12] Some historians suggest that whatever unity exists between the nations that comprise the United Kingdom, it was forged through fighting off external military threats.[13] That sense of identity is significantly undermined if its wars fail to achieve their objectives or cause more harm than good to those for whom Britain fights.

The unity of the United Kingdom is also increasingly under threat, with the Brexit vote in June 2016 and continued calls for Scottish independence highlighting how differently British citizens remember the country's past, perceive its identity in the present, and express hopes for the future. This raises the issue of what story the British government should narrate about its national identity and the role of its military in the future. This is a challenge for all states looking to project themselves onto the international stage and maintain a sense of stability for their citizens, but it is especially acute for Britain at present. Again, this makes the study of the stories British citizens tell about these issues particularly important.

Although there exists a growing body of quantitative research seeking to aggregate British public attitudes to wars, the narratives citizens use to explain their country's role in conflict remain largely unexplored.[14] It is unclear how much variety there is in the stories the British public tell about wars, or which historical events are most crucial to them. Interested observers might be able to guess at some of the key characters in people's stories, but it is harder to tell why others are forgotten. The plot of people's war stories is unclear, as is where they begin and how they think they will end.[15] International Relations (IR) scholars have shown how states construct their identities by creating singular 'national biographies' to maintain a coherent sense of self or 'ontological security' over time.[16] Such approaches have tended to try and identify a single national story or strategic culture rather than explore how these are understood through the narratives of ordinary citizens.[17]

In addressing this void, this book's ground-up, qualitative investigation represents a timely and original examination of a crucial case in contemporary foreign policy and international relations. It advances the existing literature on strategic narratives by examining the contestation and variation in how these are understood from the perspective of individual citizens. It advances research into ontological security in IR by adopting an 'everyday' or 'vernacular' approach to how individual narratives bring a nation into being as a collective.[18]

First, it asks how similarly individual citizens narrate stories of Britain's role in war. It then examines what these stories reveal about how citizens construct Britain's identity and how they evaluate its role as an international military actor. Finally, it considers how citizens selectively emplot their memories of British military history to try and make these identity claims more convincing. It departs from the assumption that narratives are a means through which people construct their identities but their stories are never wholly individual. Instead they are drawn from a limited range of narratives circulating in public discourse.[19] The stories studied derive from semistructured interviews with a highly diverse range of British citizens. These stories are examined in minute detail to see how their narrators try and make their interpretations more convincing. In this way the book brings to the fore the voices of ordinary people in ways typically absent in aggregate research into attitudes to war. This is directly relevant to academics, strategic communication practitioners, policymakers, journalists, and anyone interested in how publics interpret the information they encounter in everyday political life.

Defining Narrative

Since I suggest that researchers and practitioners in foreign policy and IR could distinguish more clearly between what is narrative and what is not, a clear definition of the concept is vital.[20] This is difficult since disagreement on what constitutes narrative persists across the social and human sciences. Many studies define it extremely broadly, or alternatively, avoid defining it at all. The variety of metaphors for narrative across political discourse is vast, including 'explanation', 'argument', 'description', 'discourse', 'frame', 'framework', 'belief', 'vision', 'value', 'perspective', 'logic', 'truth', 'life', or even simply 'content'.[21] In political communication, the idea of 'controlling the narrative' reduces it to a product of 'spin', a metaphor for 'message' or even 'news cycle'. As Riessman laments:

> In contemporary usage, narrative has come to mean anything beyond a few bullet points; when someone speaks or writes more than a few lines, the outcome is now called narrative by news anchors and even some narrative researchers. Reduced to little more than a metaphor, everyone has a 'story'.[22]

These vague conceptualisations detach the concept of narrative from the assumption on which its use is based: that there is something special about it that makes it particularly persuasive. When narrative is defined so broadly, this uniqueness is lost. Claims that we are in a new 'narrative age'[23] have limited meaning if all texts are considered narrative.

How far narrative differs from story is similarly contentious. Some argue that story is a subordinate feature of narrative;[24] others claim the opposite.[25] Some see story as a mental representation of events, but narrative as their material representation.[26] Strategic communication theorists often use scale to differentiate between the two, conceptualising narrative as a system of individual stories told and retold over time.[27]

This book deliberately conflates story and narrative.[28] It does so because as a type of text, they contain the same fundamental features. Most crucially, these features distinguish narrative text from argument or explanation. Here, narrative text consists of *a temporally, spatially, and causally connected sequence of events, selected and evaluated as meaningful for a particular audience.*[29] It is a socially constructed unit of discourse often identified as having (though not always possessing) a beginning, middle, and end, involving actors, settings, and plot.[30] Conventionally, a narrative might consist of a past that leads to a present that puts in place a possible future.[31] This often revolves around the resolution of conflict, starting with an initial situation, a disruption to this situation that creates drama, and a resolution that restores order.[32]

Narratives may not always contain all these elements. There are 'habitual' narratives, which lack dramatic sequences of events but instead describe how things typically occur over time.[33] There are hypothetical narratives, suggesting possible future outcomes depending on what policy is pursued.[34] Pragmatically, though, the more of the above elements are present, the more 'story-like' a unit of discourse will appear, and the more 'narrativity' it can be said to possess.[35]

Strategic narratives are differentiated by being deliberately designed by political actors to persuade. They are therefore defined here as *selective interpretations of the past, present, and future designed to achieve political objectives through persuasion.*[36] The formula for persuasion varies in the foreign policy literature. Freedman notes that a strategic narrative should appeal to emotion as well as reason; that it could employ dubious metaphors and historical analogies but must partly be grounded in truth lest it be discredited.[37] Casebeer, Russell, and Simpson employ the Aristotelian rhetorical proofs of *logos, pathos,* and *ethos,* arguing that an effective strategic narrative should have rational appeal (*logos*), emotional resonance (*pathos*), and be morally credible (*ethos*) in terms of its content and narrator.[38] Ringsmose and Børgesen suggest that strategic narratives for military interventions require four key elements: clarity of purpose; the prospect of success; consistent communication; and the absence of competing counternarratives.[39]

These theories of narrative persuasion are perfectly reasonable. However, none of these elements is specific to narrative. They apply equally to framing, explanation, or argumentation. After all, any argument will be more persuasive if it is communicated clearly, consistently, and doesn't face strong counterarguments. It will also be more persuasive if it combines rational, emotional, and moral appeal. These features are likely to make any discourse more persuasive; they are not unique to narrative. These theories are therefore of limited use in explaining why narratives might be uniquely persuasive.

Methodologically, researchers often start by claiming the unique persuasiveness of stories but then do not appear to separate them from other forms of discourse during empirical analysis. For example, De Graaf et al. explicitly claim that strategic narratives are 'storylines' that are distinctly different from arguments or frames.[40] But later they describe their concluding narrative typology as a collection of 'argument types'.[41] Others conflate narrative with discourse in the Foucauldian sense—a 'common language' that 'governs public discussion and debate'.[42] Thomas Cawkwell, in his recent study of British strategic communication in Afghanistan, describes narrative as 'the sum total of statements, justifications and rationales uttered by British officials over time.[43] From this perspective, narratives are 'everything politicians say' rather than specifically the stories they tell.

Arguably these contributions obscure any persuasive advantages narratives might have since they consider almost all discourse types examples of 'narration'. This creates an unusual situation in which narratives are assumed to possess an unparalleled capacity to influence human cognition and behaviour, yet the mechanisms through which they do so remain vague. As Jacobs summarises, 'the narrative turn continues to win over social scientists . . . [but] what is sorely missing is methodological refinement: that is, the attempt to delineate specific narrative processes'.[44]

I do not argue that narratives are uniquely persuasive compared to other modes of strategic discourse. They may prove to be, but this has more often been theoretically assumed than empirically demonstrated.[45] To understand better how persuasive strategic narratives actually are, research should ideally examine specific elements that differentiate them from other modes of discourse. It is necessary to separate what is a story from what is not.

Differentiating Narrative

Differentiating narrative text from other forms of communication is not straightforward, however. In reality, the lines between different modes of discourse are blurry. Narratives are often incomplete or interspersed with description or argumentation.[46] Indeed narratives can be used to make arguments, at least indirectly. As Deborah Stone notes, policymakers use stories about political problems to attribute 'cause, blame and responsibility' to others to promote their preferred policies to address the harm.[47] The very idea of strategic narrative is based on the notion that stories can be used to support a claim about what a political actor should do—be it to make America great again, break free from European rule, or create a purer society under Sharia law.

I argue that plot—the *temporally, spatially, and causally connected sequence of events*—is what differentiates narratives from other modes of discourse. Plot formation or 'emplotment' involves selecting, linking, and ordering events to create an overarching framework of meaning.[48] Selectivity is fundamental to the process, for every narrative involves the inclusion of certain episodes and the exclusion of others.[49] Plot can make apparently unconnected events seem whole, creating a unified story around an overall message, moral, or endpoint. This coherence is thought to be a key aspect of what makes narrative persuasive, regardless of how partially it represents the historical record.[50] Moreover, a story typically obscures the reasons why some events are included and others are not, potentially even from the narrator themselves. This makes narratives less likely to be challenged and harder to refute.[51]

Temporal sequencing of events is often considered the most significant aspect of plot formation, but sequencing can be spatial too.[52] For example, a story about Britain's transition from a small island nation to a global empire and back again concerns spatial change over time. Nevertheless, movement through time is commonly thought to be what most distinguishes narrative from other modes of communication. This recounting of events over time differentiates narrative from argumentation, which instead makes rational appeals to general principles about how the world is, what someone should do and why.[53]

Confusion comes because statements can allude to narratives without them being articulated. Take the statement that 'Britain should intervene in Afghanistan'. According to Jones et al., for example, all that is needed for a unit of discourse to be considered a 'policy narrative' is a named character and a policy action.[54] By this logic, 'Britain should intervene in Afghanistan' is a narrative, since it contains a character and an action. It also has a setting—another aspect of narrative—since every foreign policy action does, be it the country in question or the 'international stage'. Yet to call such a basic statement a narrative rather than an argument makes it difficult to see any way the two might be differentiated. Even if Britain's original justification for the intervention is added—to prevent Afghanistan being a base for terrorists[55]—it still appears to be argument rather than narrative. The most obvious reason is that it has no plot. However, one could infer that there is an implied plot behind the statement, a sequence of events in which Afghanistan was not a base for terrorists, has become one, and therefore Britain should act to eliminate this threat in the future. It might therefore seem reasonable to describe the statement as a narrative, despite the ambiguity this might cause.

Such thinking holds two negative consequences for strategic narrative advocates. First, since most policy statements reference what has happened in the past (often the failures of the opposition) and what will happen in the future if a given policy is followed, then it can be claimed that all political discourse is narrative in nature.[56] From this position, though, it is difficult to accept the claim that it is the unique aspects of storytelling that makes such discourse more compelling. Political discourse cannot all be uniquely persuasive.

Second, identifying narratives based on allusion rather than a concrete story risks neglect of the variety of interpretations of a given series of events. The statement 'America should use military force against North Korea' is not supported by one narrative that is universally known; multiple narratives could be used to support or oppose such a response. These interpretations risk being lost in approaches that assume that a certain phrase has a specific story behind it without investigating this further.

The vague, all-encompassing use of narratives, along with the tendency to underestimate the variety with which they are interpreted, has led some to question their utility. As Freedman theorises, narratives

> are not precise strategic instruments because they can convey a range of mes-
> sages, not all of which may be understood, and narrative devices such as meta-
> phors and irony can cause confusion. The meaning of stories can be ambiguous
> and some interpretations may undercut the storyteller. Audiences may focus on
> minor features or impose their own experience on the narrative.[57]

If this is true, then the utility of narratives hinges on an as yet unexplored question: *how similarly* do individuals interpret narratives? If the meanings of stories are ambiguous, how many interpretations are there? Narratives should not be dismissed without first investigating the extent of these variations. The stories citizens use to understand their nations' identities and roles in the world set the discursive boundaries of what policymakers can credibly say and do to legitimise their foreign policies and delegitimise those of their opponents.[58] Examining the stories individual citizens tell about Britain and war provides an in-depth perspective on these constraints.

Why British Public Interpretations of War?

The methods advocated in this book are applicable to a range of countries and contexts where researchers seek to study from the ground up the stories individual citizens tell about political issues. Here the value of this approach is demonstrated through examining how British citizens interpret war.[59] The book aims to provide a more nuanced perspective to complement a small but significant body of quantitative research into British attitudes to war, as well as present an alternative case in a field still dominated by US public opinion research.

Aggregate research into British attitudes to war has so far generated contradictory and sometimes inconclusive data regarding public views of military interventions. There appears to be little consensus about defence policy attitudes beyond a 'broad and rather generic attachment to maintaining the UK's historical Great Power status'.[60] Findings frequently contradict each other on how best to categorise British citizens. For example, Mludzinski asserts that they are more isolationist than internationalist.[61] Writing in the same year, Rogers and Eyal claim the opposite. They maintain that, notwithstanding a brief period of domestic retrenchment, the British public are 'instinctively internationalist'.[62] Davies and Johns claim an almost equal split between the two.[63] Authors have also found that compared to American citizens, the British people are 'both more pacifist and more interventionist'.[64] Indeed reflecting the uncertainty over aggregate British attitudes to war, they conclude that 'the average British citizen is neither stubbornly isolationist nor keenly interventionist, neither hawk nor dove'.[65] Most tellingly, they express uncertainty as to whether British attitudes are 'confused' or 'heavily contextual'.[66]

Being confused or having a view that changes according to context imply very different things about someone's understanding of war. The former implies incoherence, a lack of understanding; the latter suggests the ability to make subtle distinctions between one situation and the next. Or, more cynically, it might reflect the assumption that the public understand little about strategic issues and will just go along with however a given conflict is framed by the government and the media.[67]

This uncertainty about British public attitudes to war may be partly explained by methodological variation between studies. However, it also suggests uncertainty about how well citizens understand war. Descriptions of British public opinion as 'confused', 'contradictory', and 'incoherent' suggest the persistence of century-old realist assumptions that publics are too ignorant and emotional to hold meaningful views on issues such as war.[68]

Conversely, authors such as Hines et al. conclude that the public have an 'intuitive understanding' of war due to Britain's long history of military operations, even if they lack precise knowledge of the work of the military itself.[69] Towle even argues that not only do the British public respond to debates on using military force in a balanced and sensible way, they may even demonstrate superior strategic judgment to policymakers.[70] These conclusions reflect a body of research suggesting a 'prudent' and 'sensible' public, capable of making basic cost-benefit analyses regarding military interventions.[71]

Taken together, these contrasting aggregate judgments suggest the value of a qualitative, narrative approach, since it offers a different perspective on how coherent and consistent citizens' views are when they are given the opportunity to explain themselves.[72] The aim is not to identify specific attitudinal categories or statistically generalise these to the broader population; it is to uncover nuances that polls and surveys find harder to assess.[73] The aim is not to determine the proportion of the population that support or oppose war, but to illustrate how similarly citizens explain their views using stories. Doing this may provide a more accurate and subtle picture of public perspectives on war and its importance to British national identity and ontological security.

A more sophisticated grasp of how citizens interpret war may also help policymakers understand the perspectives of their citizens. As Kull and Destler showed in their study of American foreign policy, politicians have previously misread public opinion on foreign policy by assuming that a reasonable indication of the public mood can be derived from a combination of media representations, opinion polls, and interest groups.[74] The latter has always been a questionable guide to the latent views of the broader population, if indeed these can ever be accessed. Moreover, the utility of the media and polls as indicators of a population's views has been further thrown into question by recent events. The 2015 and 2017 British general elections, the Brexit vote, and the 2016 US presidential election all confounded pollsters' predictions. Meanwhile, each campaign saw concerns raised that some mainstream media organisations, such as the BBC, were overly neutral, while social media platforms, such as Facebook, fostered echo chambers in which people consumed increasingly biased and potentially erroneous content. Meanwhile the rise of populism in the West reflects the alienation of sections of society from a mainstream political establishment seen as neither understanding nor caring what they think. These issues make direct attempts to understand public views more pressing than ever.

Methodology

This study does not just innovate by bringing the stories of 'ordinary people' to light; it also does so through its novel methodology. Existing research into public attitudes to war tends to ask about specific conflicts assumed significant by the researcher. However, I was not interested in the conflicts I deemed important; I was only interested in those deemed significant to participants. On this basis, the principle behind questioning was not to ask about any war until the interviewee brought it up.[75] Only once a conflict was mentioned were people asked, 'what did you feel at the time' or 'what can you remember about why Britain intervened?' Such methods are more common in narrative and biographical research but represent an original approach when assessing public understandings of war.[76]

This open-ended approach proved particularly valuable in two ways. First, it generated a rich array of historical references, from Crimea to the Cod Wars, that participants used to make sense of Britain's wars. The task was then to identify the shared general patterns of history embedded in these stories and how the building blocks of each story were emplotted together. Similarities between individuals could then indicate which conflicts have shaped British collective identity and memory more strongly.

Second, the open-ended approach facilitated analysis of which conflicts participants chose *not* to bring up and why. This point is taken up in chapter 7, which examines the remarkable finding that a range of British citizens appear to have collectively 'forgotten 9/11' in their accounts of the War on Terror, despite the attacks being widely considered one of the few unforgettable events in recent history. Again, such analysis of what people choose to silence is impossible when the researcher determines which conflicts are the subject of discussions.

The narratives analysed in this book were derived from semistructured interviews with a diverse sample of British citizens resident in England from non-military families.[77] Since the aim was not to quantify what the British population thinks about war but instead to identify the range of stories they tell about it, generating a statistically representative sample was inappropriate but also impractical given the in-depth nature of narrative analysis. Instead the most logical approach was to interview as diverse a population as possible and then look for commonalities. Sampling was therefore purposive, based on two core qualitative research principles: range and saturation.[78] Stratified purposive sampling was used to ensure the broadest possible range of participants. This hybrid approach selects groups for variation across a given phenomenon but also provides sufficient depth to compare different groups meaningfully.[79] Individuals were sampled based on age, gender, location, and socioeconomic classification. Recruitment occurred within rural and urban populations across

England, including London, Birmingham, suburban Liverpool, a market town in Dorset, and villages in rural Worcestershire and Oxfordshire.

Sample size was determined based on the principle of saturation. This involves interviewing until one is confident that the full range of possible responses has been elicited, and is typically associated with grounded theory.[80] Having initially estimated that 40 to 50 participants might be sufficient to reach saturation, 69 participants were eventually interviewed, with 2 omitted once they were found to be active servicemen. The process resulted in a highly diverse sample of 67 individuals across the full range of the British adult population in terms of age (range 18 to 92 years), gender (n = 34 male, 33 female), and socioeconomic classification. Sample diversity was enhanced by numerous Welsh and Scottish participants, British Asians, and British Arabs, although even greater ethnic and regional diversity would have been ideal.

To enhance the validity of my interpretations of participants' stories, and consistent with ethnographic methods, it is important to acknowledge factors that might have influenced the stories people told and how I analysed them.[81] I therefore kept painstaking field notes that included noting moments where I might have shaped the content of the interview, or when contemporaneous events might have done so. For instance, as a British citizen with exclusively English relatives, I was in many ways an insider in the study population. This was something of a double-edged sword. On the positive side, it was easier to grasp the meaning participants were trying to convey; they could allude in little detail to events or use idioms that I understood, having similar cultural knowledge and experience. On the other hand, they may sometimes have chosen not to discuss certain events because they assumed I would know about them already. They may therefore have appeared less knowledgeable when actually they did not want to state what they felt was obvious. My field notes recorded a few occasions when I inadvertently positioned people relative to their British identity, unwittingly asking prompt questions such as 'what should we do about Islamic State?' rather than 'what should Britain do?'. This demonstrates the futility of claiming to be a genuinely objective observer, but also the importance of researchers in international relations acknowledging their potential influences on the research they conduct.

People's stories were also potentially influenced by events taking place at the time of the interviews. To mitigate this, interviews were conducted in as short a time frame as possible, between mid-October 2014 and mid-January 2015. Fortunately, there were no notable changes in Britain's military operations during this period that might have significantly altered the data, as could have happened if the research took place, for example, between August and October 1939 or 2001. Still, the period was notable for several events relevant to British defence policy. Militarily, it saw Britain's ongoing participation in coalition airstrikes against the Islamic State in Iraq. A month previously, the Scottish independence referendum had raised the issue of Britain's very existence. The centenary of the First World War's outbreak was commemorated in November, with many participants noting its prominence in their minds given its extensive coverage. Several 'lone wolf' terrorist attacks also occurred, including in New York, Quebec and Ottawa (October), Sydney (December), and the Charlie Hebdo attack in Paris (January). However, the fact that these took place reasonably consistently throughout the sampling period and the preceding months suggests that they did not result in significant shifts in thinking during the data collection process.

Data analysis consisted of recording, transcribing interviews in full, identifying segments of narrative, and then coding these into themes.[82] In contrast with other discourse analysis methods that tend to segment text to categorise it, people's narratives were kept intact where possible to examine their coherence and meaning as a whole.[83] Because of the study's open-ended approach, this process was not guided by formal hypotheses about the likely content of participant stories. Instead it proceeded based on a process of abductive reasoning, which involves an ongoing interaction between induction and deduction.[84] In other words, I initially identified plots and patterns in participant stories inductively and then searched for these among other participants in order to deduce which stories people share. This approach reflects the honest admission that research can rarely be wholly inductive, because no researcher arrives at their data without preconceptions about its possible content, otherwise they could not decide what questions to ask. Moving back and forth between deduction and induction in this way, the aim throughout was to provide a plausible and comprehensive picture of how similarly British citizens interpret war.

Plan of the Book

Having established the rationale for the ground-up investigation of the narratives British citizens tell about war, the book proceeds as follows. Chapter 1 sets out the analytical framework through which people's narratives are studied.

First, it establishes the relationship between the stories people tell and how these relate to the construction of national identity and collective memory. This is important in explaining why participants tell similar stories about Britain and war. It then shows how the construction of plot is integral to these processes. The chapter then explains a two-level framework through which plot will be analysed: genre—the general patterns of citizens' stories—and emplotment—the process of selecting, linking, and framing events to create these overall patterns. This makes it possible to analyse narratives from the most general account of history down to the specifics of individual events.

Chapters 2 to 5 address the narrative *genres* individuals use to describe the general pattern of British military history, and how they use these to make identity claims about Britain as an international actor. Chapters 2 and 3 address two storylines identified early in analysis as being shared almost universally across the sample: that Britain's history is a story of *Continuous War*, in the face of *Material Decline*. The *Continuous War* narrative reveals that across the political spectrum, British people see war as a routine, everyday activity, something Britain 'just does'. By comparing Britain's assumed greater willingness and ability to go to war to others, the narrative shows how military interventionism maintains the sense of self or ontological security of many British citizens over time. The second shared narrative portrays Britain as undergoing *Material Decline* since the peak of the British Empire, making it less able to fight wars than previously. Taken together, these stories reveal a pride in Britain's ongoing willingness to intervene to uphold righteous causes but concern for its increasing inability to do so.

While citizens take for granted that Britain is continually at war but less materially able to fight, differences emerge when examining how they *morally* evaluate Britain's wars. Combining these storylines about how frequent, effective, and ethical Britain's wars have been over time reveals a typology of five genres that provide contrasting overall judgments of Britain's military history. Addressed in chapters 4 and 5, these genres portray Britain as *Punching Above Its Weight*, as a *Vanishing Force*, as *Learning from Its Mistakes*, as *Led Astray*, or as a *Selfish Imperialist*. Each offers a competing vision of how Britain should use its military in the future, encompassing an extremely broad range of perspectives, from the most ardent interventionist to the most avowed pacifist. Chapter 5 finishes with an important discussion of how applicable these narratives are to different conflicts, and the extent to which similar narratives are likely to be found in other militarily interventionist states.

Whereas the previous chapters investigate the genres individuals use to account for Britain's military role, chapter 6 moves to the micro-level, considering the way individuals selectively *emplot* different wars to try and make their narratives more persuasive.[85] The focus concerns how individuals include or silence events in order to portray Britain as a *Force for Good* in the world, a prominent government framing of British defence policy. In the process, it demonstrates a novel approach to analysing narrative emplotment that may be useful both for those studying strategic narratives and those looking to construct them.

Chapter 7 then looks even deeper, considering the role of memory in the emplotment process. It reveals how shifts in the ways conflicts are narrated over time can lead people to forget events previously considered 'unforgettable'. It does this using the striking case raised earlier: that numerous British citizens appear to have collectively 'forgotten 9/11' in their explanations of why war in Afghanistan began, despite the attacks being widely considered an unforgettable event that changed the world. Instead citizens explain the war using an 'Iraqistan quagmire' narrative in which Afghanistan and Iraq merge into one seemingly endless, purposeless war, to the extent that they cannot remember how it all began. This provides a groundbreaking case of how the way citizens remember wars can shift over time and how the stories governments tell can shape this process. It also shows the unique findings that can result from the open-ended approach the book adopts.

The book concludes by discussing the implications of these findings for Britain's identity and future military role and how it is narrated. This includes the impact of Brexit and the apparent contradiction it raises between those that value Britain's international influence while appearing to have voted to diminish it. The chapter also examines Britain's present military engagements and what these suggest about how Britain's military story might develop alongside its allies in the future. It then broadens out to reflect more on how the book's approach might be useful for researchers and policymakers seeking alternative perspectives on strategic narratives and public opinion across a range of issues in international politics.

CHAPTER 1

Analysing Narratives, Identity, Memory, and War

'Narrative is everywhere, but not everything is narrative.'[1]

Narrative is not just a distinct mode of communication. It is a means through which humans construct their identities. This position is consistent with decades of narrative research in multiple fields theorising that humans understand who they are and communicate this to others using stories locating themselves in the past, present, and future.[2] These stories can provide 'ontological security', a coherent and consistent sense of self over time.[3] Alternatively, they might anticipate dramatic changes in the future.[4] From this perspective, identity is not a singular inner essence but an ongoing story, emerging through the selective emplotment of biographical experience.[5] Who we are is a question of what stories are told about us.[6]

The biographical narratives individuals construct to make sense of their lives are the product of a selection process. In theory, humans do not see their lives as just 'one damned thing after another'.[7] Instead they attempt to link together selected biographical events into a coherent pattern that explains who they have been, who they are, and who they might be in the future.[8] Highlighting certain events while downplaying or silencing others enables people to present themselves as they want to.

Memory is integral to this process. Understanding who one is in the present cannot be meaningfully done without reference to the past.[9] However, biographical narratives are not just random collections of whatever past events a person remembers in a given moment; they are typically guided by an overall

18

sense of who one is or is trying to be. This determines the events included in a story, even though the narrator may not be aware of this process in action.[10] Moreover, memory is unstable and malleable; it shapes and is shaped by how events are narrated over time. Events narrated more frequently are more likely to be remembered, whereas those that are repeatedly excluded are more likely to be forgotten.[11]

Narrative, Collective Identity, and Memory

However, when individuals narrate, they do not do so in a social vacuum; they narrate for an audience. The content they select and the way they seek to establish its meaning are shaped by the culture in which they communicate. In this respect narratives are never wholly individual. An extensive literature demonstrates that while people could theoretically make up any narrative they choose, they typically construct them from a surprisingly limited repertoire of available and acceptable narratives circulating within public discourse.[12] Rather than being created out of nothing, people's stories are constructed out of a web of existing narratives in which individuals, groups, and nations are entangled.[13] This social constructivist approach sees narratives as networked and relational social products, continuously renegotiated as they are told and retold over time.[14] Within this network, individuals can identify with families, social movements, or nations, just as states can project strategic narratives to try and shape their identity or those of others.[15]

The relationship between individual and collective memory can be theorised in a similar way. Consistent with social memory theorists such as Zerubavel and Wertsch, I contend that while it is individuals that remember and narrate, they do so not in isolation but socially. What they remember and the stories they tell about it are shaped in part by narratives prevalent and socially accepted in the groups in which they interact.[16] Consequently, the collective memories of nations are not seen here as the sum of the individual memories within them, but instead refer to 'representations of the past shared by members of a group'.[17] The media may shape how events are remembered, and as with individuals' stories, the frequency with which an event is narrated will shape how well it is remembered or forgotten.[18] Governments may also attempt to influence collective memory using museums, monuments, and rituals. By shaping the stories told about a nation's past, all of these activities can shape national identities. But I argue that collective memories or collective identities are not something a state 'has'; they are social, intersubjective phenomena residing in narrative networks.[19] By implication, similarities in how people emplot historical events in their stories can be seen as evidence of collective memory and identity.

The assumption that nations, like individuals, construct their identities through narratives drawn from collective memories makes it possible to argue that nations also derive ontological security through the way they narrate their histories.[20] Anthropomorphising the state, researchers have used this assumption to identify 'national biographies' through which countries explain who they are and where they have come from.[21] A common criticism of such research is its tendency to 'homogenize the national self' into singular, monolithic stories as they are understood by political elites, rather than explore the extent of variation in a given culture.[22] Rather than generalise in this way, this research differs by exploring the extent of variation at the individual level in a manner closer to those calling for an 'everyday' or 'vernacular' approach to security studies.[23] This enables consideration of how contested British interpretations of war are from the perspectives of its citizens.

This ground-up approach is important because states are not 'people' as such. Their identity is a product of the stories people tell about them. This is not just a top-down process, whereby the narratives elites project about their states provide ontological security for their citizens. A state's identity is brought into being by the individual stories people narrate about the collective. The extent of contestation and variation in those narratives can therefore indicate the extent to which people feel secure in their identity as British citizens.

Adopting this approach makes it important to show how one person's seemingly unique story is linked socially to others. This can be done by considering how an individual might tell the story of a terrorist attack. While describing what happened during an attack, a witness might describe the events as perpetrated by 'evil barbarians' or 'savages' who seek to undermine the 'our way of life'. This would be an *individual* narrative, in that it is recounted by a single person. However, if other observers told the same story, or portrayed the perpetrators in a similar way, one could also consider the individual's story a *public* narrative, in that it is shared by different people.[24] This appears even more obvious if the media or politicians frame the attack in a similar way.

However, the narrative may also be socially linked at a deeper level—that of *meta-narrative*. Meta-narratives are deeply embedded, overarching stories that order and explain knowledge and experience within and potentially across cultures. These have also been termed master narratives, master plots, myths, master frames, and root metaphors. They are closely related to dominant discourses and ideologies, because they can appear so deeply embedded in culture that they seem obvious, taken for granted, common sense.[25] As Somers explains:

> [Meta-]narratives can be the epic dramas of our time: Capitalism vs. Communism, the Individual vs. Society, Barbarism/Nature vs. Civility. They may also be progressive narratives of teleological unfolding: Marxism and the triumph of Class Struggle, Liberalism and the triumph of Liberty, the Emergence of Western Citizenship, the Rise of Nationalism or of Islam.[26]

In the case of the terrorist attack, the meta-narrative is one of 'barbarism versus civilisation', a post-Enlightenment narrative common in the discourse on terrorism that contrasts the historical development of secular, liberal societies with backward, barbaric, uncivilised Others whose irrational violence reflects their failure to progress to modernity.[27]

The distinction between these different levels of narrative is not fixed or rigid; an individual's story can be situated in each one simultaneously. The example simply shows how the stories individuals tell can be related socially to others, and also how narratives that are deeply culturally embedded across time and space may influence people's personal interpretations. It helps explain why people tell similar stories.

War Stories and Britain's National Identity

A research approach that examines the relationship between narrative, collective identity, and collective memory is particularly appropriate for the study of public interpretations of war. Nations make sense of who they are by constructing narratives using a limited number of historical references to formative national experiences in which they played certain roles.[28] Wars provide a source of some of the most traumatic but also glorious episodes in a nation's history.[29] Military victories and defeats are often central elements of the mythological stories that bring a nation into being as an 'imagined community'.[30]

The British military is widely considered to be integral to the constitution of British national identity due to its extensive deployment over the centuries.[31]

Consequently, studying how people narrate Britain's military past might pro-vide insights into how people explain what Britain's national identity was, is, or should be. Similarities and differences across citizens' stories may provide evidence of how far British collective identity is unified or contested.

These identity narratives are of continual political concern because they can shape what military strategies are pursued and domestic support for them.[32] As Ringmar explains, 'the narratives we construct about our state will specify who we are and what role we play in the world; how our "national interests" are to be defined, or which foreign policy to pursue.[33] Decisions to use military force are shaped by perceptions of a state's international identity and the role it should play in world politics. However, as McCourt suggests, the military roles states under-take are not simply determined by an internal need to maintain a consistent sense of self, but also because of expectations that emerge in interaction with others.[34] In turn, the role a state is perceived to have played in subsequent events can shape the ongoing narratives through which a state's identity is constructed.[35]

In this way national identity narratives are shaped by evaluations of the role a state plays in events as they play out over time. They are also influenced by a wide range of discourses. British defence policy can be seen to be shaped by Atlanticism, Europeanism, Liberal Interventionism, and multilateralism; military strategic elements such as conventional war, counterinsurgency, and the indirect approach; the foreign policy traditions of Whiggism, socialism, con-servatism, and liberalism; theories of International Relations such as realism, liberalism, institutionalism, cosmopolitanism, internationalism, Marxism, and feminism; and cultural traditions concerning the Commonwealth.[36]

Even though singular, clearly identifiable policies may emerge from this complexity, that does not mean that one should assume British citizens all tell the same story. British society is diverse and people will interpret the nation through the lens of their own experiences of the world.[37] As Kenny observes,

> it is rarer than is often supposed for any single version of the national story to achieve a position of unchallenged dominance. Invariably, different versions of the past are in competition with each other, and these narratives are usually harnessed to different ideas about the character of, and prospects for, the nation in the present.[38]

Contestation does not mean infinite variety though. As Cruz finds, national identity narratives are often constructed within dominant rhetorical frames held by collectives about themselves and their role in the world. These provide only 'a restricted array of plausible scenarios of how the world can and cannot be changed and how the future ought to look'.[39] These identity narratives, and the events emplotted within them, may change over time 'as a nation's sense of what we did and who we are changes'.[40] However, rarely is transformation extensive; it is more probable that emphasis will shift in line with new events.[41]

This implies that the general patterns of citizens' stories at a given moment are likely to reflect longer term narrative understandings of Britain's identity. It suggests the utility of an approach that considers both the overall patterns of citizens' stories and the specific events that are emplotted to support them, while paying close attention to the context in which the research takes place. Doing this may increase our understanding of the 'collective field of imaginable possibilities' regarding Britain's future role in the world as currently perceived by its citizens.[42]

Studying Narratives of War: The Importance of Plot

To assess adequately the similarities in the narratives British citizens tell about war, it behoves the researcher to differentiate between what is narrative and what is not. I argue that plot is what structurally differentiates narrative from other modes of discourse—a temporally, spatially, and causally connected sequence of events.[43] I have also established that plot is a means through which individuals and groups construct their identities through the selection and linkage of historical events. On this basis, plot is the primary focus for analysis of the stories British citizens tell about their country's role in war.

Plot does not just structurally differentiate narrative from other modes of discourse or play a key role in identity construction; it is also implicated when narratives are used to entertain or influence others. To entertain, a narrator is likely to select and highlight the unusual while silencing the banal. They may also construct plot to maximise surprise, as a breach from expectations is what imbues narrative with drama.[44] But since the study's rationale derives from the notion that understanding public interpretations of war would be beneficial in the strategic narrative formation process, the main interest in plot here is its role in persuasion.

Narrative persuasion is not just the realm of propagandists seeking to influence publics to support or oppose wars. An individual making an identity claim is in a sense trying to persuade themselves or others that the claim is valid. In doing so they are likely to select events that support the claim while silencing opposing events. At a basic level, a person recounting their day is likely to include interesting occurrences while silencing the mundane—unless of course their intent is to convey the impression that their day has been mundane. It is therefore assumed that there is no *structural* difference in how plot might be used in biographical narratives or political narratives. The only differences are the strategic intent of the political communicator and their awareness that they are deliberately designing narratives to influence others.

When considering how narratives persuade, the most common rhetorical distinction in the literature is between narrative and argumentation. Bruner famously considers them two distinct modes of thought, stating that 'a good story and a well-formed argument are different natural kinds'.[45] Both can be used to make sense of the world, and both establish causality. However, argument seeks to establish truth through formal empirical proof while narrative seeks to achieve 'verisimilitude' by presenting a plausible, lifelike representation of social reality.[46]

In everyday discourse the distinction is far from clear. The two modes are better thought of as ideal types that overlap considerably and sometimes work together.[47] The dictionary definition of argument is to 'give reasons or cite evidence in support of an idea'.[48] So when a politician decides to tell a story about their humble origins to support their claim that they understand the ordinary voter, they are using a narrative to argue. This does not mean that narrative is a subset of argument though. It simply means that argument is one of several functions that narrative can perform beyond just telling a story, including description, explanation, clarification, and instruction.[49]

Despite this overlap, a useful distinction can still be made between formal argumentation and argument through narrative.[50] As an ideal type, an argument is an inference derived from general principles through a process of logical deduction.[51] To convince someone that one is a good person, one might do so based on the following premises:

A good person is someone who helps others
Then either
    a. I try to help others in everything I do
OR
    b. I try to help others in most of the things I do

OR

    c. More of the things I do help others than harm them

SO

I am a good person.

A narrative to convince oneself or another that one is a good person would be structured differently and persuade differently from the above process. Instead of stating the premises on which an argument is based, narrative creates a framework of meaning through its plot. The aim would be to make sense of one's life as a whole, creating a selective account that emphasises positives while silencing negatives. At a basic level, the story persuades using *enthymeme*. In conventional rhetoric, enthymeme refers to a syllogism without a premise, a logical inference without all its premises stated.[52] In other words, rather than the full logical progression above, the narrative instead requires the audience to fill in missing elements. By selecting some events and omitting others, it seeks to present a plausible inference rather than a logically binding one.[53] Simplistically, therefore, the unstated, underlying logic of a story portraying someone as a good person might be as follows:

This selection of actions shows me being a good person

SO

I am a good person.

Stated so minimally, the flaw in this logic is obvious. A person may have caused considerable harm to others or acted immorally on multiple occasions, and it is fallacious to generalise from select cases. This is not the point of narration though. It does not aim to convince the audience using falsifiable arguments; it seeks to present a selective but plausible interpretation that resonates with audience understandings of the world. Events are selected in which the narrator plays the role of 'a good person' and used to support the narrative's overall claim about who they are.

Enthymeme is a similarly important plot device in the strategic narratives states construct to project their identities and justify their actions on the international stage.[54] While it has not been proven empirically that foreign policy narratives are more persuasive than foreign policy arguments, historiographers, memory theorists, and discourse analysts have all shown how states attempt to portray themselves favourably through highly selective narrations of their histories. The arguments such stories convey are often flawed in terms of formal logic, since they are typically based on similar premises to those outlined above. For example, a story told by a political leader to justify their country's role in war might also use enthymeme to make its case:

The selection of wars in this narrative helped others

SO

Our wars are justified because they help others.

Again, the logical flaws in this argument are relatively unimportant, because narrative persuasion rests not on formal argumentation but on the overall framework of meaning that plot creates. Enthymeme thus allows narrators to deliberately omit controversial events in their past with which others might disagree.[55] Bringing up past wrongdoings in a narrative designed to portray a nation favourably could undermine narrative coherence, invite disagreement, and reduce the credibility of the story and its teller. This is because the role being played in a given situation contradicts the overall identity claim being made.

In this way rather than identity and role being conflated, as is sometimes the case in constructivist IR theory,[56] roles are situation-specific behaviours that shape and are shaped by the identity narratives actors tell about themselves. If an international actor's role in a given event contradicts the identity claim of the overall narrative, it is likely to appear less coherent and convincing as a result.

Presenting a selective account of events is also helpful because it invites active participation by the audience, who can fill in the gaps based on their own understanding of the nation's past. They may have knowledge of very different events, but if they interpret the country's role in those events in a similar way, they are more likely to find the story persuasive. Since the audience participates in creating a narrative's meaning, attempts to use it to shape their views are less obvious.[57] Stories can argue, but indirectly. Plot distinguishes them from formal argumentation.

Notwithstanding this study's emphasis on plot, it is recognised that narrative persuades differently from argumentation in other ways too. In theory, argument persuades through encouraging cognitive elaboration: critical evaluation of message content.[58] Conversely, narrative is thought to persuade through discouraging critical analysis. Instead it uses transportation and identification: immersing people in a vivid story world, populated with characters with whom they can identify emotionally.[59] Drama can also absorb audiences in a story, distracting them from persuasive subtexts.[60]

Plot is implicated in these processes too. Not all narratives contain dramatic plot twists. There are stories of continuity, with sequences of events being used to demonstrate an ongoing historical trend.[61] Nevertheless, turning points in a plot are what create drama, be it the sudden fall from grace of the protagonist or their unexpected victory against incredible odds.[62] The steeper the trajectory of the narrative, the more dramatic the turnaround appears.[63] Politicians frequently exploit this by seeking to make their opponents' failures appear more drastic so that their improvements look more impressive. Donald Trump's call to reverse a supposedly catastrophic decline and 'Make America Great Again' is a classic example of this.

Character development is also a crucial aspect of narration. Indeed some argue that this more than plot is the key to making narratives compelling.[64] In fact, character and plot are closely intertwined, as the moral character of an actor is shaped by the actions attributed to them in the story.[65] Plot affects who is portrayed as the victim, 'how blame is assigned to the villain', and 'what actions are needed from the hero'.[66] Whether a country is characterised as an ethical international actor is shaped by its actions. The military interventions a state undertakes, and its conduct within them, can therefore be expected to shape public perceptions of the state's character and the roles it is expected to play. So while this study's analytical framework is plot-focused, character is also addressed, because analysis concerns how plot is used to support identity claims about the central character(s) in citizens' narratives: Britain and its military.

Analytical Framework: Genre and Emplotment

The previous discussion suggests the value of an analytical framework that considers two things. First, it should be able to analyse not just the events people include in their stories but the ones they don't. Second, it should consider how these choices are integrated to make an overall identity claim, in this case about Britain's character as an international military actor. As Bruner explains, narratives are shaped through the interrelationship of the overall story and the episodes that make up its constituent parts.[67] Considering both of these elements therefore generates a fuller understanding of citizens' war stories.

Bearing this in mind, citizens' narratives were analysed at two levels: *genre*—the overall pattern of a given narrative in terms of progress, continuity, or decline, and *emplotment*—the process through which events are selected, ordered, and framed to create the overall pattern. Combining both facilitates a broader and deeper analysis of public interpretations, from the most general story about British military history down to the specifics of an individual conflict. Genre can be used to illuminate the identity claims made about Britain and its military, while emplotment can show how past events are used to make these narratives more convincing.

Genre

The first level of analysis examines the overall pattern or trajectory of people's stories. Numerous authors have shown that while the specific events in people's stories may vary greatly, overall individuals narrate history in patterned, familiar ways.[68] Reality rarely unfolds so prescriptively. Nonetheless, the stories people habitually tell about history can reduce extremely complex events, cultures, or entire historical epochs to 'simplistic, one-dimensional visions of the past'.[69] These formulaic plotlines are not universal, objective representations of reality; they are social products, reflecting shared traditions of remembering.[70] The question is, what general stories do individual citizens tell about Britain's military history, and how many variations of these shared stories are there?

This idea that people narrate using a limited range of culturally recognisable stories forms the basis of the concept of narrative genre. Genre can be defined in many ways: as a generic category of literature, art, or film; as a specific mode of discourse, of which narrative is an example; or as a subset of narrative types, including hypothetical, habitual, (auto)biographical narratives and accounts.[71] Here, genre refers to the literary notion that there exist different types of story involving formulaic and familiar plotlines.[72]

The classic example of this derives from Frye and the claim that there are four archetypal plot structures: romance, tragedy, comedy, and satire.[73] Not all authors agree with this typology. Booker proposes seven universal plots into which all stories fit; Tobias claims that there are twenty.[74] Focusing instead on history and collective memory, Zerubavel contends that people tend to narrate history using narratives of progress, decline, zigzags, or cycles.[75] Each author acknowledges considerable crossover between genres, which can apply to both 'fictional' stories and 'factual' histories.[76]

Despite the intuitive appeal of classifying entire national discourses or even every story ever written into a limited number of genres, caution should be raised about the complexity this could hide. Even a simple alteration in the start point of a narrative can affect what story is told.[77] For example, depending on the start point, Britain's imperial history could be narrated either as a narrative of progress, decline, or a rise and fall. It could even be understood as part of a cyclical narrative, as exemplified by Toynbee's famous claim that each civilisation in history has undergone the same process of genesis, growth, and decline.[78]

Doing justice to this complexity suggests the benefit of a more open-ended, flexible approach to analysing citizens' stories, rather than attempting to shoehorn them into rigid preexisting and supposedly universal frameworks. To that end, genre is approached here in a manner closer to that of Wertsch in his narrative analysis of collective memory.[79] He too advocates the analysis of the general patterns of citizens' narratives, but rather than genre he uses the term 'schematic narrative templates'.[80] These, he explains, are 'not some sort of universal archetypes. Instead, they belong to particular narrative traditions that can be expected to differ from one cultural setting to another'.[81] They do not focus on one specific event from the past, but instead comprise a general pattern into which different events can fit depending on the specific knowledge of the narrator.[82]

Similarly, this book proceeds on the assumption that the stories individuals tell about war are constructed from a limited range of genres within a given culture, but that they do not necessarily correspond to universal archetypes. The study then proceeds inductively, with the aim of identifying the range of general stories told about Britain and its role in war. Its start point in differentiating genres is deliberately flexible: that at the most basic level, the simplest trajectories a plot can take are progress, decline, or continuity.[83] Indeed each genre mentioned above comprises variations of these. Put simply, over time things are either getting better, worse, or staying the same.

Whether a story is one of progress, decline, or continuity depends on what is being evaluated. This is crucial, because several objects can be evaluated in a given narrative. In this way, just as identity is assumed here to be multilayered, identity narratives would logically be expected to be multilayered too.[84] A person might simultaneously narrate their adult life as a story of economic progress as they gain wealth, moral continuity based on their belief that they always do the right thing, and a decline in their physical fitness. Each would be a generalisation, since there are likely to be peaks, troughs, and turning points in each case. These story lines can then be woven together to construct an overall life story that conveys a central identity claim. The aim here was to unpick these strands within British citizens' narratives about their country's role in war, rather than assuming the form they might take a priori.

Emplotment

While numerous studies have researched the genres political actors use to make sense of international events, the process of emplotment has been rarely studied in the literature on foreign policy and war. Most studies have sought to identify plots rather than examining micro-level processes through which they are generated. Authors have identified the causal and temporal sequencing of events using basic frameworks of past, present, and future; beginning, middle, and end; or initial situation, disruption, and resolution.[85] Others have addressed emplotment more indirectly. Ó'Tuathail, for example, uses Burke's dramatic pentad, analysing narratives of war in terms of actor, agent, agency, scene, and purpose, or who, what, when, where, and why.[86] An extensive framing literature examines the emphasis placed on certain events and actions in order to shape how conflicts are interpreted.[87] Meanwhile researchers in multiple fields have examined how historical accounts include some events while silencing others, exaggerate benevolence, and reframe atrocity.[88] However, rarely have these processes been combined together in a structural framework to analyse the emplotment process in depth, and not using the stories told by the general public.

Emplotment is a complex process that concerns not simply which events are included and excluded but how they are emphasised and framed. For this reason, some narrative policy analysts have avoided studying it, preferring instead to focus on character and setting.[89] Meanwhile research examining the analogies politicians and the media use to explain new conflicts tends to focus on individual event choices rather than how multiple events are incorporated into a coherent whole.[90]

Given the lack of in-depth studies of the emplotment process in the literature on foreign policy and war, the study's analytical approach draws insights from autobiographical narrative research. Specifically, it augments a framework originally deployed by Gabriela Spector-Mersel in her studies of narrative identity formation.[91] According to the framework, there are six selection mechanisms individuals use, either consciously or unconsciously, to make a specific overall point with a story. First, they *include* events that support the point of their story. They also use *sharpening* to add extra detail about events that are particularly significant, perhaps telling an embedded account about a given incident. They *clarify* the 'real' meaning of events that might have meant something different previously.[92] Meanwhile they *omit* events deemed irrelevant to the story and *silence* potentially contradictory events. They might also *flatten* the significance of contradictory events by bringing them up to explain them away. Combining these elements thus enables an individual to construct a coherent narrative to support a given identity claim.

The analysis here moves beyond Spector-Mersel's approach in two important respects. An acknowledged limitation of the framework is that its constituents are not all narrative-specific. Argumentation, after all, is also selective and involves highlighting supporting evidence and silencing contradictions, omitting the irrelevant and explaining away inconsistencies. Consequently, this study extends the framework by adding *linking* to improve narrative specificity. Clear causal and temporal linkages between events are key aspects of what makes narratives more coherent and are fundamental to the emplotment process.[93] This addition creates an augmented framework of seven selection mechanisms used to examine how people construct coherent narratives about Britain's role in war:

Inclusion: selecting facts that fit the identity claim being made.

Linking: establishing a temporal, causal, or spatial relationship between events.

Sharpening: emphasising specific aspects of an event that fit the identity claim being made.

Clarifying: explaining what an event was 'really all about', as opposed to alternative, commonly assumed meanings.

Omission: not including events that are *irrelevant* to the point of the story.

Silencing: not including events that *contradict* the point of the story.
Flattening: selecting but telling little of events that may contradict the point of the narrative. These events may be condensed and receive minimal focus. Alternatively they may be mentioned to assert their insignificance to the overall story.

A second way the book's analysis of plot advances beyond Spector-Mersel's approach is in shifting the focus of analysis from the individual to the nation, stories in which Britain is the central character. This reflects the assumption, backed up by authors such as Patterson and Monroe, that people use the same selection mechanisms whether a story's protagonist is the individual or the nation.[94]

Emplotment, Framing, and Analogies

As well as facilitating fine-grained analysis, an advantage of this emplotment framework is that it incorporates consideration of framing and analogies, both of which are implicated in narration. An analogy is a comparison highlighting some similarity between two objects or situations.[95] The book began with a classic example of this when governments seek to persuade publics to support wars: comparing the current security threat to Hitler and the Nazis. Analogies are used as a form of reasoning, frequently employed by policymakers to advocate one policy over another.[96] They argue that the current situation is equivalent to one in the past, and therefore we should either act in the same way if this was previously successful or act differently.

Despite being arguments, analogies contain a narrative element that makes them a key aspect of what can make narratives 'strategic'. They imply that the sequence of events in a present-day crisis will play out in the same way as a given drama from the past unless those involved act differently this time. They apply the causal and temporal logic of a past situation to create a script that anticipates how events will develop in the future.[97] The addition of linking to the framework is therefore doubly important. It can highlight instances where individuals' narrative understandings of war today are based on what they perceive as comparable episodes from Britain's past. It may also indicate the situations in which they might support military intervention in the future.

Framing is also closely related to narrative. Both involve 'selecting and highlighting some facets of events or issues . . . so as to promote a particular interpretation.[98] Theorists frequently disagree on whether narratives are subordinate to frames or vice versa. Just as there are different levels of narratives, frames have been conceptualised on a scale ranging from the choice of a single word to overarching 'master frames' that organise knowledge and experience.[99] Confusingly, this variation means that there can theoretically be frames within frames, narratives within narratives, frames within narratives, and narratives within frames.

When considering the specific events people include in their stories, framing seems subordinate to emplotment for a very simple reason: an event must be included in someone's narrative before it can be framed. Once selected, sharpening, clarifying, and flattening highlight or minimise certain aspects of the event to promote one interpretation over another. However, the emplotment process as a whole creates an overall story that is in itself a framing of British military history, be it as destructive, glorious, civilising, or exploitative.

All narratives frame events because they are selective. The two concepts are distinguishable because narrative involves emplotted movement through time.[100] Choosing one word over another to frame an event can alter its meaning. But narrative constructs the meaning of events by 'showing their temporal or causal relationship to other events . . . and by showing the role such events play in the unfolding of the larger whole'.[101] Frames do not necessarily contain this temporal and causal logic.[102] All narratives frame, but not all frames are narratives.

Narratives, Facts, and Attitudes

Two caveats are observed before turning to the British people's war stories themselves. First, the aim is not to compare individual narratives to an objectively 'true' historical record, even though narratives may contain 'facts' such as dates that could be considered 'true' or 'false'.[103] Instead what matters is *how* people interpret events and how similarly they do so. They may agree on the facts but disagree on what they mean.[104]

Second, while participants may well express their views during stories, it cannot be definitively assumed that the stories people tell reflect what they actually think. Citizens' narratives are likely to reflect their attitudes to a significant extent; but since attitudes can never be directly observed using any method, one can never know for sure.[105] Moreover, because the content and form of narratives are influenced by audience and social context, it cannot be claimed with certainty that a given story corresponds to an attitude held by its narrator.[106] They may wish to present themselves in a certain way in a given interaction, and what they say may not reflect deeply held views. Partly for this reason, and consistent with discourse analytic methods in general, the primary focus is on the narratives elicited themselves, rather than trying to determine the underlying beliefs they may or may not represent.[107]

Nonetheless, since narratives *can* reflect the attitude of narrators, for readers interested in what this study reveals about British attitudes to war, two features of narrative are worth looking out for. To recap, narratives are temporally, spatially, and causally connected sequences of events, selected and *evaluated* as meaningful for a particular audience. In other words, people do not just recount series of events; they evaluate them too. These evaluations explain the meaning of the story being told and the narrator's judgment of the characters involved.[108] Just as autobiographical narratives contain evaluations of one's actions in relation to moral and ethical assumptions, narratives about Britain involve moral and ethical evaluations of its actions as a nation-state.[109] Since attitudes are commonly defined as the 'categorisation of a stimulus along an evaluative dimension', evaluations within narratives can theoretically reflect attitudes.[110] Also, since stories are typically far more detailed than responses to survey questions, it could be argued that narrative methods provide a deeper understanding of the nuances of individual attitudes than surveys.

A further way attitudes can be revealed is through hypothetical narratives. As Carranza observes, people often combine stories about what has happened with hypothetical narratives about what might or should have happened in different circumstances.[111] A person recounting the fall from power of a political leader might add that 'had they listened to their constituents more they would not have been ousted'. Another might suggest that 'had they invested in the economy more, they may have stayed in power'. In each case, the hypothetical narratives, however limited, reveal what appears to be the narrator's attitude about the cause of the politician's fall. Similarly, the oft-repeated claim in British popular culture that 'had we not stood up to Hitler, we might all be speaking German right now', implies that Britain was particularly important to allied victory in the Second World War. These parallel accounts of what might have happened evaluate a narrative's events and characters and therefore can be used to infer an implicit attitude—or at least an attitude a narrator wishes to present themselves as having—even if it is not stated.[112] These alternative plots are also considered when analysing the stories citizens tell about Britain and war.

To summarise, the rationale behind this book is that to understand better how narratives might strategically persuade publics to support or oppose wars, it would be helpful to understand *how* individual citizens use narratives in the first place. This requires a narrative-specific methodology, sensitive to the subtle distinction between narrative and argument and the extent to which attitudes can be inferred from stories. To do this, the book adopts an analytical approach combining inductive, qualitative analysis of genre and emplotment: the general patterns of citizens' stories and the way they select and frame historical events to create those overall patterns. These were used with the intention of establishing a comprehensive range of interpretations of Britain's past, present, and future role in war, and to generate insights into the contested nature of British collective identity and memory across a diverse sample of British citizens. The remainder of the book presents its findings and what they reveal about perceptions of Britain's future military role in the world.

CHAPTER 2

Britain and the Banality of Continuous War

LEONARD (55–64, DORSET): I don't think war is any different from decorating your house. If you're going to make a change, why are you doing it, and what outcome do you want at the end?

An early impression when examining citizens' stories was that there is neither a generic national biography that encapsulates Britain's role in war nor infinite variation. Inductive analysis revealed a limited range of distinct interpretations of British military history, each of which portrayed Britain's international identity and role differently. People's stories diverge on who Britain is, who Britain fights, and how ethical Britain's wars have been.

In this way, public interpretations of war reflect the observations of both academics and policymakers that Britain lacks a coherent, 'hegemonic' narrative through which its military strategy can be explained.[1] Nevertheless, two recurrent assumptions across the sample were that Britain should seek to continue to play the role of a 'great power' and that military interventionism would enable it to do so.[2] This manifests itself in an enduring appetite for military strength even among those who oppose the use of force.

Few participants managed to articulate Britain's identity today, and many only explained roles it should play in general terms. Often people characterised Britain through what it was in the past or what it should be in the future. So while Britain, for example, is 'not what we were', 'not the power it once was', 'almost insignificant now', or should in the future 'set an example' of 'tolerance' and 'mediation', 'be less aggressive' or 'become great again', this was often not accompanied by a statement of who Britain is today. The difficulty in encapsulating Britain today could be seen as part of an oft-cited identity crisis in what it means to be British.[3] More importantly, it shows the significance of narrative in identity construction, since people are characterising Britain by explaining how it has changed (or not) over time.

Beyond the general idea of remaining a great power, there are notable similarities and differences across the sample in the general purpose of Britain's wars and perceptions of those Britain fights. Support for the use of military force varied greatly, from hawkish individuals who stated unequivocally that they always support every war Britain is involved in to pacifists who reject military force entirely. Some explained that war is 'often the only way of settling matters',[4] while others believe that 'probably 99 percent of the time . . . there are other ways'.[5] Still, the most commonly held view is that the main purpose of the military is defence. Polling consistently backs this up, with a 2009 National Army Museum poll finding that 70 percent of the British public felt that the primary function of the British Army was to defend home territory.[6] Even so, opinions on what exactly Britain must defend were diverse. Beyond a narrow focus on 'our shores', this included British citizens abroad; the country's way of life, values, and interests; freedom and democracy; Britain's allies; international human rights; 'those that cannot help themselves'; and 'those that ask for our help'. For many participants a solely defensive role of the military was more a theoretical ideal than actual reality. So while Bill (35–44, Yorkshire) explained that 'I think the fact that it's called the Ministry of Defence would wrap it up', Richard (65+, Worcestershire) countered that 'it's interesting that we call it the Ministry of Defence yet we seem to go out and attack'.

What exactly Britain needs to defend against is similarly varied and often vague. While some harbour fears of a resurgent Russia, Britain becoming an Islamic state, or even Germany completing a long-desired conquest of Europe, most recognise the observation made early in the 2008 and 2010 National Security Strategies that mainland Britain does not currently face an existential threat.[7] Instead, in the words of the sampled public, an international British military role is needed to protect Britain (and others) against 'malign influences', 'crackpots', 'dictators', 'lunatics', 'tyrants', 'extremists', and 'terrorists'. If Britain is the hero, these are the villains in citizens' tales of British military history.

Beyond domestic defence, responses reveal a wide range of additional military roles. These include peacekeeping, humanitarian assistance, crisis response, 'policing the world', 'defending freedom', maintaining a deterrent, supporting allies, and protecting human rights. Some are more about possessing a strong military than deploying it, including maintaining Britain's power, influence, or 'place at the top table' and ensuring the country is 'listened to'. As Fiona (18–24, London) states, 'to keep up on the world stage, having a strong military is pretty important, otherwise you kind of sink to the bottom'. These ideas confirm Gaskarth's observation that 'the capacity to exercise force has in itself huge symbolic value for an actor's authority and legitimacy' on the international stage.[8] This assumption is deeply embedded in citizens' narratives across the full spectrum of public interpretations of war.

These varied ideas of Britain's military role, mapped onto its multiple wars, provide thousands of combinations of building blocks out of which citizens' narratives could be constructed. But when asked to tell stories about Britain's role in war throughout history, people's narratives coalesce into a limited number of genres that convey general impressions of its past. Sometimes these revolve around an individual aspect of Britain's military history, such as the causes, conduct, or consequences of its wars. More often, though, citizens' stories consist of several interlocking storylines that are weaved together to create an overall pattern. This pattern conveys the identity claim at the heart of each story. This is why they can be termed 'identity narratives', because they make claims about who Britain is based on its military actions over time. The question is, how many variations of these shared stories are there and what claims about Britain's identity are encoded within them?

To answer this, the first stage of analysis was to try to disentangle these narrative strands to see if any are shared across the sample. Having identified these, analysis turned to uncovering differences in the way these stories are woven together to generate different interpretations of Britain's identity as a military actor over time. This process revealed two basic storylines that were found almost universally across participants. The first concerns a widespread impression that Britain is continuously at war, and has been throughout its history. This is termed the *Continuous War* narrative. It illustrates how, across the political spectrum, British citizens see war as a routine, everyday, almost banal activity—something Britain 'just does'. The second storyline that quickly emerged was that Britain's material capability is declining over time, making it less able to fight wars. This is termed the *Material Decline* narrative.

These are genres in their own right, since each possesses a clear general pattern. They also reveal much about how participants construct Britain's international identity. However, their main function in participants' narratives appears to be to provide a foundation of basic assumptions that people largely take for granted. As will be shown, when people narrate Britain's military history, they almost unanimously agree that it is continuously at war, but is less able to do so over time. However, they disagree widely about how Britain's wars should be *morally* evaluated. So while they may agree that Britain always seems to be at war, they disagree on whether this should continue. They may concur that Britain is less able to fight wars today, but differ on whether this is a good thing or not. These varied moral judgments produce very different claims about Britain's identity today and the role it should adopt in the future. Some see Britain's seemingly continuous war as the actions of an incomparably ethical power willing to sacrifice itself for the good of the world; others see it as an imperialist aggressor bent on economic exploitation.

These differences generated five overall genres. Each one makes a distinct claim about Britain's international identity, be it as a great power *Punching Above Its Weight*, a *Vanishing Force*, as *Learning from Its Mistakes*, as being *Led Astray*, or as a *Selfish Imperialist*. These narratives are explicated in full in chapters 4 and 5, but for reference they are summarised below. Note how the *Continuous War* and *Material Decline* storylines are embedded in each:

Punching Above Its Weight—Britain is continuously at war but has declined materially over time. However, it has always punched above its weight through its military compared to other countries and should continue to do so in the future.

Vanishing Force—Britain is continuously at war but has declined materially over time. This has eroded Britain's influence and it is no longer a great power. This should be reversed by future military investment to return Britain to greatness.

Learning from Its Mistakes—Britain is continuously at war but has declined materially over time. Britain's imperial wars were illegitimate and destructive but it is learning from past mistakes to use military force for the good of the world.

Led Astray—Britain is continuously at war but has declined materially over time. After illegitimate imperial wars, Britain was learning to use military force to do good but material decline has driven Britain to ally with the United States, which has led it astray. Acting more independently will enable Britain to be a force for good again.

Selfish Imperialist—Britain is continuously at war but has declined materially over time. These wars have invariably been illegitimate and economically motivated. Reduced military capability is positive if it makes Britain pursue peace rather than war, although this is not anticipated in the future.

The Continuous War Narrative

One of the most striking features of British citizens' war stories is how they portray war as ordinary, normal, almost banal. Wars have typically been treated as periods of exception, where ordinary political exchange is temporarily suspended.[9] On the contrary, across the political spectrum, participants narrated Britain's wars as a routine activity in which they expected Britain to participate at a given point in time. However positively or negatively people judge Britain's wars, they take for granted that it is always fighting them.

That people narrate British history as one of *Continuous War* is perhaps unsurprising given the historical record. Since 1914 there has not been a single year when the British military has not seen combat.[10] However, people's accounts suggest something more: that being persistently at war provides a daily reminder of what makes Britain morally exceptional compared to other nations.

Dennis (55–64, Worcestershire) exemplifies the *Continuous War* narrative when asked about the nature of Britain's role in the world. He narrates a linear story in which no matter what conflicts are happening globally, Britain always seems to be involved:

DENNIS: I think that Britain has taken on the role that comes from history of being involved in all the conflicts and major events, and I still think that whenever something happens Britain expects to be involved. So, you know, Ebola, they expect to be there, I suppose partly because it involves a colony that we used to have, but you know we expect to be involved in problems in the Middle East and in other places. So if there is a problem we expect to be there as one of the participants. And it's difficult at the moment to imagine a point when we would shrug our shoulders as a country and say 'not our problem, we won't get involved'.
RESEARCHER: Why is that do you think?
DENNIS: I think it's historical that we've always, for the last five hundred years, been involved in everything. Certainly in living memory for some people we were the dominant force in the world, and I think that

that hasn't stopped. I mean I don't know whether it will carry on or not, but yeah, I think that's probably why people in Britain expect to be involved in everything. But certainly it's what happens. . . . I think the truth of the matter is, you know, in my lifetime it's been what Britain does, and I've never really questioned it. You just expect Britain to be involved in all sorts of things that are happening.

Dennis's narrative conveys continuity in Britain going to war in a number of ways. He begins by explaining that throughout history there is an ongoing expectation that Britain should play a role in all major events. Explaining that this has been the case for at least half a millennium, the plot includes examples such as the Ebola crisis and 'problems in the Middle East'. He then finishes by repeating the original assertion that it is simply expected that Britain is always involved. Perhaps most notably, he explains that he cannot imagine this not being the case, and that he has 'never really questioned' it. For Dennis, Britain is always at war, and he does not expect any different.

Since Dennis is seeking to convey continuity, his story lacks the conventional narrative features of beginning, middle, and end—of initial situation, plot disruption, and resolution. It lacks a clear start point, containing only the general statement that British interventionism has been the case for 'certainly the last five hundred years'. It is remarkably undramatic. Indeed, Dennis's account could be seen to resemble argument more closely, in that he makes a claim about the nature of British history—that it is characterised by continuous war—and supports this with examples.[11]

However, just because a narrative trajectory is continuous, is based on a generalisation, or lacks overt drama, does not mean that it is not a narrative. Stories can be told in order to demonstrate ongoing traits, be it dependability, trustworthiness, or in this case bellicosity. Such stories will inevitably be less dramatic because the whole point is to convey the *absence* of change. Dennis's account is still a narrative; it merely has lower *narrativity* than accounts with a more dramatic narrative arc.[12] In fact, the story contains an animate protagonist (Britain) as well as temporal and causal links. The events selected are not temporally linked in terms of occurring one after the other. Instead they are separately linked to a thread running throughout the story: that for centuries Britain has 'been involved in everything'. The causal logic is vague but it is nonetheless present, explaining that Britain participates in so many conflicts because of an 'expectation' that it should do so.

Furthermore, drama is arguably implicit in the individual conflicts about which Dennis's story generalises. In suggesting that 'if there is a problem we expect to be there', he implies that when disruptions to the world order occur, Britain is the hero who is always compelled to try and resolve them. In this way, Dennis's account most closely represents a 'habitual' narrative, as he explains what Britain's role typically is in international dramas such as wars.[13]

The power of habitual narratives is that in generalising about the way things are, they are harder to challenge. Dennis could easily have included alternative conflicts in British history, or perhaps named none at all, without undermining his central point. As Nigel (35–44, Yorkshire) summarised, 'we've been there. Where have we not been? In every . . . most conflicts throughout time we've had a role to play in it, rightly or wrongly. But in most instances we've been there'.

Overall, the key point that marks out Dennis's account as more narrative than argument is that he does not argue deductively from general principles: he selects particular events in history, creating a coherent (if limited) framework of meaning into which they fit. He makes a claim about the nature of British military history but does so through *narration*.

The fact that Britain being at war is simply expected reveals the extent to which it is taken for granted. Supposedly this interventionist imperative 'comes from history', as if guided by some universal, timeless logic. It is just 'what Britain does' and, most tellingly, Dennis has 'never really questioned it'. This suggests a strongly mythological element to this understanding of war. Myths are defined here as symbolic stories told by a society that illuminate its key values.[14] They shape what is unquestioned or treated as common sense in a particular culture.[15] For Dennis, as with so many other participants, continuous war is normal, routine, expected. As Emma (35–44, Birmingham) confirms: 'we always seem to be in the middle of it. It just always seems that we're the ones that feel that we can take on the world, as if we're like a . . . sort of superpower I suppose'.

Clues as to what exactly 'comes from history' to drive Britain to war can be gleaned from the narratives of other participants:

> ISOBEL (45–54, WALES): I think, worryingly, that we seem to have been involved in so many conflicts. Thinking of trying to build a British Empire, as it were, and that again involves going into other people's countries, like in India and places over the years. I think that's the worrying thing about British history. We seem to have been involved in a lot of conflicts over so many years, you know. We always do seem to be involved. And I don't know whether that's good or bad.

GRACE (55–64, WORCESTERSHIRE): Well, I mean obviously over several centuries there was the imperialist drive, and people going out adventuring, wanting to conquer other lands, then having to subdue them once they'd conquered them. I think in more recent times there are a number of reasons. It might have been partly to do with wanting to be seen as big players on the world stage, and I think possibly also a certain amount of sleight of hand by other powers.

NIGEL (35–44, YORKSHIRE): Some nations tend to get involved more than others. I don't know, it's weird. You don't see South American nations getting involved in things. They've got militaries, do they get involved? Why do we have to get involved with everything all the time? I'm not sure. We tend to.

RESEARCHER: Why do you think that is?

NIGEL: I think it's because historically we've been . . . I don't know how to put this . . . a force. And we still think we are. . . . I think because we were the empire that we were, we seemed to be involved in every war that was waged around the world. And that's probably why we still think we need to get involved in every other war that's happening around the world.

In each of these accounts, Britain's tendency to 'get involved with everything all the time' is largely a product of its imperial past. It is this 'imperial hangover' that has left Britain seeking to use military interventionism to maintain the impression of ongoing global influence. Significantly, both Nigel and Isobel imply opposition or at least concern with Britain's continued great power pretensions, but these evaluations flow from the shared underlying story in which Britain is always involved.

These accounts are consistent with the dominant assumptions in the foreign policy literature that Britain's imperial past drives its persistent interventionism today, both through a material desire for continued power and influence and a perceived moral obligation to uphold international security.[16] They also show that British military interventionism is not just an elite preoccupation but is taken for granted by many citizens too. Edmunds explains that British defence policy is 'unambiguous in its acceptance of a role for military interventionism in British foreign and security policy'.[17] However, he also claims that interventionism reflects the desires of political elites rather than the public, the latter of whom are 'disengaged from elite strategic discourse' and 'sceptical of the efficacy of military force'.[18] In contrast, citizens' stories here support the contention of Rogers and Eyal that British military interventionism is certainly 'not an invention of the country's politicians alone'.[19] There appears to be 'a remarkable public consensus' about Britain maintaining an expeditionary military role in the world.[20] While some participants did question the efficacy of military intervention, few challenged the principle that war is an 'acceptable extension of national policy'.[21]

While it is almost impossible to determine all the influences on a given story an individual tells, it is worth reflecting on the extent to which the *Continuous War* narrative would have been as prevalent were this study conducted at a different time and place. Since the end of the Cold War and particularly during the Blair administration, one can trace an almost continuous stream of British military interventions, from the Gulf War, Yugoslavia, Kosovo, Sierra Leone, Afghanistan, Iraq (2003), Libya, Mali, to Iraq once more, and now Syria. In comparison, during the 1970s, Britain was involved in far fewer military interventions, and there was extensive debate about whether the military had an international role at all.[22] In a different time period, therefore, the idea of Britain being continuously at war might not have been so prevalent.

Another explanation for the prevalence of the *Continuous War* narrative concerns two ideological influences in recent years. The first is what has been described as the 'Blair doctrine', in which the former Labour prime minister portrayed a world in which increasingly globalised threats and vulnerabilities require extensive, global military interventionism.[23] As Gaskarth notes, particularly under New Labour, 'the capacity and willingness to use force were seen as a major factor in the continuance of Britain's status as a major international actor'.[24] This viewpoint perpetuates the idea of war as a foreign policy necessity.[25]

The second ideological influence is the recent dominance of what Hodges and others term the 'War on Terror' narrative.[26] Since 9/11, the threat of international terrorism has been portrayed as a long-lasting, epochal threat, and war has come to be framed in an increasingly boundless way.[27] The idea of perpetual war is reflected in Western discourse on terrorism, even if strategic communication practitioners have discarded the 'War on Terror' and 'Long War' monikers themselves.[28] This interpretation creates a permanent state of exception to combat what is depicted as an enduring, existential threat. Since people can only narrate the past from the perspective of the present, the current perception of a continuous state of war is likely to influence judgments about this being a natural state of affairs further back in British history. In Britain, decades of exposure to the threat of terrorism related to the Northern Ireland conflict adds to the sense of continuity in comparison to other states.

The stories elicited here suggest that the *Continuous War* narrative has even deeper foundations. Dennis, for example, generalises that the story has been the same for five hundred years, while others go back to William the Conqueror, or even the Britons' resistance against the Roman invasion, when explaining why Britain is always at war. As Grace (55–64, Worcestershire) explains, 'I think in many ways we're a country founded on conflict. There's probably nobody in this country who doesn't trace their ancestry back to some sort of conqueror or other'. Such accounts appear to confirm Paris's finding that the idea that Britain is a 'warrior nation' is deeply embedded in popular culture.[29] Moreover, in contrast to the 'War on Terror' narrative, these accounts portray ongoing war not as a permanent 'state of exception' but more as a 'state of normality'. It may therefore be more accurate to switch the analysis around and suggest that the normalisation of Britain being continuously at war is precisely why the Blair Doctrine and the War on Terror narratives were subsequently so resonant.

General Causes of War

An even broader explanation participants give for Britain's constant fighting is that war is human nature rather than a particularly British phenomenon. Susan (55–64, Oxfordshire) and Mary (35–44, Dorset) exemplify this interpretation in their responses to being asked to 'tell a story of Britain's historical role in war and conflict'. Their responses show that some participants can produce far more detailed stories, but the same underlying logics persist:

> SUSAN: There's been a lot of fighting over the years, hasn't there when you think about it. It's gone on all through history. How our modern royal family started back in 1066, with a battle. Everything changes with a battle, doesn't it? All different kings and queens and entering different wars seemed to be what they were at most of the time, trying to increase their territory or take another throne, or very keen to quickly raise an army and march on somewhere else. And then I suppose I mean that was all hand-to-hand fighting early on, and then the weapons got more sophisticated, guns were brought in, and the Spanish Armada, the Na-

poleonic wars, and finally bringing us up to the world wars. We've always been right there haven't we, fighting something.

RESEARCHER: Why do you think that is?

SUSAN: Human nature I suppose. Everybody wanting a bit more territory or not wanting somebody else to take your territory. Perhaps we should be more inclined to discuss these things these days rather than fighting over them.

MARY: The story is, we've been constantly involved in war and conflict for hundreds of years. It used to be to do with us expanding our empire, so it was over territory. For me, if you look at things simply, we're just little kind of furry mammals running around the world and we're battling over territory and resources . . . whether that's oil, gas, could be water in the future. . . . Basically Britain has constantly been at war, sending off what used to be just their young men but now it's their young women as well. We've been doing that constantly for hundreds of years.

As with Dennis, the trajectories of Susan's and Mary's narratives are those of continuous war. Susan initially suggests repeated war might be a particularly British phenomenon, citing seminal wars and battles in British history as examples of Britain specifically 'always being right there . . . fighting something'. Mary does not emplot specific wars, though she does reference the empire. Instead the causal linkage in both stories is based on the generalisations that, 'if you look at things simply', *wars are human nature* and are *fought for resources.* The temporal flow in Susan's story concerns changes in the technology used, while in Mary's it involves the steady change over time in which resources are fought over—from territory, to oil, gas, and perhaps water in the future. But in both cases there is continuity in the general cause of Britain's fighting. Again this is a simplification; if one examined the purpose of each of Britain's wars, one would not see such a neat pattern. However, the intuitiveness of war being fought for resources is such that observers read it into wars where resources were of peripheral importance originally, such as Afghanistan in 2001 or Kosovo in 1999.[30]

These generalisations that war is human nature can be described as a form of 'folk realism', portraying a Hobbesian world in which conflict is inevitable and normal.[31] This logic is significant because future change is not anticipated—if the world is one of continuous conflict over scarce resources, there is no reason to expect change. Such a story would have no clear beginning, middle, and end, just a continuous stream of inevitable conflict. At a more granular level, one could see the story as punctuated by a series of dramas provided by the individual wars in question. In this way, what appears as a continuous stream of violence could also be categorised as a cycle of one war after another, as Tim (35–44, London) explains:

> TIM: When you get to my age you tend to see stories repeating themselves over and over and over. The places and maybe the people change, but the central story is still the same, and events keep on happening over and over and over.
> RESEARCHER: And what sort of story is it?
> TIM: Group A, for whatever reason, has some conflict with Group B, and for whatever reason they just can't resolve it in an amicable way and it leads to conflict. It might be a fight over resources, it might be a fight over religion, territory. It's usually around those main three. These are the themes that seem to keep coming up.

Whether Britain's military story is one of continuous war or a cycle of repeated wars is a semantic debate. The impression of ongoing war is, after all, derived from Britain fighting a succession of overlapping conflicts. As the 'War on Terror' demonstrates, it may also reflect the nature of twenty-first-century war, which is characterised by ongoing, sporadic conflicts blurring together across time and space.[32] What matters is that across the sample, Britain being continuously at war is normalised, even though many other states clearly do not share this 'hyper-interventionism'.[33] From this folk-realist perspective, Britain is not abnormally militaristic; it is acting understandably given the nature of the world.

War being human nature is one of several basic assumptions people use to explain why Britain is continuously at war. But only some interviewees constructed reasonably detailed narratives to explain this. Others tended to state the general assumption without providing further detail. A particularly prominent example that Tim brought up is that war is caused by religion, echoing Cavanaugh's assertion that this myth is particularly prevalent in Western culture.[34] This explanation was common in interviewees' initial responses to being asked about the first things that come to mind when thinking about war. Kenneth (55–64, Liverpool) described religion as 'probably the cause of all war'. For

Joanne (55–64, Dorset), religion 'has been the biggest enemy of man and caused the most conflict of anything ever, outside of perhaps the Second World War'. Olive (65+, Oxfordshire) explained that 'I don't think there's ever been a conflict that hasn't been a religious one really, at the root of it'. These statements were not elaborated upon, potentially because their authors considered them common sense and no more detail was needed.

When participants did expand on why they saw religion as a cause of war, they tended not to blame Britain. Instead they portrayed Britain as stepping in to resolve conflicts that irrational religious Others had started. While Islamist terrorists are a predictably common frame of reference in recent years, for many citizens Northern Ireland represents an equally strong reference point for Britain's intervention in irrational religious conflict. In participants' words, religious wars are fought by 'lunatics', 'fanatics', or 'fundamentalists' who are 'harder to fight against' and beyond negotiation or reason.

> SEBASTIAN (65+, WALES): You may as well throw the rulebook out of the window when you bring religion into wars. . . . There is no logic, it seems to me, that you can bring to the negotiating table, that would come to a peaceful resolution for that sort of conflict.

In contrast, Britain's continuous interventionism is framed as a morally legitimate and enlightened response to the irrationality of others. In Joanne's (55–64, Dorset) words, Britain works with its allies to 'stop letting religion get in the way of common sense and safety'. These findings support Cavanaugh's observations that

> in foreign policy, the myth of religious violence serves to cast non-secular social orders, especially Muslim societies, in the role of villain. They have not yet learned to remove the dangerous influence of religion from political life. Their violence is therefore irrational and fanatical. Our violence, being secular, is rational, peace-making and sometimes regrettably necessary to contain their violence. We find ourselves obliged to bomb them to liberal democracy.[35]

Participants with more detailed knowledge of the British Empire acknowledge that Britain has imposed Christianity on others in the past. However, consistent with secular, liberal meta-narratives, it has apparently progressed beyond others so that it is no longer driven by the destructive forces of mysticism and fanaticism. Once more, though, whether war is the right response is unquestioned; it is accepted as a just response to the irrational violence of others.

Generalisations that all wars are caused by religion are easily discredited with greater knowledge of the historical record. Three of the five most cited wars across the sample—the First World War, the Second World War, and the Falklands War—are rarely if ever attributed to religion. Some participants had more nuanced understandings of the role of religion in war, suggesting that it was 'an excuse' for war rather than its cause. Validating the diversity of the sample, some even rejected the idea that religion had caused any war, arguing as Mark (65+, Birmingham) did that 'religion's got nothing to do with fighting . . . because if you've got any religious feelings at all you don't believe in fighting anyway. Let alone killing people'. As Grace (55–64, Worcestershire) put it, 'I don't by any means think that <u>all</u> wars are attributable to religion, and anybody who says that has never read a history book'.

The point here is that for participants across the political spectrum, the generalisation that religion causes war seems to be common sense. Those taking this for granted may never have given it significant thought. Consequently, they may never have sought evidence to support it. Even if they do possess supporting knowledge they may feel no need to provide it because the assumption seems obvious—what Swidler describes as a 'natural, transparent, undeniable part of the structure of the world'.[36] As Joanne (55–64, Dorset) simply asserts, 'well ever since the Crusades and God knows what else it's all been about religion, hasn't it'.

These uncritical generalisations demonstrate how those with limited knowledge of specific conflicts understand war using a limited range of myths and analogies. The rise and fall of the British Empire, for example, might be explained by the folk wisdom that 'what goes up must come down'.[37] Generic assumptions about human nature, religion, and natural resources as the cause of all wars reflect Hoggart's observations in his famous analysis of the British working classes. As he explains, people may appear to have views on political issues but they usually consist of

> a bundle of largely unexamined and orally-transmitted tags, enshrining generalisations, prejudices and half-truths, and elevated by epigrammatic phrasing into the status of maxims. . . . These are often contradictory of each other; but they are not thought about, not intellectually considered.[38]

These sweeping statements about war are not narratives as such, although by generalising about the causes of human behaviour *over time* it could be argued that they possess a temporal element that imbues them with a degree of narrativity. Even though an individual may be alluding to a narrative in stating the phrase, its content and form are not self-evident. The statement that 'wars are fought for natural resources' implies a continuous story throughout history. But different stories might be told to back this up, perhaps emphasising that their importance has varied over time. Such statements are better thought of as arguments about general causes of human behaviour that people then support using narratives of varying coherence and detail. The underlying assumptions remain vital, though, since they provide heuristics through which people interpret new conflicts as they arise.

Moral Exceptionalism and the 'Warrior Nation'

The plot of the *Continuous War* narrative conveys the general pattern that British history is an ongoing stream of conflict; but what does this story reveal about how citizens construct Britain's international identity? This question can be answered by analysing how citizens construct the characters whose actions create the plot's general pattern: Britain, its military, its enemies, and its potential allies in the international system.

Analysing these characters reveals that Britain—the story's protagonist—is typically portrayed as morally exceptional in its willingness to go to war compared to others. As Jacobs and Sobieraj argue, when people tell stories they simplify characters into binaries, casting themselves as heroes and opponents as villains to legitimise themselves and delegitimise the Other.[39] Unsurprisingly, the central binaries in people's war stories are Britain and those it fights, although there is certainly disagreement over how far Britain has been the hero or the villain throughout its history. As chapter 6 will explain, Britain is overwhelmingly portrayed as a *Force for Good*, at least in its intentions, particularly compared to the 'dictators' and 'tyrants' against whom it fights.[40] However, a small minority of participants oppose Britain's wars on principle, casting Britain as a *Selfish Imperialist* rather than a hero (see chapter 5). Independent of this, when participants agree that a given crisis calls for the use of military force, Britain is overwhelmingly cast heroically in comparison with morally inferior countries less willing to use force to defend the liberal order.

As Kinnvall explains, 'the construction of self and other is . . . almost always a way to define superior and inferior beings'.[41] Participant narratives appear to confirm the observation that a corollary of the 'expeditionary culture' within Britain is that people look down on others less willing to use military force.[42]

A notable example of this was a comparison of interventionist Britain with stereotypically neutral Switzerland. This was an unexpected comparison, particularly since polls that ask British citizens for their views on a predetermined list of countries have frequently excluded Switzerland, presumably because researchers may not have assumed it significant.[43] As stated previously, one of the novel aspects of this study's methodology was that rather than asking people about specific countries or conflicts, open questioning enabled them to bring up those *they* considered important. While the most frequent comparisons were with the United States, and Europe in general, the Swiss comparison reveals much about how military interventionism is portrayed as positive and uniquely British, with neutrality morally inferior in comparison. Sebastian's (65+, Wales) explanation of what he sees as Britain's role in the world illustrates this:

SEBASTIAN: I'm not sure what [Britain's] role is . . . in my view . . . I've just had a flash of Switzerland, you know, sitting there being neutral and everything, and I can't quite see Britain transforming into that sort of society overnight. . . . I suppose it's quite nice to have a couple of gangs of boys that can join in and keep our place at the table. I really would rather it wasn't necessary at all.

When prompted to elaborate, he continued:

SEBASTIAN: I suppose people who don't think about these things a lot, which is sort of me I think . . . when they think 'neutral', they think Switzerland. They don't tend to think of anywhere else. There are probably loads of other neutral places. And after the Second World War, the concept of Switzerland had a bit of a nasty taste to it because they seemed to be sitting back quite nicely, raking in all the money. And okay, they offered asylum to numbers of people. There was not a great deal of rightness in their concept of being neutral, so it's a difficult concept to imagine what being neutral would be like, with only the Swiss to go with.

This exchange demonstrates several salient points about British interventionism. While Sebastian does not clearly evaluate Britain's military role, his brief narrative about Switzerland during the Second World War paints neutrality as selfish and lacking 'rightness' in comparison. He also considers neutrality as intrinsic to Swiss culture and not just a policy decision. It is a 'sort of society' that he cannot imagine Britain ever becoming. Neutrality is thereby portrayed as inherently Swiss, while military interventionism is by implication inherently British. That a more neutral stance would require 'societal change' demonstrates Sebastian's perception of the importance of military interventionism to British national identity. If true, it explains why there is so much disquiet at the idea of Britain withdrawing from an active military role in the world. His explanation of Britain's need to 'keep our place at the table' reiterates that Britain's military interventionism is a necessary condition of great power status. His follow-up that 'I really would rather it wasn't necessary' reveals a preference for a world without the need for military strength, but more interestingly it shows that the need to do so is taken for granted. Neutrality on the other hand is unnatural, sedentary, immoral, un-British. As Joanne (55–64, Dorset) bluntly states when asked about the importance of possessing a strong military:

JOANNE: I think if you want to remain a country that believes in right and wrong, and that wants to be able to help people that can't help themselves, then it's quite important. But if you just want to be a Switzerland, then get rid of it and put the money into something else.

While the Swiss comparison is instructive for its juxtaposition of neutrality and interventionism, Europe was most often chosen as being particularly pacific or indecisive compared to Britain. Consider the following examples from Florence (55–64, Oxfordshire) and Stephen (65+, Birmingham):

FLORENCE: I think as a nation, my understanding . . . we seem to have engaged in conflict where we have felt we have almost been pushed to the limit where we could no longer ignore the situation. So it's either been in defence of our country, or it's been in defence of some high moral standpoint. I wouldn't in my view call us a war-mongering nation. I don't think we're war-mongering, or are we? Nor are we like Sweden or other European countries. Nor are we afraid to get involved.

STEPHEN: Europe is very lukewarm, <u>very</u> lukewarm on military in my book. . . . If we'd got a decent European army and everyone pulled together, we'd be pretty good I reckon. But we've got so many nationalities—I don't know how many there are in Europe, 20 odd countries probably, and I'm afraid they're not inclined to go out militarily, most of them. There are a few. In fact our better ones are people like the Commonwealth, Australia, Canada, New Zealand. They will help. Yeah, I'd like to see a stronger military I have to say.

Florence tells a generalised story in which Britain's repeated conflicts have been defensive and thus morally justified. She then seeks to position Britain's military interventionism in a moral position between overly aggressive 'warmongers' and overly pacific European countries such as Sweden that are 'afraid' to act. Stephen meanwhile generalises that many European nations lack the inclination for war, unlike 'better' nations who are more willing to help Britain such as Australia, Canada, and New Zealand. These Anglophone and former Commonwealth states are consistently viewed more favourably by British citizens according to polling data.[44] Because these nation-states were largely formed out of migrants from the British Isles, they tend to be included in the idea that the Anglosphere above all others is the protector of the liberal order.[45]

As well as characterising other nations as more faint-hearted than Britain, another explanation for why Britain is always at war is that other powers take advantage of its unique moral conscience. This is borne out by Emma's (35–44, Birmingham) response when asked her opinion about Britain and military intervention.

EMMA: I think it's good that [Britain's] doing it. Obviously if other countries are in need of help and they haven't got the resources themselves then, you know, if our troops can do that, fine. But are other countries helping as much as us who are perhaps in a strong position? Are the countries themselves who are having our help, are they trying to help themselves? You know, is it equally balanced or is it taking advantage of our good nature really and our resources, financially.

The series of questions Emma asks are not narrative as such. But in the context of the *Continuous War* narrative, they show how the 'good-natured' central character (Britain) is juxtaposed with others less willing to contribute.

These may not be the villains against whom Britain fights, but they are morally inferior for failing to pull their weight. Again, the principle that Britain *should* intervene is accepted uncritically, the only debate being its relative contribution compared to others.

The notions that Europeans are militarily and morally inferior, and that Britain is contributing disproportionately and is therefore being 'taken advantage of', have both featured in debates concerning Brexit and the related negotiations. Media commentary on negotiations in the initial months after the Brexit vote frequently used the metaphor of a card game, with the hope that Europe may 'fold' if Britain stands strong, just as it did against the Germans in 1940.[46] The idea that Britain invests in the EU while receiving little in return was played on successfully by the Leave campaign before the referendum, where it was claimed that Britain was sending £350 million a week to Europe while ignoring that Britain's rebate made the true figure much lower.[47] Indeed the assumption of Britain being taken advantage of was sufficiently strong that, paradoxically, the strongest votes for Brexit came in areas most economically dependent on the EU.[48]

The persistence of these assumptions in the face of contradictory evidence reveals the power of myths to trump facts. One of the most common descriptions of Britain's international military role across the sample was that of the world's 'peacekeeper'. This might seem reasonable given that in 1995 Britain was the leading contributor to UN peacekeeping missions. As of March 2016 it was 53rd globally, deploying fewer than 300 troops worldwide.[49] No participants seemed aware of this, however, instead assuming that Britain contributes more than other countries.

For some participants the assumption that Britain 'stands alone' in its unique willingness to intervene to help others means that they appear wholly unaware that Britain has fought alongside others in recent military interventions.

MEGAN (65+, OXFORDSHIRE): I do feel sometimes it's the British troops that go into other countries to help fight their war, when I'm thinking 'where are other countries?' They don't ever seem to be mentioned. Whether it's the reporting of the war I don't know. Where are the French, the Germans, the Dutch? We hear about America going to war or pulling out, because they pulled out of Afghanistan much earlier than we did, and I thought 'thanks'. They left us to it.

Megan's account makes claims that would be revealed to be false with further knowledge. Asking where the French, Germans, and Dutch are ignores their active (though less prominent) role in the International Security Assistance Force (ISAF) mission in Afghanistan. Her statement that America pulled out of Afghanistan before the British is false, given that America retains an extensive military presence in the country and still had combat troops there at the time of the interview.[50] She does make an interesting point about the reporting of Britain's wars, which tends to emphasise British independence and leadership while downplaying collaboration or reliance on other countries.[51] As Wallace notes, Britain's cooperation with the French has been extensive in recent years and is a laudable diplomatic achievement. Nonetheless, the importance of independent military capability to British national pride means that this cooperation is marginalised by the government and mainstream media as it means admitting needing the help of others.[52] Instead the stronger impression is that Britain stands on its own in its willingness to aid others. For Sophie (18–24, London) this is obvious: 'if they don't then kind of who will?'

These accounts support the mythological notion that an inescapable, deep moral impulse prevents the British people from being able to turn away from those in need. Florence (55–64, Oxfordshire) explains this impulse even more clearly when asked when military force should be used:

FLORENCE: I believe there does come a point where there's something so insanely inhumane and cruel going on somewhere that we can't in all honesty and in all faith, stand by and see something so shocking happening to people. But then again, there seem in the world to be so many instances of that that I don't know quite how our resources could stretch to it. But I do think there is something about, as a nation, being unable to stand by and watch unimaginable suffering and, you know, oppression occurring somewhere. We can at least express ourselves through intervention.

Florence articulates well the dilemmas British people supposedly face when it comes to intervention abroad. While she implies that 'defending our shores' is fairly obvious, she also claims that Britain is simply incapable of being able to stand by (unlike others) and let bad things happen to people. Again, there is no question that Britain should play such a role; the only issue is whether 'our resources could stretch to it'. From this perspective, Britain is continuously at war because of the 'many instances' of atrocities and inhumanity that oblige it to repeatedly intervene. Britain is a *Force for Good* in a world so full of conflict that it cannot avoid trying to help even if it wanted to. Even though many state that the ideal British role might be mediation rather than military action, the nature of the world requires that it step in.

Continuous War and British Ontological Security

The suggestion that Britain constantly goes to war because of a deep-seated moral compulsion implies that the *Continuous War* narrative provides British citizens with a sense of ontological security. To recap, ontological security theorists posit that humans possess an inherent desire to maintain a consistent sense of self, particularly in challenging situations.[53] They achieve this by telling stories that portray continuity in their identities over time.[54] In theory, the most difficult situations to explain are those when their actions, or those of others, undermine this sense of identity, causing anxiety.[55] As Linde suggests,

> the most problematic areas in the national life story are those for which the nation has no generally accepted formulation of what happened and how it can be seen as the story of the actions of a good people.[56]

By implication, to understand the significance of the *Continuous War* narrative to Britain's international identity, the most informative examples are likely to be those where Britain has threatened to disrupt this narrative by nonintervention. This can be assessed by analysing how participants evaluate the wars contained in their stories. Narratives do not just consist of selected sequences of events; these events are *evaluated* as the plot progresses. These evaluations generate the overall pattern of the story; one cannot identify continuity, progress, or decline without evaluating whether the focus of the story is improving, deteriorating, or staying the same. If the *Continuous War* narrative is significant because it shows that the British perceive themselves as being uniquely compelled to intervene militarily to help others, then decisions not to intervene potentially undermine this narrative identity claim.

A particularly notable example in participant interviews was the parliamentary decision not to intervene in Syria in 2013. If it were true that the British are continuously at war because they are 'simply incapable' of letting atrocities take place, then there would have been unanimous public support for intervention in Syria rather than the overwhelming opposition that there was at the time. The decision not to intervene was heralded as an isolationist shift in British foreign policy. Indeed some participants here expressed relief about nonintervention in Syria, seeing it as 'something new' (Mabel, 55–64, Scotland), a 'proud moment' (Lily, 18–24, London) that showed that Britain had learnt from the mistakes of Iraq and Afghanistan not to intervene in costly foreign conflicts. The subsequent complexity of the Syrian war then reinforced the judgment that Britain was right to stay out of it. Nonintervention appeared to rupture the *Continuous War* narrative, with Britain stepping back rather than charging in.

This was far from the dominant view in this study though. Far more participants drew the lesson that earlier, more decisive action would have been preferable, as it is now 'far too late' to help. Across the sample a variety of people expressed regret and frustration that with 'so much suffering and misery being caused', Britain in hindsight 'should have done something' and 'needed to intervene'. Indeed Syria was the most cited conflict when interviewees were asked about wars in which Britain should have intervened but didn't. Despite the likelihood that many expressing these views would have opposed intervention at the time, responses ranged from remorse to outright anger that Britain dithered, rather than stepping in resolutely when others were unwilling. As Joanne (55–64, Dorset) vents, 'I'm very angry about Syria. Nobody really helped. When people are being slaughtered and tortured for no reason . . . I get very angry when we don't do something more quickly'. Instead Britain has had to passively observe unimaginable suffering without being able to exert meaningful influence on the conflict. Having been concerned previously that 'our conscience pushes us too far' (Vincent, 65+, Lancashire), Britain seems to be 'backing off when we should be there, because we don't want to get our fingers burnt again' (Daisy, 65+, Worcestershire). This hesitancy, brought on by exhaustion after Iraq and Afghanistan, has left Britain in a situation 'where we won't do something where maybe we ought to' (Grace, 55–64, Worcestershire).

These responses suggest that nonintervention in Syria in 2013 may have not just disrupted the *Continuous War* narrative but also undermined Britain's ontological security as a state that is uniquely willing to use its military to help others. Standing by and watching the suffering of Syrian civilians has fostered shame among its citizens that Britain should have done more to help.[57]

The desire to intervene to help is interesting because it stands in contrast to widespread appreciation among participants that doing so might not be strate-gically beneficial. If people think Britain should use military force to help oth-ers, it is logical to assume that they believe that it can achieve humanitarian benefits. The general utility of force is broadly accepted across the spectrum of British citizens. As in elite foreign policy discourse, the main terms of the de-bate rarely concern whether Britain *should* intervene, but on how to do so and whether Britain can afford it.[58] Few question the principle of military interven-tion itself.

That said, a wide range of citizens expressed concern about the efficacy of military intervention in recent conflicts. With British air power deployed against Islamic State in Syria in recent years, nonintervention in 2013 seems like a minor blip in the *Continuous War* narrative rather than a turning point. Yet it does appear to reflect public recognition that military intervention has proved ineffective in achieving benefits for vulnerable populations recently. Britons have observed prolonged wars in Afghanistan, Iraq, and Libya and their effects on the current strategic situation Britain faces. They appear to understand well the complexity of many recent conflicts in the sense that 'getting rid of despotic dictators with your military force may end up creating more problems'.[59] As Danielle (35–44, London) comments on Syria:

DANIELLE: You see a country whose people are being absolutely repressed and destroyed and divided, and if it was as cut and dry as there was some baddie holed up in a house somewhere then I'd say 'yeah, take him out'. But as we can see with the Taliban, that doesn't work really, because yes, in a sense we took down Saddam Hussein and Osama Bin Laden, but it hasn't really made a blind bit of difference. If anything it might have got a bit worse.

The example of nonintervention in Syria thus demonstrates a tension onto-logical security theorists have identified between actions undertaken to main-tain one's physical security and actions to maintain one's sense of identity.[60] A number of participants appear conflicted between the desire for Britain be seen as a country who helps others with the recognition that military intervention in Syria might be counterproductive. Resolving this does not necessarily suggest an end to the *Continuous War* narrative, merely a shift in the scale of the inter-ventions through which its plot is sustained.

To conclude, while citizens evaluate Britain's military role differently, they commonly narrate British history as a story of *Continuous War*. This typically takes the form of a parsimonious narrative which explains that when conflicts occur, it is routinely expected that Britain steps in to try and resolve them. This story typically possesses low narrativity; there is a clear general pattern but few narrative structures. Partly this is because narratives aiming to convey continuity over time inherently lack the plot twists and drama created by moments of change. It also seems that because participants see Britain's involvement in war as so ordinary and common sense they feel little need to provide much detail.

The nature of Britain's interventions and the extent of public support vary from one conflict to another. Nonetheless, across a diverse sample of the British public, citizens appear to take Britain's regular use of military force for granted, unquestionably assuming it to be a legitimate and natural instrument of policy, something Britain 'just does'. The normalcy of British military intervention is partly a product of the country's interventionist historical record, but participants also explain it as due to an obligation to intervene deriving from Britain's imperial past. Some see continuous war as not just a peculiarly British phenomenon but the general product of a world characterised by conflict because of human nature, religion, or the quest to control natural resources. A further ideological influence on perceptions of continuous war is the sense of an enduring state of exception engendered by what might still be termed the War on Terror.[61]

Most crucially, though, closer examination reveals that the *Continuous War* narrative is significant to British identity because it portrays Britain as a morally exceptional 'warrior nation' in its willingness and capability to intervene compared to others. In this respect, the *Continuous War* narrative could be seen as portraying military intervention as a form of what Michael Billig terms 'banal nationalism': an everyday, habitual reminder of what differentiates Britain from other nations.[62] Military intervention is a routine activity that enables British citizens to maintain a consistent sense of self or ontological security over time, even if other things change. Disrupting this routine through nonintervention risks undermining the ontological security of the many who see going to war as 'a necessary and inescapable function' of who Britain is and how it acts.[63] Even participants who see military interventions as increasingly ineffective or oppose them on principle nonetheless anticipate that Britain will continue to undertake them in the future. They may not agree with war, but they expect it.

This reflects the power of the *Continuous War* narrative. It appears to be sufficiently deeply culturally embedded that it fixes the terms of British defence policy. This explains De Waal's comment that reexamining whether Britain should continue to go to war 'risk[s] being treated as an attempt to overturn 1000 years of British history, rather than as a normal and natural fact of political life'.[64]

Regardless of how strongly citizens accept the *Continuous War* narrative, it is not the only understanding of Britain's wars that they share. They tell another story almost universally: that Britain is steadily losing the material capacity to exert meaningful influence on contemporary conflicts. This narrative concerns not Britain's tendency to use its military but its capability of performing this historically (self-) ordained role. It is the narrative of Britain's *Material Decline.*

CHAPTER 3

Britain's Material Decline

Small Island Syndrome

NICHOLAS (45–54, LANCASHIRE): We may be rubbish and we can't make things anymore, but at least we can go abroad and kill people efficiently.

No account about Britain's current military role can escape the issue of decline. Having once ruled an empire 'on which the sun never set', it seems obvious that Britain is not as powerful as it was during imperial times. For participants who could recall when 'one-fifth of the world was pink', but now see Britain's overseas territories consisting of 'a few scattered islands', it is almost trite to say that Britain is not what it once was. The corollary of the British tendency to view the world through the lens of its imperial past is a fixation on how far it has fallen since. For some authors, declinism is so endemic in the British psyche that it is frequently exaggerated to the point of being 'overblown, ill-focused and quite often absurd'.[1] Others counter that Britain's apparent decline has been interpreted far more diversely than a universal, paralysing soul-searching across British society.[2]

In the vast literature on the subject, Britain's postimperial decline is rarely questioned.[3] Commonly the narrative resembles a tragedy in which a great power is brought low, the only major disagreements being over its beginning, causes, and inevitability. Authors disagree on whether the decline began after losing the American Revolutionary War,[4] the 1870s and 1880s,[5] after the First World War, or more commonly after 1945.[6] Some frame imperial decline as 'planned obsolescence',[7] while others see it as the inevitable result of the industrial bases of other nations catching up with Britain after the industrial revolution.[8] Critics lambast the British political establishment for ineptness and poor economic policy or wider society for decadence and neglect.[9] Britain's decline is also often portrayed as part of a rise and fall narrative, or even as part of a broader cycle of the inexorable rise and fall of all empires throughout history.[10]

Decline, and how to explain it, is also a central preoccupation for policymakers looking to justify British defence policy. A combination of the increased cost of military technology and successive administrations reducing military expenditure has shrunk the British military. The media commonly report reductions in numbers of Britain's soldiers, aircraft, and ships, often in minute detail.[11] When people see these cutbacks, decline seems a logical conclusion. Given that maintaining Britain's great power status has been a preoccupation of successive British governments, managing, averting, or simply denying decline has been a perennial concern.

Reconciling Britain's declining military capabilities with its ambitious interventionism is a strategic dilemma, but it is also a narrative one, particularly if one agrees with Freedman that strategy is meaningless if not communicated effectively.[12] The task is to create a narrative that resolves the tension between two storylines: the story of the continuously interventionist 'warrior nation' and the story of its reduced material capability. Doing this requires a clear understanding of public perceptions of how, when, and why Britain has declined, the villains of the story, and what should be done about it in the future.

The Material Decline Narrative

The *Material Decline* narrative concerns Britain's reduced ability to conduct global military operations based on the reduced size and strength of the armed forces. It is inextricably linked to the country's economic strength in that, alongside political will, Britain's military strength is largely a product of what its economy has been capable of sustaining at a given point in history. The plot of the story is that since the peak of its imperial power, Britain has become economically weaker and lost its empire, reducing its ability to sustain a global military presence. Today it needs the help of allies when it wants to go to war.

The emphasis on *material* decline stands in contrast to *moral* decline, on which people's stories disagree. The distinction makes sense given that these have been previously identified as the drivers of British foreign policy—a material desire to maintain power and influence and a moral obligation to uphold international security.[13] However, while it is commonly agreed that Britain has materially declined, whether it has morally declined, progressed, or stayed the same is contested in citizens' stories. Those particularly nostalgic about the empire tend to tell a story of Britain the *Vanishing Force* (see chapter 4). In this account, material decline is the product of a moral decline, with weakened political leadership and a general societal malaise eroding Britain's preeminent position. In contrast, in liberal interpretations (see chapter 5), Britain's material decline has been accompanied by moral progress. This is because reduced capability to fight wars reduces violence, moving humankind toward a more peaceful world.

In most cases participants narrated a linear story, beginning with British imperial dominance and decline thereafter. This oversimplifies British history: decline was arguably far from linear, considering that Britain was more active in its colonies in the decade after the Second World War than before it, saw unprecedented economic growth in the 1950s and 1960s, and was more militarily prominent under the 1980s Thatcher government than the decade before. It is also debatable whether Britain was ever as powerful as conventional wisdom suggests. Barnett, for instance, asserts that Britain's dominance was 'more a matter of rhetoric, more a façade of power, than hard political, strategic or economic fact'.[14] But, as mentioned previously, people tend to reduce the past to general patterns rather than complex narratives. Moreover, these genres appear to be grounded more in myth than in detailed historical analysis. What matters here is that from the perspective of the early twenty-first century, a diverse range of British citizens narrates the 'gist' of Britain's modern military history as one of global dominance followed by linear decline.[15]

Significant events commonly cited by participants included the world wars for their deleterious effect on the British economy and the Falklands War, which is particularly symbolic as the last time Britain was materially capable of fighting a major war alone. A few older participants mentioned Suez, with the 1956 crisis symbolising Britain's weakness in becoming subservient to the United States, and the 1968 retreat from 'East of Suez' heralding Britain's global military retreat. Eurosceptics cited Britain joining the Common Market as the precipitant of further decline, even though the decision to align more closely with Europe was more a product of Britain's decline than its cause.[16] Again, the accuracy of the historical record is less important than the power of myth to shape perceptions. This is further shown by the fact that those lamenting decades of British economic decline overlook a remarkable increase in their standard of living in the same period.[17]

While some participants named specific events, most accounts were more partial and vague. Rarely were interviewees specific about when Britain's fall began. Instead Britain's past was often simply referred to as 'empire', then compared to the present.

> MARY (35–44, DORSET): I think we think we're important. I don't know how important we are. You know, obviously we have been important once. You know, we ruled the empire. I think we're probably a country with fading powers. We're a tiny little island. I don't know economically how important we are on the world stage.

Many participants struggled to define who Britain is in the present. They could only characterise Britain today in relation to the past using vague terms and limited detail. Britain today was 'not the force we were', 'almost insignificant now', with powers that are 'fading', 'sadly reduced', leaving the country 'emasculated', or as 'weaklings' who are 'not big players' with 'not a lot of say' and who are 'not listened to' any more. What Britain has actually lost was often similarly nebulous, including 'power', 'prestige', 'influence', 'clout', 'weight', 'force', 'dominance', 'credibility', and 'respect'. Participants frequently interchanged these terms without clear differentiation between their meanings. In academia the exact meaning of terms like power and influence is explored extensively but their everyday usage 'tends to be imprecise, loose and lazy'.[18] Here they are loosely interpreted as metaphors for power, describing Britain's general ability to get others to do what they would not otherwise do.[19] This exchange with Daisy (65+, Worcestershire) typifies such responses:

> RESEARCHER: So what do you see as Britain's role in the world as a country, and has that changed at all in your experience?
> DAISY: Well we try and keep the peace don't we. We are trying . . . but I don't think we've got the strength or the economy to be the world peacemakers that we've tried to be. . . . . I don't think we've got that capacity anymore but we want to still feel we have, but I don't think we've got the clout we used to have.
> RESEARCHER: What are your views on that?
> DAISY: I think it's sad that we are just a little island and we've got to learn that we aren't the big players any more. We've got to learn to take it on

the chin. I think it is sad that we're not what we were. We haven't got the empire behind us which made us the strength that we were.

(. . .)

DAISY:.Are we seen as the weaklings now? I think a lot of people do see us like that, that we want to be strong but we're just little puppy dogs trying to be the big growling dog. I think we've lost an awful lot in the last 30 years. When you think what we achieved after the wars, we were a force to be reckoned with, but I don't think we are any more. I think we're pushed around quite a bit as a country.

RESEARCHER: Could you elaborate a bit more on that?

DAISY: Erm . . . well, as with Europe at the moment, I don't think a lot of states . . . are fearful of us anymore. I think we can say what we want to say but I don't think we have any weight behind us. I think we've lost an awful lot.

Daisy's account uses many of the terms outlined above, seeing Britain as no longer a 'big player' but instead as 'weaklings' without the 'clout', 'strength', 'capacity', or 'weight' it used to have. The exchange is not structured as a coherent narrative but one can be pieced together from Daisy's responses. That is, Britain's achievements in the world wars made her a 'force to be reckoned with', a country of which people were 'fearful'. However, since losing its empire, Britain has 'lost an awful lot' and no longer has the 'weight' or 'clout' to assert itself. Today it tries to 'keep the peace' but lacks the economic strength to do so. Instead it is 'pushed around quite a bit'.

Metaphors such as 'weight' and 'clout' are particularly significant because they enable those with limited knowledge to understand complex issues such as defence policy. This is because they can be used instead of specific events to construct the plot of a given narrative.[20] In this case, they are examples of the anthropomorphic 'state as person' metaphor, whereby international state behaviour is understood in terms of hand-to-hand combat such as boxing.[21] Participants can substitute these metaphors for concrete events, narrating Britain's decline as a story in which it used to be able to 'throw its weight around' and 'give people a bloody nose' but now it no longer has the 'weight' or 'reach' to do so and must 'take this on the chin'. This allows others to understand their overall point without requiring specific knowledge. Such metaphors are therefore a significant piece of the puzzle in showing how the British people understand war.

Realism and British Decline

The logic underpinning the *Material Decline* narrative is that economic strength determines a state's power and influence. This could derive from territory, resources, or trade, and facilitates military strength. Thus at the height of the British Empire, the country had power, influence, authority, and was listened to. Even if Britain was ignored, it could coerce unilaterally, because militarily it was a 'force to be reckoned with'. In this way, the *Material Decline* story is based on a traditional, realist conception of power based on hard elements such as territory, economic resources, and military strength. It is because economic decline has eroded these that people claim that Britain is not taken seriously enough.

> SEBASTIAN (65+, WALES): The prevailing view from the government in power at the moment is that we are a formative influence on world policy, and you know, we can stand up in the United Nations and say 'Great Britain thinks this' and people take notice . . . but I'm not sure many people do these days.
>
> NATHAN (45–54, DORSET): I think [having a strong military] is very important, I really seriously do. I think it is, because it is part of the reason the rest of the world takes us seriously. Because economically we're not a midget, but we're not what we were. And if we want to have a space on the global stage to bring what we perceive to be good, sensible British values, by which I mean the liberal end of that—with a small 'L' please—then we need to be taken seriously.

Interpreting citizens' perceptions of Britain's material decline is more complicated, though, because many also value aspects of 'soft power' as alternative sources of credibility and influence. Many participants explained how Britain retains residual influence through its language, education system, technological innovation, and cultural institutions such as the BBC.[22] In most cases, however, these are used more as examples of British superiority but are insufficient to fully offset material decline. Britain might have superior capabilities to others in certain areas, but economic and military power are considered the 'real' source of a country's strength and prerequisites for credibility even as a humanitarian actor.

KYLE (18–24, LONDON): I basically think that Britain's time of being a super-power is over. We're a tiny, tiny country . . . and we have the same prow-ess as America but we don't have the economic clout, the militaristic backing. And I feel if we cannot support that then we should keep our mouth shut for a bit.

FELICITY (45–54, DORSET): Erm . . . I don't necessarily think Britain should have a role. What I do think is that Britain thinks it has a role. The Brit-ish Empire ruled what, a quarter of the world at its biggest, and in many ways many British people still think in that way. But we haven't got the power that we had, we haven't got the influence that we had. We cer-tainly don't have the political clout any more. Alright, we might still be the sixth richest economy in the world, but we're in no way in the same league as the United States, China, the Soviet Union, well, Russia, or even the European Union. As a part of the European Union, we've got clout, and . . . we've probably got more influence because such a large part of the world is English speaking. We probably punch higher than our weight because of that, because of the sheer fact that we speak Eng-lish. But we should stop mistaking cultural influence for political influ-ence.

Both Kyle's and Felicity's responses are underpinned by realist logic, even though they acknowledge 'cultural' sources of British influence. Kyle explains that Britain may have similar 'prowess' to the United States, but what matters more is economic and military 'clout'. The plot of Felicity's response describes the past as 'empire', with the present being Britain's position as the world's sixth biggest economy. Interestingly she assumes that Britain used to be a 'super-power', a term typically limited to the United States and Soviet Union in the Cold War. This could be seen to illustrate the popular tendency to overestimate Britain's imperial dominance. This steepens the narrative trajectory of its de-cline, making it seem more dramatic. While she does not mention the military, her narrative is important in revealing the assumption that Britain's decline is economically driven. She does not state this explicitly, but it is implied through the comparison of when Britain ruled 'a quarter of the world' with it 'not being in the same league' as other larger economies.

Felicity's account becomes more nuanced in its differentiation between what she describes as 'political influence' and 'cultural influence'. She reiterates that Britain may have disproportionate 'cultural influence' through the English language, but then explains that 'political influence' through relative economic strength is more important. This reveals her scepticism with the idea that Britain could use soft power to replace hard power. Indeed few citizens found this idea convincing, despite its recent prominence in policy and academic circles.[23]

British Decline across the Political Spectrum

The narrative of *Material Decline* is sufficiently uncontested that it is found across the political spectrum, spanning multiple interpretations of Britain's ideal military role. Stereotypically, concern with a decline in Britain's image, power, and status is associated with the 'nostalgic Daily Mail and Telegraph reading publics' of the political Right.[24] Nonetheless, it was found across the sample here. Participants expressing liberal sentiment explained that Britain's material decline has made it less likely to be listened to, not in coercive 'gunboat diplomacy' terms, but as 'the ones people turn to' to mediate international conflict. Even self-identifying pacifists reluctantly accepted that the antidemocratic forces of the world might necessitate a militarily strong Britain. There is a sense that the weaker Britain is economically and militarily, the less people are likely to pay attention to what it has to say, whether trying to coerce or attract others.

Samuel's (65+, Dorset) response when asked about how Britain should respond to Islamic State led to a *Material Decline* narrative typical of older, more conservative participants:

> SAMUEL: . . . If you look at our situation over the last twenty years, our governments that we've voted in have reduced the armed forces to a level that doesn't align with most people's views of what Britain was about. It just doesn't match any more. So then, you have to cut your cloth don't you. You have to say 'well is this job too big for us, as we are currently set up?' But I conclude that the response that we are carrying out is more in line with our capabilities than the response that we had to Afghanistan 13 years ago. So I suppose it's the right thing. It's the best we can do I guess.
>
> RESEARCHER: I think that's a very articulate way of putting it. You mentioned that these forces cuts are not what Britain's about for most people. Could you possibly elaborate on that?

SAMUEL: Well I think in the back of most people's minds we will say upfront we know Britain's not a major world power any more, you know, it's all over, the Commonwealth's gone, our powers are gone, we're not what we were, but at the back of your mind you probably haven't given up completely on that idea. And we do have a sort of historical and probably inherited feeling of superiority. And of course we're not . . . and probably never were to be honest, but we thought we were.

Samuel's response suggests how some see military strength as fundamental to British identity. By claiming that cutbacks have left the military at a level that 'doesn't align with most people's views of what Britain was about', he implicitly associates Britishness with military strength. He reinforces this later, stating that 'for hundreds of years, nobody had any doubt that you didn't mess with the British'. Also, when asked about when Britain should use its military: 'I still have in me, I'd say everybody does, that when . . . somebody twists the lion's tail, we've got to have at them. And er, you can't help it'. Taken together, these comments present military interventionism as a natural, inescapable, almost instinctive part of being British.

This emphasis on the naturalness of military strength explains Samuel's dolorous language in describing Britain's decline. Apparently, 'it's all over', Britain's 'powers are gone', suggesting a finality that leaves it irrevocably insignificant. There is no recognition that Britain remains one of the world's leading economies and military powers, just a lament that a glorious past is 'all over'. He specifically cites the last twenty years, explaining that Iraq and Afghanistan were particularly influential for him since 'the poor guys that went there weren't properly equipped, supported, didn't have the money, didn't have the country behind them. It was just a disaster'. Interestingly, Samuel demonstrates sound understanding of the strategic importance of reconciling ends and means, acknowledging that limiting Britain's response is the 'right thing' given its more limited military capabilities. But the fact that this is only 'the best we can do', and the fact that he suggests that people have not given up on the idea of Britain as a 'major world power', suggests a strong degree of nostalgia.

While for Samuel, Britain's material decline is regrettable as it is no longer the imperial power it once was, the following story by Bridget (25–34, London) shows that Britain's material decline is also concerning from a liberal internationalist perspective:

BRIDGET: Once upon a time . . . Britain was a leading power, supported by its Commonwealth. So all these huge, huge swathes of land and their populations. And it felt like there was deep loyalty. And with that we continued to just . . . everybody looked to us as a nation. . . . And that made us feel safe to a certain extent. But that power's dissipated. And I think with it has come democracy, a blurring of the social strata, the lines. It's right that we don't have power over those other countries and nations anymore, but with it we have lost an awful lot of our power. I think we still have respect but I don't know that anyone looks at Great Britain anymore and feels fear . . . as in the leader of an aggressor, say. I don't think Putin looks at Britain and thinks we're his biggest problem.

RESEARCHER: Yes, that's probably true. What do you see as the future of Britain, its military and its role in the world?

BRIDGET: Where it is now, the mediator, peacekeeper, er . . . considered, so if and when we have to enter conflict again, it has impact because it's so rare for us to go in, to do it anymore. So I think considered, yeah, thought through. And when we have to do it I imagine we'll do it well.

Bridget's story once more demonstrates how Britain's material decline underpins citizens' narratives about Britain and its military. The plot is simple again, with the past as 'empire' and present-day Britain as having 'lost power'. Unlike Samuel's account, though, the empire is evaluated negatively. Therefore while she thinks it is right that Britain no longer rules other countries any more, she suggests that Britain is now less secure and less able to influence others. She suggests that Britain is still respected, though not feared, particularly by other 'aggressors'. The reference to Putin is unsurprising given that conflict involving Russia in Ukraine was taking place during the interview period. The story positions Britain as a defender of the liberal order against aggressive Others, suggesting that military strength is a useful deterrent, whether it is used or not. The British people apparently 'felt safe' when the country held more territory, with material decline engendering insecurity. A similar viewpoint led MccGwire to question whether Britain's Trident nuclear deterrent is more a 'comfort blanket' than a 'weapon of war'; just as Barnett described the empire as a 'psychological prop' rather than a genuine source of economic power.[25]

As well as suggesting that material decline has eroded how secure British citizens feel, Bridget's narrative implicitly calls for a strong military in the future, and she reinforces this later. Her suggestion that ideally Britain would remain a 'cautious' and 'considered' 'mediator' or 'peacekeeper' of world conflict might suggest she does not prioritise military strength. However, her argument is still underpinned by the realist logic that Britain needs to be respected or even feared in order to be 'listened to' as an arbiter of international conflict. Later on she also describes a strong military as 'very important', not just to 'protect our shores' but also to maintain Britain's 'respect' and 'international standing' as 'an organised society that values people's liberty'. So while Bridget may not necessarily favour using military force aggressively, she believes that military strength is good for Britain and the world.

Concern about Britain's material decline is also found on the political Left. Even self-identifying pacifists who dismiss Britain's wars as actions of an exploitative imperialist reluctantly accept that the antidemocratic forces of the world might necessitate a militarily strong Britain.

FATIMA (35–44, OXFORDSHIRE): I think in the current . . . well, when has it not been current to look imposing to other countries . . . I think it is necessary within the systems that the countries of the world are governed in. You know, you need to have this force behind you. I don't really support that, and I think if there was a better way of doing that . . . I'm not really sure how, but by not having huge militaries, and kind of this huge dependence on this 'my army's bigger than yours', I think that would be a much more beneficial way for everybody, if we pursued more peaceful outcomes. But, as we don't do that, probably having quite a strong military is important. I wish we didn't have to have it, but I can see there are pluses and minuses to having it, and . . . I don't know, it's useful in disasters.

ISOBEL (45–54, WORCESTERSHIRE): I mean I don't really agree with war at all really, but we don't live in an ideal world so they're always going to be there, there's always going to be conflict.

(. . .)

ISOBEL: I'd like to say [the military] shouldn't ever be used, but that's not going to work is it, because it seems we're always going to have a need for war.

PETER (25–34, DORSET): I think it is [important to have a strong military], considering the nature of the modern world and the amount of conflicts and things. But at the same time the idealist, pacifist part of me would like to say 'no'. But I realise how stupid that might be.

While none of these responses mentions Britain's decline, they imply that it is potentially bad for Britain if it cannot defend itself or others. Fatima and Isobel both renounce war, comparing a hypothetical scenario about a world free of war with a conflict-ridden reality. This illustrates that while citizens may not support using military force, the importance of military strength is widely accepted. Even if ideally the military might not actually be used, it is 'necessary within the systems that the countries of the world are governed in'.[26] Both material decline and the need for military strength are seen as common sense.

Small Island Syndrome

Like the *Continuous War* narrative, the *Material Decline* narrative constructs Britain's international identity in a certain way. The notion of being a 'small island' was a particularly notable characterisation. Being an island nation is long recognised as fundamental to British national identity; symbolising its distinction from Europe and the need to be an outward-looking trading nation.[27] Specifically, being a *small* island, though, represents a potent symbol of material decline. Having once ruled the world's largest ever empire and been the dominant global economic and military power, the notion that Britain is now only a small island reflects a sense of inadequacy and insecurity that drives attempts to maintain its power and status. A strong and active military is a way of compensating for this diminished size and stature. While Sanders referred to this as 'Great Power Syndrome',[28] it might be more aptly described as 'Small Island Syndrome'.

The 'small island' characterisation provides a reminder that narratives are organised spatially and not just temporally. So far, the main focus has been the temporal aspect of material decline, with the idea that since a peak in British power, it has steadily lost territory, economic strength, and military capability. Yet states and empires are bounded in space, so to talk about how they change over time is to talk about space.

In some citizens' stories, Britain's status as a 'small island' is used as evidence of its purported exceptionalism:

BRIAN (65+, DORSET): We have such an extraordinary history, for this tiny little island, barely visible on a projection of the world on a map, and yet we have gone around changing vast swathes of the world. Not always for the better, but overwhelmingly for the better, and the legacy that we've left behind is incredible.

Brian's point that it is hugely impressive what the 'tiny little island' has achieved seems reasonable. Britain's historical achievements appear impressive, noting that it is contentious how positive its 'incredible legacy' is.[29] As Danielle (35–44, London) suggests, 'it's quite spectacular how such a small country, island, managed to make such a huge impression across the whole planet'.

The problem with Britain's apparently immense legacy is that it becomes an unavoidable source of comparison with the present. As Hansen notes, the empire can be described as a 'temporal Other', a constant and inescapable reference point to when, in Kyle's words (18–24, London), Britain 'used to be <u>the</u> power'.[30] Britain's empire can also be described as a 'spatial Other' compared to the 'small island' of today. Most national myths rely on a heroic golden age, or perhaps one to come.[31] But if Britain today is only ever compared to when 'a fifth of the world was pink', narratives of despondent decline are inevitable.

In reality, Britain is not a small island but a collection of over one thousand islands that make up the United Kingdom of Great Britain and Northern Ireland. In participants' stories, the 'small island' notion is more important metaphorically, connoting insignificance rather than geographical area.

> FELICITY (45–54, DORSET): I think that we were a small island until Tudor times, when the British navy was built up. Obviously it was mainly against the Spanish, wasn't it. And it was with the building of the British navy that we started to become a superpower.

Felicity shows that not all participants narrated British history as a linear decline from the days of empire. Some went further back, recounting Britain's rise and its fall. For Felicity, Britain's smallness reflects its power and status— Britain was no longer a small island once it became a 'superpower' thanks to the Royal Navy. This spatial construction was far more common in laments over Britain's subsequent decline, with 'only [being] a small island' reflecting its fading power, influence, or economic strength:

> MARY (35–44, DORSET): You know, obviously we have been important once. We ruled the empire. I think we're probably a country with fading powers. We're a tiny little island.

DAISY (65+, WORCESTERSHIRE): I think it's sad that we are just a little island and we've got to learn that we aren't the big players any more.

The corollary of the 'small island' metaphor is that the 'Great' in Britain is also used metaphorically to denote Britain's status. Technically, the term refers to the major island of the British Isles, on which mainland Scotland, Wales, and England are situated. However, in nationalist sentiment it takes on a different meaning, symbolising Britain's power and influence, not its topography. As Teresa (55–64, Worcestershire) explains, 'I don't think we're perceived as Great Britain by the rest of the world, but I think there's a lot of people here who still think that we are Great Britain'.

As well as reflecting Britain's decline, for some being a small island implies vulnerability. This does not necessarily make military sense; while being an island might increase susceptibility to blockade, it provides a strong barrier against invasion from which Britain has repeatedly benefited. But if the constant reference point is that Britain used to be so much more than a small island, the sense of vulnerability is likely to be heightened. For some this justifies Britain's extensive armed forces. Consider the following two responses when people were asked how important it is for Britain to have a strong military:

EMMA (35–44, BIRMINGHAM): Very. Very. Because really, we could be very vulnerable, being a small island. So we are really exposed to attack, aren't we. So I think we would be very vulnerable if we didn't have the military.

MARK (65+, BIRMINGHAM): A good many people disagree with having the nuclear submarines. But when you've got a small island like ours I think it's necessary to have such things. You've got to make the enemy afraid of you. And that's the only way in the modern world.

Being a small island does not necessarily imply the need for a strong military. Iceland has no standing armed forces and according to Prime Minister Geir Haarde in 2006, 'no military tradition' or public interest in possessing one.[32] Nonetheless, the idea seems common sense among British people for two reasons. First, countries with imperial pasts such as Britain and France may perceive military strength as particularly important.[33] The responses here support this, indicating that the loss of empire may have heightened feelings of insecurity beyond what is strategically rational. Second, fighting off invasion is a foundational aspect of British national identity, be it through stories of the Roman invasion, the Norman Conquest, the Spanish Armada, the Napoleonic wars, or the Battle of Britain.[34] At its most extreme, this is manifested in the erroneous nationalist myth that Britain has never been invaded, which persists despite dozens of incursions into Britain over the centuries:[35]

> SAMUEL (65+, DORSET): . . . the most important fact is we know that the British Isles have never been invaded by anyone. Now if that can't give you a feeling of superiority, I don't know what can.

Today, although it is widely recognised that an invasion of Britain is unlikely,[36] the idea that 'there will always be threats' persists.[37] As Mabel (55–65, Dorset) explains, 'the last ten, fifteen years at least have proved the unexpected happens and . . . yes, you want to feel that there was something in place that would help your country not be invaded'. In Ray's (45–54, Birmingham) words, if Britain isn't defended with a strong military, if someone invaded 'it will just be a walkover'.

As well as defending the imperially weakened 'small island', a strong military is vital to Britain compensating for its loss of power and influence in world affairs, even if this requires a different role.

> BRIDGET (25–34, LONDON): I suppose I feel like we're kind of mediators. I don't think . . . we're not Russia, we're not the USA. We don't have the power that I imagine, or certainly aren't viewed as having the power that we were viewed as having back in the First and Second World Wars. We're just a little island and I don't think anybody's that afraid of us.

Again, in Bridget's response, Britain being 'just a little island' is symbolic of a country no longer feared. But as she later implies, if Britain is to have the authority to 'mediate' or act as 'peacemaker', it requires the 'respect' that comes from military strength.

> BRIDGET: [A strong military is] very important. . . . We're a very small country, we're an island. Those are the very obvious practicalities of it. We need to protect our shores so to speak. But I think it's also our standing within the international arena. I suppose it does feel like short man syndrome almost. We don't have the scale, we don't have the land, the vast

areas of land. But I think it helps maintain the respect that I believe other countries do have for us.

Bridget's metaphorical description of Britain as suffering from 'short man syndrome'—whereby a male compensates for diminutive stature by acting more assertively—seems a particularly apposite way of describing Britain's military interventionism. It describes well the sensitivity, particularly of the British political Right, to being 'emasculated' through a decline in power and status.[38] With short man syndrome, one would expect a highly defensive response to any perceived sleight about size or strength. It is hard to imagine stronger evidence of Britain's 'small island syndrome' than the remarkably defensive response by Prime Minister David Cameron to a claim by an aide of Russian President Vladimir Putin in 2013 that Britain was 'just a small island' to which 'no one pays any attention':

> CAMERON: Let me be clear—Britain may be a small island but I would challenge anyone to find a country with a prouder history, a bigger heart or greater resilience. . . . Britain is an island that has helped to clear the European continent of fascism and was resolute in doing that throughout World War II. Britain is an island that helped to abolish slavery, that has invented most of the things worth inventing, including every sport currently played around the world, that still today is responsible for art, literature and music that delights the entire world. We are very proud of everything we do as a small island—a small island that has the sixth-largest economy, the fourth best-funded military, some of the most effective diplomats, the proudest history, one of the best records for art and literature and contribution to philosophy and world civilisation.[39]

Cameron's reply reflects the symbolic importance of the 'small island' in narratives of Britain's decline. Such a response might be expected of a national leader looking to present his country favourably, particularly one from a Conservative Party seen as having a 'militaristic background and slightly jingoistic history'.[40] Nonetheless, the suggestion of Britain's insignificance clearly touched on a nerve, or one would not expect such a defensive, hyperbolic reaction.

At first glance Cameron's response is a fairly typical nationalist narrative, containing many myths previously identified as underpinning Britain's perceived exceptionalism, including its unique historical legacy and the inherent superiority of the British people in terms of heart, resilience, inventiveness, and creativity.[41] It emplots events from British history selectively, highlighting examples of British moral exceptionalism such as its leading role in abolishing slavery, while silencing the fact that up until abolition Britain transported more slaves than any other state.[42] In emphasising that Britain was 'resolute' against fascism 'throughout World War II', it implies that Britain is morally superior to the economically larger powers of America and the Soviet Union, whose participation against Germany only began in 1941. Hyperbolic claims such as Britain inventing 'most of the things worth inventing', along with the patently false claim that Britain has invented 'every sport currently played around the world', demonstrate the rhetorical importance of myth over factual reality.

The most striking aspect of Cameron's narrative is that he felt the need to reassert so strongly Britain's contemporary relevance in the face of relative material decline. His highly defensive response goes far beyond what would be needed to remind a potential adversary that Britain retains hard power and the will to use it. It also reads as an attempt to alleviate feelings of ontological insecurity among domestic audiences by reminding them of British greatness. To that end, Cameron frames the 'small island' characterisation not as a metaphor of Britain's insignificance but as a sign of its exceptionalism. It does not represent change compared to empire, it represents continuity. Britain has always been a small island and has always been great. While some see Britain only having the fourth-largest military and sixth-largest economy as part of its sad decline from primacy to being a *Vanishing Force*, for Cameron it demonstrates that Britain retains capabilities that vastly outweigh its size. Since Britain's military strength is ranked higher than its economy, and it is supposedly more resolute in using it than others, it enables Britain to 'punch above its weight', an idea explored in the next chapter.

Reconciling Continuous War and Material Decline

To conclude, no single narrative accounts for British citizens' understanding of their country's role in war. There are, however, two storylines shared across the diverse sample studied here: first, that Britain is a country continuously at war, and second, that it has undergone a material decline since the peak of empire that makes it progressively harder to maintain this interventionism. People do not agree that these storylines should necessarily continue, and they have different ideas about how Britain's use of military force might change in the future. Nevertheless, these genres provide a baseline of commonsense assumptions about Britain's ongoing tendency but diminished capability.

The *Material Decline* narrative, like the *Continuous War* narrative, often lacks detail, because participants see the idea that Britain is weaker than it used to be as obvious. Ordinary citizens do not appear to engage with debates about whether Britain was ever as powerful as it is portrayed as being; overwhelmingly they convey the simple linear narrative that Britain used to be a dominant global power and now it is not what it once was. The spatial element of this narrative is particularly significant, with interviewees juxtaposing when 'a fifth of the world map was pink' to Britain today being just a 'small island'.

It may be that if participants were then asked to provide more detail from earlier in British history they would explain Britain's rise to imperial power too, in which case the narrative trajectory would have been a rise and fall. However, more significant is that when given the freedom to narrate Britain's military history in any way they liked, the widespread response was simply to contrast 'empire' with Britain's strength today. This suggests that while the *Continuous War* narrative constructs Britain's identity through comparison with other countries, the *Material Decline* narrative primarily constructs Britain's identity through comparison with its own imperial past. Other countries are relevant too, since the concern expressed is that being materially weaker gives Britain less influence over them.

Combining the *Continuous War* and *Material Decline* narratives produces the idea of the 'strategic deficit', whereby British expectation of an interventionist military role becomes increasingly divorced from its material capability.[43] Indeed Barnett suggests that this gap between pretensions and capabilities has been a persistent flaw in British military strategy since 1945.[44] Resolving it is a material challenge, for there is a need to reconcile strategic ends with the means available. It is also a rhetorical challenge though. To reiterate, a basic narrative consists of an initial situation, a problem that disrupts it, and a resolution that reestablishes order.[45] From the initial situation of Britain's imperial strength, the problem is that Britain's desire to maintain an interventionist military stance is being challenged by relative material decline. Participants agree on these storylines so far. They disagree on how the tension between them should be resolved.

Intuitively there appear to be three solutions to resolving the 'strategic deficit'. The first two are suggested by the loaded nature of the term 'deficit', which implies an insufficiency that must be eliminated. First, Britain's hard power could be raised to match its lofty ambitions. Unsurprisingly favoured by military elites, but also imperial nostalgists wanting the 'Great' to be put back in Great Britain, this solution calls for an end to cutbacks and a significant increase in military expenditure. With it being unlikely that Britain could significantly increase its hard power through economic transformation, increased military strength would reinvest Britain with the 'real' power and influence it should apparently never have lost.[46] Whether the military is used or not is secondary to the 'clout', 'weight', 'force', and 'credibility' Britain would have again. This is the idealised future of those who tell the story of Britain the *Vanishing Force.*

The second solution is most readily associated with recent governments and involves accepting Britain's diminished economic power and instead focusing on maintaining its qualitative superiority. This would be done through a 'smart' combination of soft power, such as cultural influence, and hard power in the form of its military.[47] This is embodied by the metaphor of Britain *Punching Above its Weight.* The military remains vital to this, particularly since survey research has shown that the British public still perceive it as the country's greatest source of international influence.[48]

The third solution is to reduce ambitions to match Britain's diminished material capabilities, accepting a more limited role in the world. This solution was occasionally expressed in people's stories, though polling evidence suggests limited support for this idea among the broader public, since it would undermine the ontological security of British citizens who value the idea of Britain as a great power.[49] Participants hoping for this perceived an insecure, conflict-ridden world, but appeared to accept reluctantly that it may be preferable that Britain plays an active military role rather than less morally upstanding powers. But even staunch opponents who see Britain's wars as nothing more than a selfish crusade to exploit others appear to retain hope that Britain can maintain a leading role through mediation and humanitarianism instead.

The way the strategic gap between Britain's intentions and capabilities is resolved will have direct implications for the ontological security of those who see the British as a 'warrior nation' intent on remaining a great power despite only being a 'tiny little island'. Citizens are torn between seeing Britain as uniquely willing and able to step in and accepting economic reality that suggests it should step back. To understand better how citizens think Britain should resolve this tension, it is necessary to add a layer of complexity and consider how their narratives *morally* evaluate the rightness or wrongness of Britain's wars.

CHAPTER 4

Punching Above Its Weight or Vanishing Force

Five Narratives about Britain and War

RESEARCHER: What do you see as the role of Britain's military?
DIANE (18–24, LONDON): Erm . . . well overall . . . I think peace probably, but through fighting.

Britain seems to be always at war. However, it is less capable of fighting wars than it used to be. These statements summarise the continuity British people perceive in their country's involvement in conflict but the decline in its military strength. Since these points seem to be common sense, stories conveying them tend to possess low narrativity; they contain few narrative structures and their plots tend to lack detail. Why explain something that seems obvious?

These may be the dominant interpretations when the focus of people's stories is on the quantity of wars Britain fights or its ability to fight them. However, they are only two strands of Britain's military past about which narratives can be constructed. The stories British people narrate about war rarely stop at the frequency or intensity at which their country fights: they evaluate the rightness or wrongness of its wars too. This is unsurprising. If identity is multilayered and constituted through narrative, then logically the genres people use to convey Britain's international identity will be multilayered too. If one assumes as I do here that narrative genres are not universal archetypes but generic, culturally specific patterns that can be weaved together, then analysis of genre can reveal the different strands or storylines that underpin public interpretations of war.

Combining material and moral considerations reveals significant contestation in interpretations of Britain's wars. People may agree that Britain always goes to war but they disagree on whether they have been right to do so. They take for granted that Britain has materially declined but disagree on whether being less able to fight wars is a good thing or not. Inductive analysis revealed that these differing perspectives coalesce into a typology of five public narratives (See table 1 overleaf). Each story passes judgment on Britain's military past while advocating ideal ways force ought to be used in the future. The *Continuous War* and *Material Decline* narratives are embedded storylines within each but they are evaluated differently in each case. Likewise, each genre casts Britain's identity, as the central protagonist, differently: as *Punching Above Its Weight*, as a *Vanishing Force*, as *Learning from Its Mistakes*, as *Led Astray*, or as a *Selfish Imperialist*.

After summarising each story, this chapter examines the first two narratives, which characterise Britain as *Punching Above Its Weight* or as a *Vanishing Force*. Both interpretations are nationalistic and somewhat militaristic, in that they see military force as a justifiable means to promote British power and influence, are imbued with imperial nostalgia, and assume Britain's exceptionalism compared to others. These similarities mean that, when combined, they appear to correspond to what authors such as Wallace have described as the dominant defence narrative of the political Right.[1] In fact, they represent distinct narratives with different plots, organising metaphors, and judgments of Britain's military past, present, and future.

A Typology of War Stories

Britain Punching Above Its Weight

The first narrative portrays Britain as *Punching Above Its Weight*. Since the phrase was coined by former foreign secretary Douglas Hurd in 1993, it has become one of the most prevalent framings of British defence policy by politicians, the media, and academia.[2] Here it was the second most frequent narrative, identifiable in just over a third of the sample (34 percent). The plot explains how Britain, a pivotal world power, has undergone relative decline since its imperial heyday, and yet due to its superior historical experience, liberal democratic values, culture, and the inherent ingenuity and moral fortitude of its people, always manages to *Punch Above Its Weight* in world affairs. This is one reason why it is continuously at war.

The point of the story is to convey moral continuity; that Britain has always

Table 1. Typology of Narrative Genres British Citizens Use to Describe Britain's Role in War

Britain's Identity	Punching Above Its Weight	Vanishing Force	Learning from Its Mistakes	Led Astray	Selfish Imperialist
Frequency (out of 67)	23 (34%)	14 (21%)	26 (39%)	8 (12%)	9 (13%)
Narrative Trajectory	(flat line)	(downward line)	(upward line)	(up then level line)	(low then slight rise line)
Plot	Continuous	Decline	Progress	Interrupted progress	Continuous
Moral Evaluation	Force for good	Force for good	Becoming a force for good	Becoming force for good then led astray	Force for ill
Tendency to go to war	Continuous War				
Capability of going to war	Material Decline				

Note: These figures add up to more than 100 percent because some participants' narratives contained more than one storyline.

been a *Force for Good*, an example for the international community. Material decline is seen as inevitable and something to be managed and compensated for in other ways. This includes the maintenance of a disproportionately strong military and being seen as more willing to use it for righteous causes than others. Military interventionism is portrayed as natural and positive. Regarding the future, the nature of interventions appears to be changing from sending 'boots on the ground' to more limited deployments of special forces, air power, and military advisors. Nevertheless, military interventionism is still important to ensure Britain exerts disproportionate global influence. What is good for Britain is assumed to be good for the world.

Britain the Vanishing Force

The second narrative, and the third most common (21 percent), characterises Britain as a *Vanishing Force*. This is a tragic tale of moral and material decline.

The main frame of reference for this nostalgic, nationalist narrative is the British Empire, which is portrayed as fundamentally liberal and benevolent. Since that peak of Britain's strength, it has unnecessarily surrendered its dominant position and is now steadily vanishing into obscurity. Not being the force it once was, Britain is once more a small island, neither able to exert its positive moral influence on the world nor adequately look after its own citizens.

In this interpretation, Britain's continuous involvement in war is again seen as natural and positive, as heroic Britain above all others has the resilience and trustworthiness to counter the illiberal powers of the world. Meanwhile, its material decline should never have occurred. It is the fault of successive generations of politicians eroding Britain's inherent advantages and a growing societal malaise since the end of the Second World War. This decline is not to be accepted or managed. Instead there should be a return to British greatness through an increase in hard power to match the inherent superiority of the British people. Economically, some assume this could be done through leaving the EU and returning to being a global trader, as Britain was in imperial times. Military reinvestment is particularly vital to ensure that once more Britain has 'real power' to influence world affairs.

Morally, as with the *Punching Above Its Weight* narrative, the underlying assumption is that Britain is a *Force for Good*. The difference is that this story ties Britain's ability to do good to its material strength. The logic is simple: the less force Britain has, the less good it can do. Material decline has therefore been mirrored by a moral decline.

Britain Learning from Its Mistakes

The third and fourth narratives are both liberal interpretations, focusing on Britain's progress in building a more civilised and peaceful world after its violent imperial past. The most prevalent narrative (39 percent) sees Britain as *Learning from Its Mistakes*. Once more Britain's past is one of continuous war, but these wars have become less imperialist and more humanitarian. Britain is steadily learning to use military force for the good of humanity rather than to advance narrow, selfish interests.

On the one hand, Britain's material decline is evaluated negatively as it means Britain cannot so easily perform a global humanitarian role. It is also perceived positively, though, since it has led Britain to consider how to use its military more judiciously. Having not been a *Force for Good* as a colonial power, the two world wars were formative experiences where Britain learnt to use its military to benefit the world. In the future, it is hoped that Britain will use its historical experience to mediate or arbitrate international conflict and be a 'peacemaker' rather than an aggressor.

Britain Led Astray

The plot of the fourth narrative, in which Britain is *Led Astray*, begins in the same way as the third: Britain follows a violent imperial past by steadily learning to use military force more discriminately, helping others rather than just itself. But rather than a narrative of moral progress, this story involves a rise and fall. The Second World War is the peak of Britain's global moral role as a 'defender of freedom'. Thereafter, Britain is *Led Astray*, interfering in conflicts it shouldn't and doing more harm than good. This is most powerfully exemplified by recent wars in Afghanistan and Iraq. This is partly a function of Britain's material decline, which has forced it to ally with America, a more gung-ho, selfish power that is allegedly less discriminate than Britain in using military force.

Those that see Britain as being *Led Astray* tend to take no issue with Britain's continuous military interventionism per se but express concern that following the United States into conflicts undermines Britain's moral credibility. The hope for the future is that by distancing itself from America and becoming a mediator and peacekeeper rather than an aggressor, Britain may rediscover the liberal path of using military force for the good of the world. In both this and the *Learning from Its Mistakes* narrative, Britain's *intentions* have always been to be a *Force for Good*, even if it has not always succeeded. The destruction wrought by Britain's wars is a result of it being 'misguided' or 'clumsy' rather than illiberal intent.

Britain the Selfish Imperialist

The previous four stories are based on the assumptions that military force can be positive and that Britain has always been a *Force for Good*, at least in its intentions. However, a small minority (13 percent) told a different story: that of Britain the *Selfish Imperialist*: a violent, exploitative *Force for Ill*, using its military for selfish, typically economic purposes. As with the *Punching Above Its Weight* narrative, it is a story of continuity, but all Britain's actions are assumed to be morally wrong. The plot projects a continuous stream of imperialist violence throughout British history that is likely to continue as long as vested interests underpin decisions to use military force. While acknowledging Britain's material decline, the economic focus is more on Britain's exploitative tendencies, be it the pursuit of power, colonies, oil, or the perpetuation of the arms trade. Imbued with Marxist influences, it serves as a counternarrative to government claims that military interventions are humanitarian.

Narrations of the future in this story often juxtapose an ideal world without war with reality in which war is human nature. The story's proponents may fundamentally oppose Britain's wars, but they acknowledge that a militarily active Britain may unfortunately be necessary. Still the hope is that Britain uses its military minimally and for humanitarian purposes. However, this interpretation anticipates no progress in this regard, particularly while a supposedly militarist and nationalist British political establishment values military force as a source of power and influence.

Before setting out this typology in depth, two caveats should be noted. First, as with any typology, these categories are simplifications to some extent. Typologies are rough theoretical constructions 'designed to describe some empirical *tendency*'.[3] Reality is invariably more nuanced and crossover between genres is inevitable.[4]

Second, the claim is not that an individual only uses one story to interpret Britain's role in war. They may be aware of several different explanations for war and use different ones to explain individual conflicts. For example, someone may perceive that Britain is generally *Learning from Its Mistakes* in becoming more humanitarian, but then might interpret a given conflict as 'all about the oil'. What matters is that when asked to tell one overall story about Britain and war they chose one genre and not another.

The Punching Above Its Weight Narrative

The idea that Britain 'punches above its weight' is one of the most common themes in contemporary British defence policy. The market research firm Ipsos MORI has even used the metaphor when polling the public on what Britain's international posture should be.[5] At best it is a 'familiar idea' that intuitively encapsulates Britain's expansive international ambitions.[6] At worst it is seen as a 'horrible cliché' symbolising delusions of grandeur and an outdated, unrealistic strategic approach.[7] Either way, the pervasiveness of the phrase reflects what has been described as an 'instinctive' British assumption that it should look to project power globally.[8]

The idea behind the *Punching Above Its Weight* narrative is that Britain has always exerted disproportionate influence in the world and should continue to do so. Britain's economic power may have declined since the empire, but it retains influence far beyond its material capabilities that enables it to play what is described by McCourt as that of a 'residual great power'.[9] A story imbued with nationalist sentiment, Britain is portrayed as exceptional for achieving significantly more than other countries of equivalent physical size or economic weight. Just as it is impressive that a smaller boxer stands his ground or defeats heavier opponents, it is impressive how such a small island can have such a profound global impact.

Popular as the metaphor is in encapsulating British defence policy, it is far from unique to Britain. It is commonly used to describe any areas where states have developed comparative advantages. Commentators on Singapore and Australia also claim that their armed forces enable them to punch above their weight.[10] Academics have also deployed the phrase to describe other social phenomena, be it Cuba's use of sport to improve international cooperation or New Zealand's international promotion of breastfeeding.[11]

In Britain the idea of punching above its weight is most typically tied to military matters. Proponents suggest that Britain's military capability provides a level of hard power that compensates for relative economic decline.[12] However, claims that Britain punches above its weight extend far beyond its military to incorporate other areas of supposed British exceptionalism. According to David Cameron in November 2010, this 'unique inventory of assets' includes the English language, its time zone, universities, the BBC, the British Council, British museums, its civil and diplomatic service, as well as its networked position at the heart of the UN, G8, G20, NATO, and the Commonwealth.[13] Britain's contribution is also attributed to the ingenuity and resilience of its people. As Cameron boasts, 'few countries on earth have this powerful combination of assets, and even fewer have the ability to make the best use of them'.[14]

Punching Above Its Weight as a Story

The *Punching Above Its Weight* metaphor is not in itself a narrative. It is an organising idea, a slogan or symbol upon which narratives can be built.[15] As with any metaphor, it renders the world more easily understood, but through selectivity, highlighting certain things while obscuring others.[16] Specifically, it invites focus on ways Britain is apparently doing more than other countries but downplays areas where Britain's contributions are comparatively limited. This shapes what events are included in participant narratives and how they are framed. Whether Britain actually contributes more than others is less important than the perception that it is. As will be shown, it evokes stories grounded as much in myth as reality.

People's *Punching Above Its Weight* stories tend to have certain characteristics. In terms of plot, to recap, narratives typically contain an initial situation, a problem or a series of 'complicating actions' that disrupt that situation, and a resolution that reestablishes order.[17] Typically the initial situation is Britain at the height of its empire, with unparalleled influence on world affairs. A series of unavoidable events then causes Britain's relative material decline. Unlike in the *Vanishing Force* narrative, though, decline is seen as inevitable rather than the fault of British politicians or wider society. This is because Britain's position of dominance arose from technological advantages that were always likely to be superseded once countries with larger industrial bases caught up. It was the enduring creativeness and fortitude of the British people that enabled the country to wield disproportionate influence. Having accepted Britain's material decline, it should be managed by maintaining international influence in as many other ways as possible. One of these is the relative strength and qualitative superiority of its military, and the country's greater willingness to use it to uphold the liberal order than others. The plot shifts focus away from Britain's decline, instead generating the overall impression that Britain has always exerted disproportionate influence on world affairs.

The *Punching Above Its Weight* narrative is therefore a story of continuity, underpinned by the idea that Britain has always been more of a *Force for Good* than others. Britain's material strength may have waned and may decline further in the future but this does not matter while the country achieves more influence than its size would suggest. Part of this is historical, with Britain's imperial experience supposedly endowing it with unique understanding of other cultures and diplomacy. Britain may not be what it once was, but it nonetheless retains 'enormous residual respect', is 'highly regarded' as a 'role model . . . for democracy', a 'voice of reason', with a 'patriarchal role' through its 'incredible legacy', 'extraordinary history', and 'amazing heritage'. Militarily, Britain's supposedly superior cultural understanding underpins the mythological assumption that its armed forces understand how to conduct counterinsurgency operations better than any other power.[18]

The Logic and Appeal of Punching Above One's Weight

The underlying logic of the *Punching Above Its Weight* narrative makes it appealing for several reasons. First, it is judged relative to others. If every country contributed the same amount of men, materiel, and expertise to military interventions, then no one could be said to be punching above their weight. Thus Britain's international contribution must rest on comparison with others' less significant efforts.

The comparison with others is both quantitative and qualitative, though the latter is arguably more important. Quantitatively, Britain could be said to be *Punching Above Its Weight* if its international ranking in a given category exceeds a proxy for 'weight': for example, population size, land area, or economy.[19] Britain therefore, as Cameron's earlier statement emphasises, punches above its weight by having the world's 6th largest economy and 4th largest military despite only having the 22nd largest population and 79th largest land mass.[20] The narrative's setting is thus a realist world in which states vie for relative power, indicated by international rankings in various categories.[21] A material focus does not fully capture the importance of the metaphor though. After all, if military force is used as the measure of 'weight', then Britain is not punching above its weight; it just has more weight in that area because it has chosen to invest in it.

The qualitative dimension is arguably more significant both conceptually and rhetorically. A boxer punches above their weight if they outperform those in a higher weight category. This cannot easily be done through height, for while a taller boxer might gain 'reach', they would typically sacrifice muscle mass to compensate for their larger frame. Punching above their weight is thus typically done through greater speed, skill, or resilience. What matters most is qualitatively superior performance to others. By this logic, a state punches above its weight if it achieves more influence than traditional calculations of hard power might suggest. Britain therefore punches above its weight through all the ways it supposedly outperforms others. Even if its military is smaller than ever, its technical or tactical superiority still mean it has disproportionate influence. Additionally, Britain's influence is bolstered by various sources of 'soft power', be it through cultural institutions, language, diplomacy, or education.[22]

Framing Britain as punching above its weight throughout history is appealing for politicians for several reasons. First, the policies it prescribes are cheap. Adding sources of soft power to the inventory of Britain's capabilities appears to give it more influence without further investment, enabling it to do 'more with less'—an attractive idea in an era of austerity policy.[23] Military cutbacks are more easily justified if one assumes other sources of influence can fill the gap.

An even more important reason for the *Punching Above Its Weight* narrative's appeal is that by focusing on Britain's disproportionate qualitative contribution, it shifts attention away from the country's relative material decline and any policies that may have caused it. Britain dropping down the rankings of economic and military might doesn't matter, because its relative performance compared to others has always far exceeded its population or geographical size.

The *Punching Above Its Weight* narrative therefore sustains the myth of Britain's exceptionalism despite material decline. For example, when Britain was ranked top of *Monocle* magazine's global soft power survey in 2012, the *Daily Mail* exclaimed that 'the sun may have set on the British Empire, but this country is once again the globe's most powerful nation by at least one yardstick'.[24] The importance of international influence to British ontological security was shown even more starkly in the *Times*, expressing desperate relief that 'Britain wins esteem at last as a global force' in coming top of the 2015 Soft Power 30 Index.[25]

Where the Military Fits In

While soft power is increasingly seen as an important way Britain punches above its weight, its military is particularly vital.[26] Quantitatively, by maintaining a disproportionately well-funded military relative to the country's size and population, Britain theoretically possesses more 'clout' than its economy alone provides. Qualitatively, it is widely assumed in Britain that the military is technically superior, more disciplined and conscientious than all others. As Mallinson claims, 'no army has so consistently fielded such all-round good soldiers'.[27] Theoretically, this enduring qualitative superiority and Britain's fortitude in being willing to use it compensate for Britain's weakening relative economic position. This can help it remain a 'pivotal power' in world affairs.[28]

The following response from Nathan (45–54, Dorset) epitomises how the military fits into the *Punching Above Its Weight* narrative:

NATHAN: I think we probably punch above our weight, because with the cuts that have happened recently we don't have that many soldiers, in all honesty. We just don't. But we do go hand in hand with normally America, the superpowers, the NATOs, the UN, we're always there. We're not hanging back, we're always there. And that's a source of pride for me, I like that. I wouldn't want to do it myself but I like the fact that we do. Our role in the world . . . I think maybe because of the empire, a lot of the developing world, which is where the problems are going to arise of course, the new problems, do look to Britain, and I think they maybe give us more importance than we necessarily deserve these days. But what we do have is a hundred per cent volunteer, professionally trained and <u>mostly</u> well-equipped army, professional army, which an awful lot of these other countries don't have. They have conscription, or they're just bands of bandits, banded together loosely under an idea. So we do have an extremely efficient army, and I think we should use it sparingly but when it's necessary we should use it.

Nathan's response succinctly explains the importance of the military to Britain's ability to *Punch Above Its Weight*. First, he alludes to the *Continuous War* and *Material Decline* narratives, as he explains Britain's tendency to be 'always there' and 'not hanging back', despite military cutbacks. Despite the decline, the story of Britain's global influence is one of continuity, through the enduring qualitative superiority of the military and the country's courage in using it. This is a source of pride for Nathan. Demonstrating that a country can only punch above its weight in comparison to others, he compares Britain with the developing world. While Britain's army is a 'professional' and 'extremely efficient' group of 'volunteers', he broadly dismisses other countries' militaries either as 'bands of bandits' or as less virtuous because only conscription compels them to fight. This implies that Britain's military is better organised and morally superior. Interestingly Nathan says that it is other countries that 'give us more importance than we necessarily deserve'. Critics might see this as rather delusional, and that it is Britain's sense of self-importance that drives its attempt to play a patriarchal international role.

Nathan's claims about Britain's military superiority are even stronger in a later response, where he narrates two hypothetical scenarios to explain why the military is so important to maintaining Britain's international relevance:

NATHAN: I think we still perceive ourselves as having a voice militarily in the world certainly. Economically, if America wants to do a trade deal with Japan and China that doesn't involve us, they're not interested. We're not relevant which is quite true. But militarily if America wants to do something it will consult with us. Firstly, because we've got a better army than them, be it vastly smaller, and secondly because they know it gives them international credibility. Because out of the UN it's pretty much always in my lifetime been America, it's been us, the French send a few nurses . . . I'm joking but you know what I mean. We'll go and do it, and we'll do it well, as a rule.

Here Nathan explains that to America, Britain is economically 'irrelevant' but militarily vital. He says that the British not only possess a more skilled military than the United States but they are a more legitimate international actor too. Both claims are contestable, but they were reiterated by other participants, who variously described the United States as more 'gung-ho', 'self-interested', 'naïve', 'hot-headed', less 'tactical', less 'sophisticated', and less 'diplomatic' than the British. The French, meanwhile, are portrayed as weak and feminine, based on the expectation that they will only 'send a few nurses'. This comment, albeit delivered in jest, reflects a broader stereotype that the French are militarily inferior and expected to capitulate compared to strong, brave Britain, a trope in British popular culture associated with the French collapse against Nazi Germany in 1940. If that was Britain's 'finest hour', then it can be made to appear even more exceptional by contrasting it with the capitulation of its allies.[29]

The overall impression is that the British military may be small but it is morally and technically superior to the United States, more courageous and steadfast than the French, and vastly more efficient than any force the developing world can put together. By implication, in the interests of the world it is vital that Britain spearheads any military intervention deemed in the interests of the international community.

Regarding the future, the *Punching Above Its Weight* narrative calls for Britain to continue playing a disproportionate role in the world. However, with continued economic pressures and public scepticism of the efficacy of expeditionary military interventions, it is hoped that this can be done through more limited operations that harness the military's technical superiority.

LUKE (55–64, BIRMINGHAM): We've always been a nation of a good force within the world. This is why I think we're asked to go in first. I don't think our force is as good as it was or it will ever be. I think the quality will be there but the quantity won't be there because of how much it takes. The price of conflicts has hit us hard and I don't think we'll have the . . . well they're all cutting back on the people that we have in the forces. And I think the quality will be there but not the quantity again.

FELICITY (45–54, DORSET): I think the only way that we can have an effective role is to specialise, to become the advisors more than the fighters. Our military is very well trained, very well disciplined, in comparison to everyone else's. It still has its faults but in comparison I think the discipline shown by our military is exceptionally good. And we would be best to be the advisors I think.

These statements demonstrate that quality rather than quantity will be the key to Britain remaining a force for good in the future. Felicity is more specific, arguing that the best course for Britain is to use its military expertise to advise others rather than as direct combatants. Her response shows why the recent trend of sending military advisors, as Britain did to Ukraine in early 2015, is a particularly appealing type of intervention. With only a few soldiers, each of which is assumed to be superior to everyone else's, theoretically Britain could exert influence on a conflict vastly greater than its material contribution—the very essence of punching above its weight. Sending 'brains on the ground' rather than 'boots on the ground' achieves this influence without British military casualties. It is more politically palatable and upholds British ontological security as a state that can still exert disproportionate influence on world conflicts.

These responses also highlight how Britain *Punching Above Its Weight* is grounded as much in myth as reality. It is hard to find evidence that Britain is always 'asked to go in first' as Luke claims.[30] On military advisors, citizens seem to assume that Britain above all others is being asked to help and that others are unwilling. None provides evidence to support such assertions, but that does not matter; they are just taken for granted based on the perceived moral and technical superiority of Britain's military. Even if other countries send advisors too, since Britain's military is considered superior it would be expected to exert more influence anyway, regardless of reality. Since the objective quality of a soldier is hard to determine, not least for an ordinary citizen, this view is particularly hard to challenge.

Criticism of the Punching Above Its Weight Narrative

Despite the prevalence of the *Punching Above Its Weight* narrative, it is not without criticism. Edgerton considers it a particularly inappropriate metaphor to describe war, since the lightweight boxer, even if they punch above their weight, will likely be eventually defeated against a significantly heavier boxer or multiple opponents.[31] In his interpretation, the future of the story is British exhaustion through overextension.

There may be some truth to the latter assertion, and strategic theorists routinely criticise British policymakers for conducting defence policy based on pride and prestige or to 'feel like we're doing something' rather than sound strategy that reconciles military means with political ends.[32] Nevertheless, the metaphor remains an enduring theme of British defence policy because it maintains the idea of Britain still being exceptional despite material decline. Showing the country apparently *Punching Above Its Weight* reassures people that even if Britain weakens, it remains special in some way.

Perhaps the most significant criticism comes from elsewhere on the British political Right, where a different story is told: that of Britain the *Vanishing Force*. From this alternative perspective, the claim that Britain *Punches Above Its Weight* represents illusory 'anaesthetizing rhetoric' with no basis in reality.[33] It is used by a generation of incompetent politicians to relabel British impotence and obscure their complicity in a catastrophic, self-imposed decline.[34] Today's political leaders are lambasted for simultaneously denying decline in public while privately acknowledging it as inevitable and to be managed. Militarily, the chasm between rhetoric and reality is shown by the claim in 2010 that the military would experience no 'strategic shrinkage' while severe cuts to the armed forces were actually occurring.[35] While Britain's soft power is acknowledged as a source of national pride, the idea that it could replace hard power is seen as flawed, simply a rebranding of cultural influence that Britain already possesses.

The Vanishing Force Narrative

The *Vanishing Force* narrative is a nationalistic and nostalgic interpretation of British military history. Of the 14 who narrated it, all but one were over 55 years of age. While the *Punching Above Its Weight* narrative emphasises continuity in British exceptionalism from its imperial past, the *Vanishing Force* narrative stresses how far Britain has fallen since 'Britannia ruled the waves'. What matters is not that Britain has the sixth-largest economy or the fourth-largest military, but that it used to be first in each category. Britain's small contributions to recent interventions in Ukraine and against Islamic State are not signs of a country outperforming others but are remarkably modest contributions of a once great military power wracked with self-doubt and withdrawing from the world.[36] The setting is a world in which Britain should be a global leader. Instead, without Britain's leadership, it is a more dangerous place, beset by threats to the liberal order that the country did so much to forge. Britain, a nation of inherently superior Anglo-Saxons, should never have been allowed to diminish in this way. Future policy should reverse this decline to put the 'Great' back in Britain once more. Elements of this narrative were highly prominent in pro-Brexit discourse before the June 2016 referendum.

The Vanishing Force Plot

The plot differs from the *Punching Above Its Weight* narrative in several ways. That story portrays Britain's actions as morally right and minimises Britain's decline. Conversely, the *Vanishing Force* story exaggerates Britain's decline, emphasising how great the country once was and the parlous state into which it has apparently fallen. It also differs in tying Britain's ability to do good to its material capability. Britain might be a *Force for Good* in general, but the 'force' and the 'good' are directly correlated: the less force Britain can exert, the less good it can do. Britain's material decline is both a product and a cause of a moral decline. Britain is therefore less able to lead internationally, to its detriment and that of humanity in general. The military are portrayed as heroes, vital to the preservation of both the British state and the liberal order. Their decline further erodes both the country's international influence and national security.

The start point is the same as the *Punching Above Its Weight* narrative: Brit-

ain at the peak of the empire, which is framed as liberal, comparatively benevolent, and is a constant reference point throughout. After this peak, the plot
takes Britain from global dominance to international insignificance. Unlike the
Punching Above Its Weight narrative, relative decline was not inevitable; it
should never have occurred. The British, often conflated with the English by
tellers of this story, are characterised as uniquely innovative, resilient, and democratic, attributes that led them to global ascendancy. However, these advantages have been squandered by political leaders and the public who have
wrongly accepted a diminished role in the world.

The Second World War often features in this interpretation, not just as Britain's 'finest hour' but because it crippled Britain's economy, precipitating decolonisation. It is also important in preceding the establishment of the welfare
state, which is seen as eroding the resourcefulness of British society. The Falklands War is also particularly symbolic, as the last time Britain could undertake
a unilateral expeditionary war. The present is seen through the reference point
of whether Britain's military could undertake such an operation again. Meanwhile Britain joining the European Common Market is a key event for those
who see Britain's decline as a product of a loss of sovereignty to Europe and
'dilution' through excessive immigration.

The Villains of the Story

As Britain should supposedly never have declined as much as it has, multiple
villains are blamed for causing its fall from greatness. Politicians are blamed
particularly strongly, although there are two interpretations as to why. The first
is that they have inadvertently caused Britain's decline through ignorance and
incompetence. The second is more conspiratorial, claiming that the liberal political Establishment has intentionally eroded Britain's power because of its rejection of the aspects of the past that made Britain great—particularly the empire. Immigrants are blamed for 'diluting' British greatness. Finally, the EU is
cast as a villain for undermining British sovereignty. The characterisation of
British citizens is more complex. They are heroes for their assumed superior
ingenuity and fortitude. They are victims who have had their inheritance of
international leadership unjustly diminished. They are also villains, blamed for
a societal malaise that has eroded the popular will to keep Britain in the forefront of world affairs. Moving forward, it is hoped that by confronting these

malign influences, Britain could return to its rightful place at the top of the international order.

Poor Political Leadership

The first cause of Britain becoming a *Vanishing Force* is the poor decision-making of successive generations of inexperienced, self-interested politicians who are vastly inferior to their illustrious predecessors. Past leaders such as Winston Churchill, Lloyd George, Margaret Thatcher, and even Enoch Powell are exalted, while contemporary politicians are blamed for throwing away Britain's superior position. These ministers of inferior character have wrongly accepted decolonisation and decline as something to be managed, unnecessarily eroding Britain's power and prestige. Consider the story Vincent (65+, Lancashire) tells in response to a follow-up question about his views about Afghanistan:

> VINCENT: Well, I thought very often that going into Afghanistan, I could see the point of it. The threat of terrorism to this country, the way it could have come, I could see the point of that. And I could see the point of intervention. What annoyed me considerably was these bloody fools we had at the time that took us into it, where the services that went were ill-equipped, ill-armed, on stupid statements, 'oh a shot won't be fired'. I get so annoyed about it.
>
> RESEARCHER: And what annoys you particularly about it?
>
> VINCENT: The poor leadership generally, and the poor political leadership. I could see the sense, I know it sounds horrible, about the horrendous loss of life, looking back I could see the sense of the First World War, I could see the sense of the Second World War very much more so. We seemed to be led in those days by men of experience and principle. We're now led by little boys who have come up through the party apparatchiks, whether it be the Conservative Party central office or the bloody trade unions or the Labour movement. Consequently nobody has any experience of what life is about.

Vincent can see the point of even the most destructive wars. His concern is not whether Britain should fight but the political leadership that sends ill-equipped soldiers without a full understanding of the violence involved. This perceived decline in British leadership was found among other participants too. They venerated past leaders as 'statesmen' with 'strength' and 'conviction' who had a 'sense of duty' and 'served the people', while portraying today's political class as immature 'little boys', 'a bunch of wimps' who are 'careerists' with 'no personal experience' of 'what it means to go to war'. As Matt (65+, Worcestershire) laments, 'there's nobody that strikes me as having character'. According to Luke (55–64, Birmingham), 'I don't think you could trust <u>one</u>, to be perfectly honest'.

Distrust of politicians is neither new nor unique to those who see Britain as a *Vanishing Force*.[37] More significantly, compared to politicians, participants trust the military to act with integrity to protect and serve the country. As Vincent continues, 'I think the one institution to be really proud of, and the one institution that works, whatever job they take on, of course, is the military'. Based on this view it is easy to see why military cutbacks have left some despairing at Britain's future. As Shaun (55–64, Dorset) asserts, Britain's current military role has been

> diminished, <u>embarrassingly</u> so. I think the cutbacks in the military are obscene. We were probably the strongest nation considering our size, and I think cutting back on the military was a huge, huge mistake.

During recent wars in Iraq and Afghanistan, this trust of the military but distrust of politicians has led to the well-established phenomenon of public support for British soldiers but not the wars they are fighting.[38]

> PETER (25–34, DORSET): I've got nothing but respect for troops, and I think what they do is exceptional, it is courageous, it is amazing, but I think the reasons we go into war, and the people who send people to war, I think it's fucked for want of a better word.

Indeed the level of militarism among some who see Britain as a *Vanishing Force* is such that they would see decisions on war taken out of the hands of politicians altogether and exclusively made by the military. As Terry (55–64, Worcestershire) underlines, 'I think parliament should leave the army and, well, the forces, to do their work rather than get involved', as unlike politicians, 'they know what they are talking about'. To involve politicians would leave Britain's security and prosperity in the hands of those who have made Britain the *Vanishing Force* it is today.

Societal Malaise

Britain becoming a *Vanishing Force* is also blamed on the moral degradation of society since the end of the Second World War. This idea of cultural decline emerged particularly strongly in the 1960s, based on factors such as the cult of the gentleman amateur, the tendency toward passivity and 'muddling through', resistance to technological innovation and entrepreneurship, and a perceived decline in moral standards.[39] Interviewees raised similar themes, describing British society as having become too 'complacent', losing its 'backbone', becoming more 'wishy-washy' and 'lethargic', with overreliance on the welfare state eroding the resourcefulness and creativity that had led Britain to imperial greatness. Older participants who lived through the Second World War contrasted it with the present, as a time when 'everybody helped each other' and 'we all did our bit'. In comparison, they doubt whether today's more decadent society could achieve the victories and stoically endure the hardships of yesteryear.

> DAISY (65+, WORCESTERSHIRE): I think we've been too complacent. I think it's the way our state is made up and this welfare state. Alright, you do need a welfare state but I don't think you can keep . . . I think you've got to put the emphasis on the right things. And I think we've been a little bit spineless since the war. I think you can become complacent, and the Great War and the Second World War, we achieved marvels, but I think we've been slowly disintegrating since then, really. Because I think it is complacency. 'We've won', you know, 'we're the greatest', but you've got to keep yourself up there haven't you.

Excessive Immigration

'Dilution' due to immigration was also cited as a reason for Britain becoming a *Vanishing Force*. From this nationalist perspective, the inherent superiority of Anglo-Saxons has been 'watered down' by others of inferior stock. Politicians are also blamed for policies that facilitated immigration in the first place.

Consider Shaun's (55–64, Dorset) and Beatrice's (65+, Lancashire) responses when asked what being British means to them:

SHAUN: Being British . . . I'm very proud of being British. I think that what we have here . . . although slightly corrupted, and I don't mean corrupted in the sense of financial, it's just been spoilt, but being British is having firm belief in truth and justice.

(. . .)

RESEARCHER: You mentioned there Britain being spoilt. Can you elaborate on that?

SHAUN: Yeah. I do have pretty strong feelings about immigration. I think it needs to be controlled and tightened up. I think we've fragmented . . . no, diluted ourselves greatly. But that's been going on . . . I mean the 'rivers of blood' speech by Enoch Powell, I mean hell he told us this was going to happen. And if you go back to the empire, we were the biggest empire in the world. If you looked at the globe it was the British Empire. I mean there was the French Empire and what have you, but we gave everyone British passports basically, so what do you expect.

BEATRICE: Well [Britain] used to be great didn't it. I think the great has been taken out of Great Britain now. It's erm . . . multicultural.

In both of these responses the narrative is clear. Britain used to be the 'biggest empire in the world'. It then 'gave everyone British passports', or in other words enabled mass immigration. Thanks to this decision, Britain is no longer great but instead has been 'diluted' and 'spoilt' by multiculturalism. Shaun's dismissive rhetorical question of 'what do you expect' portrays the inferiority of those coming to Britain as so common sense that it should have been obvious that mass immigration would lead to Britain's fall.

It is not immediately clear how these accounts are relevant to Britain's use of military force. Nevertheless, different participants make both a material and moral link between excessive immigration and Britain's military will and capability. Materially, the logic is that immigrants generally cause excess strain on Britain's limited resources, thereby undermining military investment. As Iris (65+, Oxfordshire) explains, Britain used to be 'proud and very strong' but it has since been 'swamped' by 'too many foreigners loading themselves into this country, bleeding the systems dry, filling up the schools and hospitals, and battening on the services, and they just can't cope'. The expansion of the EU is also blamed, creating ever-increasing groups of immigrants looking to 'take advantage' of Britain's resources.[40]

The result of this supposed additional economic strain is that Britain's military strength has been 'sadly reduced' so that it is unable to conduct the independent operations that apparently made the nation great.[41] As the last major independent British military expedition, the Falklands War is particularly symbolic in this regard. As Terry (55–64, Worcestershire) asserts, 'if the Falklands kicked off again we would need massive help. We wouldn't be able to do it on our own anymore. We haven't got enough firepower'.

The moral link between immigration and Britain's willingness to use military force is less obvious but reflects a similarly exclusionary ethnic nationalism.[42] The following exchange with Terry (55–64, Worcestershire) shows how he thinks immigration has eroded Britain's motivation to go to war, to its moral detriment:

> TERRY: I personally think we are a massive leader really, and people do come to us. But I don't know . . . I think in probably twenty years we're going to be overrun by . . . by other nationalities, I'm not too sure. Quite interestingly actually if we went to war now, how many Muslims shall we say and other people . . . people who are British or maybe want to be British, suddenly have to fight for Britain, it would be interesting to see if they actually, you know if there was conscription or anything, whether they'd actually turn up or not. I don't think they will. I don't think they will.

Later, when asked about how the decision to go to war should be made, Terry goes further, using a hypothetical narrative to explain why he believes that immigrants are inherently more pacifist and less bellicose than 'true British' people.

> RESEARCHER: How do you think the decision to go to war should be made?
> TERRY: Well . . . I think there's a fine line isn't there. You get to a certain stage when you think right, there's nothing else we can do, we've got to bomb the hell out of them now. That's my view.
> RESEARCHER: How far do you think the public should be involved in that process?

TERRY: Well I think the problem you've got with the public is at the moment 90 percent of the public here aren't English. And you know, you're going to have immigrants and foreign people, especially in London, I mean we're all outnumbered. I don't know if you're going to get a true British answer to it. If you involve the public I don't think you're going to have a good cross-section of people.

RESEARCHER: What would that 'true British answer' be do you think?

TERRY: Probably go to war I would say. Yeah I would think probably protect our country and go and do it. Whereas I think a lot of the other people that aren't pure British will be saying 'don't, try and do it peacefully'. I think you can do it peacefully to a certain stage then you go 'that's it', you know.

Terry's comments are based on a hypothetical narrative of what would happen in the future if and when Britain has to fight another war. He anticipates that, unlike 'true British' citizens, foreigners and particularly Muslims would be less willing to fight and would prefer to resolve matters 'peacefully'. This is apparently a bad thing as, in his view, a peaceful approach is only sufficient up to a point, whereas the 'true British answer' would be to go to war. The obvious hyperbole that '90 percent of the public here aren't English' demonstrates how the decline at the heart of the *Vanishing Force* narrative tends to be exaggerated.

In this extremely nationalistic and militaristic interpretation of Britishness, the warrior nation is tied to a narrow, ethnocentric distinction between 'pure British' and others, to the point of undermining democracy by excluding ethnic minorities to get a 'true' British view on war. Using military force, even to 'bomb the hell out of them', is both courageous and morally right to 'protect the country', compared to the perceived degeneracy of pacifism. Immigrants have not just put Britain's limited resources under strain, but they have also weakened Britain's moral stance since they are assumed to be less willing to defend Britain in a future hour of need. This controversial interpretation rests on a selective reading of British history, given the extensive contribution of other nationalities to Britain's military efforts over the centuries.

From this perspective, the very definition of a British citizen is one that is willing to fight for their country. Just as politician Norman Tebbitt notoriously saw support for the English cricket team as the mark of an assimilated citizen, for Terry, what matters is support for war.[43] British politician Enoch Powell invoked similar sentiment in 1981, claiming that nationality is ultimately determined by 'the nation for which he will fight'.[44] Accordingly, to be considered British, immigrants must embrace the warrior nation.

The Erosion of Sovereignty

Another perceived cause of Britain becoming a *Vanishing Force*, for which politicians are again blamed, is the loss of British sovereignty, both through joining the EU and through the imbalanced military alliance with the United States. Sovereign autonomy is a defining feature of any nation-state. However, Britain's 'imperial hangover' means that being able to act independently on the world stage appears particularly important. For a nation with, in David Cameron's words, the 'proudest history' of all,[45] cooperating with or following others is a far cry from the halcyon days when it seemed that Britain could 'send a gunboat' to any corner of the world and get its way.

Joining the EU is perceived to have contributed to Britain becoming a *Vanishing Force* in several ways. First, the perception that Britain has been ruled and regulated excessively by Europe undermines its sense of independence. This is more an issue of identity and pride than one of military strategy, for rarely has EU membership constrained *when* Britain chooses to use military force; cooperation with the United States and NATO has long been far more important.[46] The issue is that Britain was once a great empire and is now allegedly ruled by Europeans who are considered inferior in being less able and willing to go to war to defend freedom. Second, the EU is blamed for continuously leeching money and enabling mass immigration, thereby exacerbating Britain's material decline and by implication its military strength. As was shown during debates before the Brexit referendum, rational calculation of the costs and benefits of membership was marginalised in a Eurosceptic discourse where the EU was assumed to drain Britain's resources while offering nothing in return.

> BEATRICE (65+, LANCASHIRE): It all boils down really to us not having enough soldiers, not a big enough army. . . . Osborne did his best to cut everything down to create a better country for ourselves, but now the money's been taken off us by Europe, asking for more and more money. It's not fair.
>
> IRIS (65+, OXFORDSHIRE): Well we've done an awful lot of supporting [Eu-

rope] but I feel that we haven't got the support back. I think everybody's expecting us to produce money and help support and do this that and the other, but when it's reciprocal everybody disappears.

If Europe has contributed to Britain's *material* decline, proponents of this narrative perceive the 'special relationship' with the United States as undermining Britain's *moral* position. Here the *Vanishing Force* narrative intersects with the *Led Astray* narrative, in which following America into conflicts such as Iraq is perceived as undermining Britain's credibility. Participants certainly see the value of alliance with the United States for Britain's international influence. However, the imbalanced relationship symbolises the fall in Britain's ability to act independently. So, despite the material benefits of the alliance, the more Britain slavishly follows the United States, the more it appears to be diminishing as an independent actor. As Shaun (55–64, Dorset) suggests,

we shouldn't ally ourselves to America too much. I mean we should have the confidence to stand on our own two feet. We should do that more, and I don't think we do that as much as we used to.

This hints at the ideal future proposed by those who see the country as a *Vanishing Force*: a return to a strong, independent Britain.

Putting the 'Great' Back in Britain

In the future, the only way to prevent Britain becoming even more of a *Vanishing Force* is to put the 'Great' back in Britain. This can only be done through significant reinvestment in the only sources of true power in international relations, and those that made Britain great under the empire: economic and military strength. Maintaining military investment to enable Britain to *Punch Above Its Weight* is insufficient. Furthermore, investing in soft power is a flawed attempt to sustain Britain's global position 'on the cheap' that will not return the country to greatness.[47] Only a significant increase in hard power will keep British citizens safe and give Britain back the influence it and the world needs.

Participants often explained this by narrating two stories, contrasting an ideal scenario with a pessimistic tale of what they expect. In the ideal scenario, Britain becomes independent from the EU, massively reinvests in its military, and becomes a global trading nation again. With the inherent superiority of the Anglo-Saxon people and Britain's unique historical experience of managing relationships with other states, Britain could be great again.

> VINCENT (65+, LANCASHIRE): I think we should get out of Europe, and I think we should go back to what we were . . . global traders. You know, God almighty, we're a nation full of inventiveness, we're industrious. The ideas socially and industrially, technological-wise, we really are, we're leaders. And I think that if we unshackle ourselves from Europe, I think that's the way we should go.

People contrasted this ideal scenario with the pessimistic expectation that it is too late to reverse Britain's decline, that it is 'all over',[48] and that the country is in 'such a dreadful state' that the future will only see further drift, decay, and the symbolic death of the warrior nation.[49] Military interventionism, which both Terry (55–64, Worcestershire) and Shaun (55–64, Dorset) have argued is part of what being British is 'all about', will sadly no longer be something Britain is willing or capable of doing independently. Because of this, Britain will vanish into irrelevance as a country that others simply ignore.

> TERRY: I mean we were profound, and I think now we're more peacekeepers, and I think in the future we're just going to be part of an American army. Or not so much an American army but it's going to be a coalition basically. We're not going to be going out on our own or anything. I don't think a) that we've got enough people and b) I don't think everybody's necessarily going to want to go anyway.

> RESEARCHER: What do you see as the future of Britain's role in the world and that of its military?
> SHAUN: The way things stand, not very much I don't think. I think we've become too small. And the trouble is, because we're so small, at NATO we're not being listened to because we can't put our money where our mouth is. And that goes back again to what I said, we need to have a strong military presence because if there is a time where conflict is there, if we've got the power and the strength and the weight to do it, I think we would be listened to more. But I think that we're not listened to as much as we used to be, and I don't think we're the force that we used to be within NATO, unfortunately, and within the EU.

As well as bemoaning that the death of British military interventionism would undermine Britain's ontological security, being a *Vanishing Force* is also seen as threatening the survival of the British state unless reinvestment occurs. The threats Britain actually faces are rarely named; there is just a sense that 'more army, navy and air force patrolling more areas' would make people feel more secure.[50] For those that blame Britain's decline on immigration, a stronger military is a means to prevent British society being taken over by outsiders and 'infiltrators'. This is particularly associated with Islamist extremists, which according to Croft have become an 'internal Other' against which Britishness is defined.[51] In an extreme manifestation of this fear, Mark (65+, Birmingham) foresees that in another 30 or 40 years' time 'there'll be such a mixture of races, there won't be such a place as England or Scotland' and Britain may even have a 'Muslim government'. Even though it is difficult to see how a stronger military may prevent the growth of Islamist ideology domestically, participants perceiving this threat still see the military as vital. As Iris (65+, Oxfordshire) claims, a stronger military is essential to

> stop the terrorists taking over the world and to stop the infiltration of more terrorists into this country, and in a wider sense, try and stop the infiltration into the schools of all this awful propaganda, which I find quite frightening.

How this would work in practice is secondary to the assumption that Britain's military is the one institution that has reliably protected the country over the centuries. It is hoped that it might be able to defend both Britain and Britishness.

Summary

One of the most prevalent narratives of British defence portrays the country as a uniquely experienced, capable, and ethical military actor that has always *Punched Above Its Weight*. The general pattern of the story conveys continuity in Britain playing a disproportionately influential role as a *Force for Good* throughout history. The plot's causal logic is that Britain's material decline was inevitable after the empire. Despite this decline, Britain has maintained its extensive global influence through its superior historical experience, liberal democratic values, the inherent ingenuity of its people, and especially the quality of its armed forces and its ongoing willingness to use them to help others. This narrative upholds British ontological security through the idea that military interventionism enables the country to remain special despite being less powerful than previously.

The prominence of the *Punching Above Its Weight* narrative among the sample reflects its prevalence in elite discourse on British defence. However, it is far from dominant among citizens' interpretations of Britain's wars. It is contradicted by a competing narrative in which Britain is a *Vanishing Force*. This nostalgic narrative of precipitous decline also assumes the inherent superiority of the British and that their military is a *Force for Good*. Even so, its military is unable to perform this role adequately because of a devastating and unnecessary material decline that has eviscerated the armed forces, leaving Britain increasingly insignificant in a world it should still be leading. Far from being inevitable, Britain's fall from benevolent imperial greatness is due to decades of political ineptitude and a societal malaise exacerbated, according to some, by excessive immigration. The resolution of this narrative requires a massive increase in military strength to put the 'Great' back in Great Britain again.

There are clear similarities between these narratives. They are both nationalist and to some extent militaristic interpretations that persistently compare the current state of Britain to its former empire. They both frame the British nation as exceptional for the superiority of its liberal democracy, its moral fortitude, and its military capability. They both emphasise the importance of military strength to Britain's extensive power and influence, although they can also be criticised as being underpinned by 'delusions of grandeur' rather than realistic assessments of British influence and capability.[52] Because of these similarities, there is considerable hybridity when people narrate them. For example, despite telling the *Vanishing Force* story in which hard power is the key to any British resurgence, Vincent (65+, Lancashire) shows that he favours a number of the soft power elements that enable Britain to *Punch Above Its Weight*, such as education and training. As he hopes, if people 'think of the nice experiences they've had and how we run things', they might think 'well, this really is how we should be doing it in our own country'. Setting an example through public diplomacy is for him a 'very, very important' source of influence and national pride, but since Britain does this already it cannot replace the extra hard power Britain needs to return to greatness. In this respect, proponents of the *Vanishing Force* narrative dismiss the idea that Britain continuously *Punches Above Its Weight* as empty rhetoric with no material basis.

These are but two of the typology of five genres narrated by a diverse sample of citizens about Britain's past, present, and future role in war. The focus now turns to what are loosely termed 'progressive' interpretations, which emphasise not how far Britain's power and influence has declined but how far Britain has succeeded in moving away from its violent past toward a more peaceful future.

CHAPTER 5

Progressive Narratives of Britain and War

DANIELLE (35–44, LONDON): How is the world ever going to progress if all we do is respond with military force?

If the twin drivers of British military interventionism are material influence and moral obligation,[1] they are prioritised differently by its citizens. Some citizens' historical accounts are more concerned with how successfully Britain has maintained its material power throughout history, and they take for granted that this power has been fundamentally benevolent even when used violently. The *Punching Above Its Weight* and *Vanishing Force* narratives are examples of this. Others are less concerned about how much military power Britain has and are more interested in how it has been used to forge a better world. Their judgments vary greatly.

This chapter completes the book's journey through the genres British citizens use to narrate their country's role in war by outlining three narratives that can be broadly described as 'progressive', in that they focus primarily on how far Britain has used its military to help build a more peaceful and democratic world. In these stories, Britain starts as the villain: a *Force for Ill*. The British Empire is evaluated negatively, as exploitative, oppressive, and violent. The narratives then diverge on how far Britain has learnt to become a *Force for Good* over time. In the *Learning from Its Mistakes* narrative, the country has progressed from its imperialist past to using military force for more humanitarian purposes. In a variation of this, the *Led Astray* narrative explains how Britain was making progress from its violent past but has been led astray by following the United States into destructive recent conflicts. In the final narrative there has been no progress. This is the story of Britain the *Selfish Imperialist*: an exploitative oppressor whose wars have only ever been motivated by self-serving, economic interests. Narrators of each story hope for a future without the need for war. However, they vary in how optimistic they are that this could ever happen, either because they see war as human nature or because they believe that political actors will always seek economic benefit from it.

The Learning from Its Mistakes Narrative

The *Learning from Its Mistakes* narrative is a story of linear progress in which Britain moves from a violent past to a more peaceful future. The plot is simple. Britain continuously participates in wars throughout history, but the nature of the wars changes. Starting generally with the empire, Britain's wars are exploitative and oppressive, but over time Britain learns from these mistakes and becomes more circumspect, increasingly using its military for the greater good. The story is grounded in liberal internationalist ideology, set in a post-Enlightenment world in which liberal values are assumed to be universally desirable and the future is one of ever-increasing freedom, peace, and prosperity.[2]

The idea of learning from mistakes is not just a liberal idea; it pervades all aspects of human behaviour. Seeking to do things better over time is so embedded in human learning and development that it remains almost entirely unquestioned. It seems profoundly obvious in Western liberal thought that humans should look to advance technologically or build more peaceful societies. Yet it is similarly obvious that a military would look to learn from past mistakes and get better at prosecuting war. Gas chambers and atomic bombs reflect technological progress in efficiently ending human life. From a liberal perspective, progress in war is more about developing more discriminate weaponry and tactics to minimise casualties, reducing the humanitarian impact of war, or ideally eschewing military force altogether. By doing this over time, Britain is seen as becoming more civilised, particularly compared to its opponents. They are demonised as barbaric Others who use violence indiscriminately.[3]

The *Learning from Its Mistakes* narrative closely resembles the 'Whig' interpretation of British history, in that it flattens out inconsistencies in the past to produce a simplified tale of linear progress.[4] Citizens must either omit wars that suggest a backward step in Britain's ethical use of force or alternatively reframe them to avoid disrupting the overall pattern. Historians might see this as 'bad history' for emphasising sweeping generalisation over nuance and complexity.[5] Here it is more analytically significant that of all the stories people could tell about Britain and war, many choose a progressive narrative rather than continuity or decline.

Empire: From Pillaging Outlaw to Silver Knight

To tell a story of progress, the past must obviously be evaluated negatively compared to the present. Once more 'empire' is the simplified frame of reference used to describe Britain's past. In the *Punching Above Its Weight* and *Vanishing Force* narratives the empire is viewed nostalgically as liberal and benevolent. In the *Learning from Its Mistakes* narrative it is exploitative and repressive. It may have been the zenith of British power but it was also the peak of British oppression. Imperial Britain is described as 'arrogant' and 'aggressive', using its military in pursuit of 'conquest and domination' and 'grabbing resources', 'subjugating', 'bullying', 'exploiting' others, and 'imposing our way of thinking' and religion throughout the world. As Florence (55–64, Oxfordshire) explains:

> FLORENCE: We've bulldozed our way around the world in the past in a very high-handed [way] . . . and I don't think we can ever forget, however much we'd like to, some of the bullying, cruel, heinous ways we've treated other people in the world. . . . I'd like to think there has been some progression in that way, and that we no longer go imperiously round slaying people in our path and being the big bully. I don't think we can forget that, and I think actually that we are no longer that same nation. But I do think that we can't take the moral high ground when it comes to history.

Having used its military for these regrettable ends, the most common watershed in people's stories is the Second World War, when the country learnt to use military force for the 'greater good'. Thereafter, decolonisation precipitated material decline but also moral progress. Britain's wars progressively became more considered and humanitarian, participating in wars 'for the right reasons', such as 'freedom', to promote 'more democracy worldwide' and to 'improve other countries'. Danielle (35–44, London) epitomises this interpretation:

> DANIELLE: I always think of our first discoveries in the world. I don't like to think of it in these terms but . . . we weren't great in those days. When

you think of England branching out, discovering, I often think of it as quite violent, aggressive, greedy, destructive. I think . . . that has changed. You know you think of the world wars and we were actually very brave as a country. . . . I think maybe we started as massively aggressive, hard, back when we were conquering things left, right and centre and have just gradually scaled back, scaled back, scaled back, and now I don't think of us—maybe I'm wrong—I don't think of us as . . . just hitting a country, going in there, 'bang bang bang'. I just think of America like that . . . I think of us more as a tactical, diplomatic kind of country now. Not going in there all guns blazing, trying to be a bit more thoughtful in our approach.

Accounts of Britain's progress were also underpinned by a meta-narrative of human growth and maturation. Such perspectives dismiss Britain's tendency to 'subjugate others' as backward and 'Victorian' (Kenneth, 55–64, Liverpool) compared to its more mature and considered approach today.

NEIL (65+, WORCESTERSHIRE): We were an aggressive group of people. There was no doubt about that. We liked the military. We loved to dress up in uniforms, and we were reckoned to be, you know, 'the Boer War, we'll go and sort out those damned farmers'. Afghanistan, 'we'll go and sort out these Pathans'. 'We won't let them run the world', etcetera, etcetera. The French in Canada, 'we'll knock them off'. 'Montcalm, bastard. Let's get rid of him'. Then gradually you begin to grow up. And you realise that things can't be done quite like that and certainly the watershed was the Second World War, where although we did stand alone, briefly, I think any thinking person would realise we couldn't stand alone forever. So you gradually begin to realise you've got to think realistically about what your army can do.

By framing Britain's progress in terms of growth and maturity, imperial violence is dismissed as immature and uncivilised, whereas a more discriminate approach to war is more advanced. Neil does not explicitly explain Britain's current role, but he later expresses a preference for a military working 'as a benevolent police force rather than aggressive go-getters'. So after the immaturity of imperialism, Britain is apparently growing up into a more responsible international actor.

Characterising Britain: Always Trying to Help

By suggesting that Britain's present position derives from an immoral imperial past, the *Learning from Its Mistakes* narrative challenges Britain's ontological security as an ethical international actor. Indeed for many participants, characterising Britain as an exploitative oppressor clashed with their sense of Britishness, be it stereotypes such as 'fairness' and 'tolerance', being 'really good with other cultures', or being 'willing to give a helping hand'. If, as Leonard (55–64, Wales) suggests, the British 'are all products of the empire, whether that is the good or the bad', then evaluating it negatively potentially undermines Britain's sense of self. Some participants were explicit about how the empire prevents them from seeing Britain the way they want to. Kenneth (55–64, Liverpool) laments that 'I would like to think we're the good guys, put it that way. . . . Not always true in the past, unfortunately'. Danielle's regret (35–44, London) is even clearer, explaining that 'I don't like to think of it in these terms but . . . we weren't great in those days'.

People resolved this tension between ethical aspirations and imperial reality by characterising Britain as always having fine motives but simply making mistakes. Narrators moderated their criticism of British imperialism by claiming that it always *tried* to be a force for good, even if it sometimes failed. Violence and oppression were errors due to 'clumsiness' and 'immaturity' as part of Britain's 'misguided', 'crass', and 'ill-thought-out' drive to civilise.

> KYLE (18–24, LONDON): [Britain has changed] from the pillaging outlaw and highwayman of the past to the silver knight. We've made our fair share from war in the past, we've solidified our place at the table as it is. I'd say we still are a superpower now, because of what we've done in the past. We've made our influence known, the way we used to be <u>the</u> power. But now we don't have that, and I'm glad of that. We're not an enforcer anymore. We're just mainly there to defend, I hope. I hope that's the case. Sometimes we're a little bit misguided, but generally we're trying our best, I hope.
>
> IRENE (55–64, WORCESTERSHIRE): I suppose [Britain was] a bit of an aggressor for a very long period of time. A nation who didn't really consider other nations to have any rights or . . . powers. And then perhaps that did change to a nation who was trying to do what was right in the twentieth century, as well as protecting itself, and not always getting that

right but . . . well definitely not always getting that right, but trying to improve things. And I'd like to see it now as working for . . . world peace and a world that people can live in safely for the future.

These stories give the impression of a country with fundamentally good intentions 'trying [its] best' to build a better world, even though it sometimes does more harm than good. The causal logic is that the destructive consequences of Britain's wars are unintentional. It has always tried to bring civilisation, freedom, and democracy but has not always succeeded.

Framing British military history in this way has obvious appeal. It renders Britain less accountable for its past wars. It justifies imperialism, even as it criticises its consequences. Britain's actions are framed as 'blunders' rather than being 'calculated' (Lily, 18–24, London). It has apparently learnt from these mistakes and therefore occupies a higher moral plane today. This also upholds Britain's national identity as a fundamentally liberal nation despite a history of acting in far from liberal ways.[6]

This interpretation also reinforces Britain's military activism by suggesting that war can still play a positive role in international politics—a key tenet of liberal interventionism.[7] Far from rejecting war outright, 'as long as lessons remain learnt, we can use war to achieve what war needs to achieve' and 'make things better' (Ida, 55–64, Liverpool). With echoes of Vegetius, Diane (18–24, London) further exemplifies this perspective when asked about the role of Britain's military: 'Erm . . . well overall . . . I think peace probably, but through fighting'.

The Future: A Different Kind of Exceptionalism

The idea of *Learning from Its Mistakes* is vital to how narrators of this story perceive the future of British military interventionism. They typically juxtapose a hypothetical narrative of their ideal future with the reality of what they expect. While many begin with the optimistic notion that war may be unnecessary in the future, they expect it to persist due to human nature. They also anticipate that Britain will remain continuously at war. However, they hope that ideally Britain would use its past experiences to become a mediator or peacekeeper rather than a direct combatant.

ISOBEL (45–54, WORCESTERSHIRE): I'd like to see Britain get more involved with talks with people of different countries or in various conflicts. I'm not sure we do enough on that front, in trying to bring people together. I would like to hope that we weren't going to be involved in too many more military conflicts, but I have a feeling that we probably will. Because some places you can't ever see being at peace, I think. Not troops on the ground in some places necessarily.

DANIELLE (35–44, LONDON): I would like to think we remain very important . . . even in mediation. I'd like to see us less as ground troops going in there bombing left, right and centre. I'd like to think of us more as a kind of . . . protection rather than attacking, so being in an unstable country and trying to protect citizens. It's very airy-fairy, silly, unachievable I'm sure. You know, actually being there to protect civilians and try and mediate and try to rehabilitate countries.

KENNETH (55–64, LIVERPOOL): I think we're quite expert at warfare so we should be seen as someone who can train others for sure and provide expert advice and a force to join with others if needed, without being aggressive in any way. That sounds a bit idealistic, doesn't it? It's never going to happen.

Each of these perspectives idealises a leading role for Britain at the heart of contemporary conflict. They hope for a reduction in Britain's use of force, although eschewing it altogether is dismissed as 'a bit idealistic', 'silly', and 'unachievable'. This again demonstrates how embedded military interventionism is in Britain. Instead it is framed as a reluctant necessity that would hopefully fall short of putting 'boots on the ground'. The ideal alternative, in Faith's (18–24, Cumbria) words, is that the British play a 'patriarchal' role as 'the ones that are consulted when things start to go wrong'. Such a role has obvious appeal for it would enable Britain to remain a central power in world affairs.

In this way, Britain's exceptionalism pervades the *Learning from Its Mistakes* narrative, but it is special for a different reason. Rather than being exceptional for conquering a fifth of the world, it is unique in having the knowledge and will to drive the world toward peace. This is supposedly because Britain's past experiences give it the expertise and moral authority to lead international efforts to resolve conflict.

RESEARCHER: What do you see as Britain's role in the world?

KENNETH (55–64, LIVERPOOL): Well it's certainly not subjugating the natives anymore. It should be about . . . arbitrating things. An expert witness if you like on the way it could be done. I mean we've got experience of subjugating peoples and ruling empires and things. We should know how different nationalities in different countries work. We should know a bit more than other people I suspect. So we should be there as mediators in the world perhaps.

As Kenneth shows, Britain's supposed moral authority to be at the centre of international conflict resolution derives from its imperial experience of 'subjugating' others. This may seem odd. If repressing others gives an actor moral authority to mediate conflict, then despots throughout history could be seen as the ideal people to officiate international disputes. Here the idea of *Learning from Its Mistakes* is particularly important. It implies that Britain has recognised the destruction imperial violence has caused and has learnt to forge a more ethical path. Ironically, this perspective rejects the humanitarian, civilising imperatives that drove imperialism but retains the same paternalistic assumptions that Britain knows best how to guide less fortunate nations toward a better future.[8] With additional experience defending the world from despots and dictators, it may also be uniquely placed to provide advice and military training for those that wish to overthrow regimes that threaten their own populations and international security.

The second reason Britain is thought suitable for a patriarchal role over world conflict is the assumption that it possesses an unparalleled understanding of other cultures, derived from colonial rule. This is both due to the breadth of its empire and because British imperial rulers were purportedly more culturally aware than other powers. Therefore Britain 'knows a bit more than other people' about how 'different countries work'.[9] Again, this myth is broadly accepted but easily countered; Britain's repeated failures in Afghanistan could easily be interpreted as showing that its hubristic assumptions of superior cultural understanding far exceed reality.

By assuming that Britain can achieve influence over future conflict vastly disproportionate to its material strength, the *Learning from Its Mistakes* narrative intersects with the *Punching Above Its Weight* narrative. It also plays into the established idea of Britain at the centre of global spheres of influence promoted by leaders from Churchill to Cameron.[10] The idea of the tiny little island stepping in to resolve seemingly intractable conflicts would be the epitome of overachievement relative to its size.

The corollary is the apparent desolation when Britain is excluded from international conflicts, as it was during negotiations between Russia, Ukraine, France, and Germany to resolve the Crimean crisis in 2015. For supposedly 'taking a back seat', David Cameron was derided by senior military figures as a 'bit player' and a 'diplomatic irrelevance'.[11] The assumption that Britain must 'have a place at the top table' (Sebastian, 65+, Wales) regarding any major conflict was unquestioned. But there appeared to be little reflection on whether the international community ascribes Britain the same moral authority.

International actors are not the only ones who question whether Britain has the moral authority to become the arbiter of international conflict. A number of respondents expressed concern that Britain has strayed from the path of liberal progress and its credibility has been significantly damaged by recent wars. These citizens tell a different story: that of Britain *Led Astray*.

The Led Astray Narrative

The Britain *Led Astray* narrative is a story of interrupted progress. Like the *Learning from Its Mistakes* narrative, it is underpinned by the liberal, civilising meta-narrative in which humankind is (or at least should be) moving toward a more peaceful world. However, rather than a linear trajectory, Britain has undergone a rise and fall, with moral progress followed by a recent decline that may or may not be temporary.

The plot is initially the same as the *Learning from Its Mistakes* narrative. After using military force for immoral imperialist ends, Britain starts using it for humanitarian causes and the greater good. This progress peaks with the world wars, in which Britain succeeds in defending freedom in an existential struggle against tyranny. Thereafter, Britain is led astray, interfering militarily in the affairs of others in an attempt to help but often making things worse. The most commonly cited examples are recent interventions in Iraq and Afghanistan. These wars have been ineffective militarily, offered little humanitarian benefit, and damaged Britain's credibility as an ethical international actor. This leaves Britain less willing and able to play a leading role in international conflict, whether as a combatant, peacekeeper, or mediator.

DEBORAH (35–44, WALES): I'd probably tell a story . . . of how we did the right thing twice, how in the First World War we joined in to help, and in the Second World War we fiercely defended people's human rights and borders and countries, and how good triumphed over evil. And then I think in the story Britain would lose its way slightly. We've tried to help people on other occasions but the people didn't really want our help or didn't need our help, and perhaps we left things worse than we found them.

ROBERT (35–44, DORSET): Well I think we've got a fairly proud history from back to the Second World War and First World War. Maybe not so much before that, with the likes of Crimea and obviously building the empire. I don't totally think we were great . . . doing those things. But again it's money, power and wealth. But after the Second World War, and in my time, we seem to be constantly getting into squabbles and wars that don't seem to really finish and tend to go anywhere. They don't tend to achieve anything.

Deborah and Robert combine specific wars with generalised statements about the pattern of British military history. Both cite the world wars as Britain's most justifiable conflicts. Deborah mentions nothing before this. This leaves it uncertain whether she evaluates the British Empire positively or negatively. Even so, her statement that 'we did the right thing twice' in the world wars implies that Britain did not do so previously. Robert is more explicit that some things that occurred as Britain built the empire were 'not great' and economically motivated rather than humanitarian. After the moral peak of the world wars, both generalise that Britain's wars 'don't tend to achieve anything' and have 'left things worse' rather than 'helping people'. Once more both assume war to be natural and something that can and should 'achieve' things such as 'helping others' and defeating 'evil'. They note regretfully that Britain's wars now seem to do more harm than good.

While neither cites specific wars where Britain has been led astray, both name conflicts associated with the War on Terror elsewhere in their interviews. Robert describes Iraq, Afghanistan, and Libya as 'mistakes' and 'disasters' that he may have supported initially but haven't 'solved anything'. Deborah explains that she now associates war with 'suspicion of motives' and 'inaccuracies in truth' since Britain 'broke the law by going against what the UN said' over the

2003 Iraq War. For her, it symbolised a shift whereby in Britain's wars 'the motives aren't always to defend innocent people anymore'. In fact, Iraq contradicted her perception of the sort of international actor Britain should be. As she recalls, 'when I was much younger . . . there was something about the UK always being seen to be doing the right thing. And to then be the actual ones breaking the law, that doesn't sit well with me'.

By suggesting that Britain is no longer 'doing the right thing', these stories potentially undermine Britain's ontological security as a *Force for Good* in the world. Proponents of the *Led Astray* narrative avoid this by arguing that Britain is only partly to blame. Apparently it did not actively choose to intervene in these costly conflicts; it did so passively and honourably to fulfil its obligation to its major ally: the United States.[12] However, the United States is supposedly a more immoral and selfish military actor that is really economically motivated. Maintaining the alliance therefore leads Britain to be 'dragged into things that maybe we shouldn't be'.[13] As Deborah continues, 'it seems like America decides it's going to do something and then its special friends get pulled along with them'. So America is the villain that has led Britain astray, along with the British politicians who have slavishly pursued the special relationship. Britain's moral credibility has been undermined as a result. This causal logic is unique among this typology because it limits Britain's agency in its decisions to use military force.

Competing Atlanticisms: British Agency and the Special Relationship

To understand why citizens see Britain as being *Led Astray* by the United States, it is beneficial to examine participants' competing interpretations of the transatlantic relationship. 'Atlanticism' in some academic studies represents a key tenet of British foreign policy and strategic culture.[14] However, this does not mean there is a single Atlanticist narrative that explains the link between the two powers. Participant stories suggest a variety of interpretations of the 'special relationship'.

The United States is portrayed as a different character in each story here. Rarely does it feature as Britain's enemy; the wars between the two are scarcely mentioned, be it the War of Independence or the 'forgotten' war of 1812. Overwhelmingly citizens' accounts portray the alliance as natural and transhistorical. Particularly in the *Punching Above Its Weight* narrative, the former colony and its master are depicted as natural bedfellows, sharing language and culture as bastions of the liberal democratic order. But since Britain is now materially weaker, alliance with the United States enables Britain to project power and influence disproportionate to its material capability. In other words, to stay special, Britain must maintain the special relationship. In the *Vanishing Force* narrative, alliance with America is a sad necessity, a damning indictment on a government that has allowed Britain to decline. The alliance does benefit British power and influence, but following it too closely erodes British sovereignty by appearing to be America's 'poodle', 'puppet', 'lapdog', or 'servant'. In the *Selfish Imperialist* narrative, the United States and Britain are considered similarly immoral allies interested only in maintaining their energy supplies and arms industries through selective military interventions. In the *Learning from Its Mistakes* narrative, Britain and the United States are heroic allies in mutual pursuit of a more liberal, democratic world.

Although America's role differs in each narrative, the way it is compared with Britain is broadly similar. Materially, citizens consider the United States unquestionably superior and beneficial to British security and influence. Morally, intellectually, and culturally, though, they consider Britain superior. These contrasting judgments contribute to a wide range of views on the past, present, and future of the 'special relationship'.

Blaming the United States

The United States plays a particularly prominent role in the *Led Astray* narrative. The other stories emphasise Britain's active decisions to play a leading role in international conflict. In the *Led Astray* narrative, the United States has become the driving force behind recent Western military interventions. Britain is merely a dependent ally obligated to follow along. The underlying cause of Britain's dependency is its relative material decline since the Second World War. Because of this, Britain could no longer maintain its great power status unilaterally. While economically this eventually led Britain toward Europe, in defence it sought to project power indirectly through its 'special relationship' with Washington.[15]

Since this preferential relationship hinges on Britain being a more reliable ally than other powers, the country is particularly obligated to follow America's lead. Over time, playing the role of steadfast ally has become so important to Britain's international identity that abandoning historical allies to fight alone has become almost unthinkable.[16] As Mary (35–44, Dorset) suggests:

> MARY: If America says it's going in somewhere and Britain says we're not going to send in troops, then that's, you know . . . it just can't be done. We can't be their allies and then say we're not going to support them by also sending troops.

Framing Britain's recent wars as principled commitments to allies is an important rhetorical aspect of the *Led Astray* narrative. It reinforces Britain's ontological security as a reliable, moral force in the world, ideas that can be traced back to its commitments to protect Poland in World War II and Belgium in the First World War.[17] It also distracts from the implied loss of agency in British strategy. In reality, British defence policy is primarily determined by its relationship with Washington, although this is too politically unpalatable for politicians to admit.[18] Instead they tend to frame failure to follow allies into conflicts as dishonourable, cowardly, and profoundly un-British, something that, as Mary says, 'just can't be done'. This stance paints Britain as a dependable, ethical actor while obscuring its subservience in military decision-making.

The erosion of sovereignty through becoming little more than a 'transatlantic groupie' is a concern in both nationalist and liberal sentiment.[19] For those who view Britain nostalgically through the *Vanishing Force* narrative, slavishly following the United States is problematic on principle. Britain, as a proud country with a great history, should 'be individual' and 'think for ourselves as a nation' rather than just 'doing whatever America says'. As Grace (55–64, Worcestershire) emphasises, 'I don't think we should have that kind of relationship with <u>any</u> other country. We are a sovereign state, and I don't think we should be regarded as being at anyone's beck and call'.

In the *Led Astray* narrative, though, the concern is that recent US-led interventions have been highly destructive, ineffective, and, in the case of Iraq in 2003, illegal. This has eroded Britain's moral credibility, driving it off the liberal path of using its military to forge a better world. Moreover, this reputational damage has eroded its influence, making it less likely to be 'listened to' as a mediator of international conflict.

> DEBORAH (35–44, LONDON): Well I think we need to be careful that we don't continue to meddle in situations and leave them worse. I think if that

was over a long period of time to continue, Britain would be seen as a troublemaker and little sidekick to America, and I think there is a danger of that already at perhaps some points. But still I think we hold onto the fact that we are deemed to be fair-minded people and I think that is still the case at the moment. I think the world still perceives Britain to be like that. I just think in the future we could lose that image by making bad decisions.

FIONA (18–24, LONDON): The special relationship . . . we're just kind of seen as America's . . . whatever they say we do. So it kind of takes away from the good that Britain does in the world like give money to other countries. It takes it away because we're just seen as a country that will intervene and just not be as beneficial because of our relationship with America. And I feel that's detracted away from our power in the world.

In both responses Britain's image is of paramount importance. The United States is viewed as a villainous character that goes to war for the wrong reasons. Association with it undermines Britain's reputation as a 'fair-minded people' that are trying to help.

Looking beyond the *Led Astray* narrative, these stories typify the broader sample because they assume Britain's moral superiority to the United States. While none doubts America's material dominance, the *Led Astray* interpretation assumes that ethical Britain has been corrupted by a less sophisticated and more self-interested America. This belief long predates the Trump administration and is not just a product of recent wars. Some cite the world wars as examples where Britain stood up to be counted from the outset, whereas America only joined in far later. As Brian (65+, Dorset) states, 'Americans turn up late for any war. And then think they've won it'. Or as Joanne (55–64, Dorset) puts it, 'they want us to be allies when we can help them out but I think they're quite slow at being allies when it's the other way round'. These sentiments again illustrate perceptions of Britain's superiority, be it in military skill, cultural sophistication, ethical awareness, or reliability.

FELICITY (45–54, DORSET): We still think of ourselves, I think, as a more effective and morally sound policeman than the United States. They're the gung-ho ones, we're the sensible ones.

TONY (25–34, BIRMINGHAM): I think to have America on our side is not a bad thing. . . . Typically they're the brawn, they're the muscles, we're the intelligence, you know. That together would be extremely powerful.

STUART (35–44, LONDON): I'd say the British have a better understanding of the world and also international affairs compared to America. I keep teasing my friends in the States saying they're more intolerant and na-ïve.

MEGAN (65+, OXFORDSHIRE): I think to be brutal I think to some extent they lack the sophistication in thought of some Western Europeans.

While the alliance is clearly beneficial for British hard power, many questioned America's credibility and trustworthiness:

FATIMA (35–44, OXFORDSHIRE): I don't think they've always got everybody's best interests at heart. I think if push came to shove they would quite easily betray us.

IRENE (55–64, WORCESTERSHIRE): Well . . . my view is that we shouldn't have gone along with them with the Iraq war. . . . People saw America's involvement as not very . . . unselfish. It was intended not to benefit people, it was intended to benefit America. And yes, it just seemed the wrong thing to do.

SAMUEL (65+, DORSET): Well, I've lived a lot in the United States and I know that the United States is not a friend of anybody's. The United States is very self-interested and looks after number one.

There is certainly historical irony in seeing a selfish, economically motivated United States dragging Britain into war. A century ago, Americans felt they had been drawn into the First World War by a manipulative, imperialist Britain. Today, though, portraying the United States this way reduces Britain's culpability for the destruction caused by recent conflicts such as Iraq, Afghanistan, and Libya. These interventions are in turn framed as honourable commitments to its major ally, to avoid telling a story in which Britain has little military agency. Just as in the *Learning from Its Mistakes* narrative, Britain is depicted as a *Force for Good*, at least in its intentions. Its American ally is the one that is misguided at best and exploitative at worst. As Richard (65+, Worcestershire) generalises, Britain 'usually go[es] in for good reasons', whereas 'of course the Americans go in to safeguard their oil supplies'. Nevertheless, since association with the United States appears to bring material benefits as well as moral costs, the alliance is a double-edged sword. It brings physical security at the risk of undermining ontological security. This produces uncertainty about the ideal future relationship between the two countries.

The Future: A Return to Liberal Progress?

The future of the *Led Astray* narrative is uncertain. With its moral credibility damaged, Britain is at a turning point. The liberal idea of becoming an international mediator of conflict first requires a return to the path of progress. This necessitates a more considered use of military force. This is deemed more likely if Britain distances itself from the United States and is more discriminate in following it into conflict. Just like the *Vanishing Force* narrative, the assumption is that Britain is better off when thinking independently, based on the belief that it understands international affairs better than its allies. But it is unclear whether this will occur or whether Britain will continue to get dragged into conflicts that cause more harm than good.

Military interventionism is not rejected entirely though. Deborah, who earlier hoped that Britain would no longer 'meddle in situations and leave them worse', reiterates that 'I would never suggest that we turn away from a country who is in need'. Indeed concern was expressed that Britain being led astray has undermined its moral conviction to act decisively when humanitarian imperatives demand it.

> GRACE (55–64, WORCESTERSHIRE): We've had all sorts of interesting conflicts in all kinds of parts of the world . . . some more justified than others. We invented the concentration camp. We have committed a great many atrocities in a great many places. We have no room whatsoever to stand on the moral high ground. I think we've . . . to some extent at least learnt from our mistakes. I think my biggest concern now is that the pendulum has swung again. Because we made a complete mess of the Iraq situation, and that and Afghanistan have really sickened public opinion, I think now that we're possibly in a situation where we won't do something where maybe we ought to.

Grace's account illustrates the uncertainty in the future of the *Led Astray* narrative. After a mixed past involving numerous atrocities, Britain was *Learning from Its Mistakes*, but having been *Led Astray* it is unclear whether it will continue to intervene to support humanitarian causes. This ambiguity reflects the contingent nature of the *Led Astray* narrative. Each account examined here is the product of a particular time and place. However, this is particularly noticeable in the *Led Astray* narrative, which is evidently a product of the twenty-first-century War on Terror in which Britain has followed the United States into multiple conflicts. If Britain chooses to follow a different path to America in the future, in a few decades the *Led Astray* narrative might merely be a minor blip in a broader tale of progress, or even omitted altogether.

How the *Led Astray* narrative develops will depend largely on how Britain responds to Brexit and to the Trump administration. The Brexit vote engendered an immediate call to move closer to Washington, until Trump's seemingly erratic foreign policy behaviour led to calls for Britain to distance itself from his administration.[20] Clear divergence between British and American foreign policy has also emerged, with Britain refusing to follow the United States in withdrawing from the Iran nuclear deal in May 2018. What is striking in citizens' accounts here is how Trump's 'astonishing ignorance of some major world issues' reflects continuity in British understandings of the United States and not change.[21] The interviews informing this study took place almost two years before Trump was elected, long before he entered the international consciousness as a serious political figure. Regardless of how far observers agree with his approach, the one source of agreement is how different it is to previous US leaders. Yet based on the ideas underpinning the *Led Astray* narrative, Trump's foreign policy behaviour is not new; it merely reinforces existing ideas that Britain has a more considered, sophisticated understanding of international affairs than its Atlantic ally. This shows how narrative analysis at the individual level can reveal sources of continuity beneath what on the surface appears to be profound change.

The Selfish Imperialist Narrative

The final narrative in the typology casts Britain as a *Selfish Imperialist*. It is distinctive because it portrays Britain as a *Force for Ill* and not a *Force for Good*. The country is the villain of the story: an exploitative, (neo)colonial power that primarily goes to war for economic gain. The plot consists of a continuous stream of wars fought for Britain's own benefit. In this tale of 'celebrated imperialism to this day', Britain 'interfer[es] as much as possible in other people's affairs' in pursuit of its own interests.[22] The setting paints a world in which war should in theory not take place, but it does so because of humankind's inherent greed and its desire to dominate and exploit others.

Ideologically, this story combines elements of Marxist economic logic and a rejection of the civilising narrative of the White Man's Burden.[23] Britain is characterised as a 'colonial oppressor', plundering the wealth of other countries for the benefit of its capitalist system.[24] Claims that its interventions protect human rights are just a new form of 'humanitarian imperialism' to impose putatively universal Western values on others.[25] These combine in an anti-imperialist narrative that applies to Britain's military past, present, and future.

Judgments of the British Empire reflect Gott's claim that it was a 'horrendous creation', 'established through "bloodshed"' and a 'prolonged nightmare for the majority of its subject people' that persists today.[26] This perspective is encapsulated by Lily (18–24, London), when prompted about an earlier statement that there are 'so many things not to be proud of' in British history:

> LILY: On the things not to be proud of? The British Empire I suppose. I read something recently that there's twenty-two countries in the world that Britain's never invaded apparently. . . . The consequences are that certain parts of the world are obviously kind of incredibly . . . what's the word . . . disadvantaged. It's like they were given a massive handicap because we went there, colonised them, took natural resources, slaves at one point, financial resources.

This damning judgment of the empire is also found in the *Learning from Its Mistakes* and *Led Astray* narratives. The difference in the *Selfish Imperialist* narrative is that the pattern of exploitation continues today. Throughout Britain's military history it has imposed its 'political system', 'religious beliefs', and 'ideals' on others while depriving them of economic resources. It has persistently intervened in countries to 'try and make them more Western',[27] while 'taking natural resources and minerals . . . but then not leaving anything sustainable for [other] econom[ies] to grow'.[28]

Future progress is not anticipated either. Armed force is again seen as something that 'in an ideal world we wouldn't need', to be used only for humanitarian purposes and defence—to 'support people rather than dictate'. But as long as there are economic incentives to prosecute war, continuity is seen as inevitable. It is a pessimistic outlook on the future, in which Britain is expected to remain continuously at war.

This continuity is demonstrated by Dan (45–54, Dorset), whose narrative spans a millennium of apparently continuous British exploitation:

DAN: If we go back to Richard the Lionheart, we were over there imposing on the Middle East. Now clearly there was no oil there at that time, but we wanted to impose our system on them. We look at the British Empire, when we went around the world and imposed our rule everywhere, and imposed our religion everywhere, and we imposed things on countries. We have oppressed, we have oppressed many, many times. . . . We go back to the British Empire and we went around the world and we routed places, and stole their mineral wealth and all good things from them, and then buggered off. And I think it's very similar today. It's about cash.

Lewis (18–24, London) also generalises that the overall pattern of British military history is one of 'mass interference' that he expects to continue. His account reflects on what he learnt about British imperial history in secondary school:

LEWIS: And what you're learning in history, you're celebrating imperialism when really it's horrible and we were removing people's autonomy, infringing on their independence, but we're the head of the world, so it's great from our point of view. So [in the] past we celebrated imperialism, followed by World War One, World War Two, a sort of complex defence of our culture, identity, our state. Erm . . . followed by mass interference in other countries, from the India-Pakistan independence, to Sri Lanka, to many countries in Africa, the Middle East at the moment. And in the future I can't see it changing at all, to be honest . . . and I think it's quite a bleak outlook on what it's going to be like. But recent experiences of the last ten or so years show me that I don't really trust Western foreign policy, and to some extent it's created more harm than good.

Two exceptions to the continuous narrative of British exploitation are the world wars. Dan suggests these might have been 'purer' and 'appropriate' interventions, while Lewis describes them as 'defensive', 'justified', and 'something that had to be done'. This might give the impression of a rise and fall narrative, with immoral imperial oppression followed by moral progress in the world wars and then an ethical decline thereafter. However, the world wars are framed more as exceptions than indications of progress or decline, the only wars that were 'genuinely a case of defending freedom'.[29] Despite these exceptions, narrators of this story share the general logic that Britain's wars are really materially driven. As Dan states, 'It's big business. It's all about money. It's all about money'.

A Common Counternarrative

The *Selfish Imperialist* narrative was relatively rare across the sample. It was identified in 9 out of 67 interviews (13 percent), although few generalised that the entirety of British military history was one of continuous imperial exploitation. Most saw some positives in Britain's military past and appeared reluctant to characterise it unreservedly as a *Force for Ill*. Likewise, economic motives were rarely considered the sole explanation of Britain's wars. Instead they were frequently considered one factor among many, alongside issues such as humanitarianism, sovereignty, power, and influence. Grace (55–64, Worcestershire), whose responses mainly fit the *Punching Above Its Weight* and *Learning from Its Mistakes* narratives, exemplifies this. In doing so she also shows how multiple storylines can be evident in an individual's interpretation of Britain's wars.

> GRACE: I think there are an awful lot of conflicts [that] are economic, dressed up as other things. I think there was at least an element of that with the Iraq War. . . . I think there was an economic aspect . . . because oil did seem to figure in it. And again throughout history, the British Opium Wars against China, that was a completely appalling conflict which was entirely based on the fact that we wanted to sell them lethal drugs. So this is why I haven't got a hugely high opinion of Britain's historic role in the world. And I think most war is to some extent economic because it's usually about land-grabbing, and why do you want land if it's not for economic reasons?

Grace's assumption that war is often materially motivated appears theoretically sound given that, as IR theorists emphasise, economic interests drive policy preferences.[30] Moreover, Britain's economic strength today derives partly from benefits accrued through its empire. Land brings people and resources and has done so throughout history. It is unsurprising therefore that citizens may not choose to tell the *Selfish Imperialist* narrative but still understand its logic that economic considerations are a key factor in decisions to go to war. Just because a participant tells one story about Britain's wars does not mean they do not recognise other interpretations. As with all narratives, what matters is that they have chosen one explanation that they see as more plausible than its alternatives.

Bearing this in mind, the *Selfish Imperialist* narrative most frequently appears not as a coherent narrative of British history overall but when people questioned whether specific wars were actually economically motivated rather than humanitarian. As Chomsky observes, Western countries almost invariably justify their wars by claiming that they are humanitarian.[31] But the political climate is currently characterised by intense distrust of politicians and scepticism about the efficacy of using military force in this way.[32] This leads people to question whether humanitarian rhetoric is genuine or whether it obscures an underhand agenda. This is particularly true of 'wars of choice' where no explicit national interest is at stake.[33] In such situations, economic motivations provide a commonsense, ulterior explanation when distrusted governments claim that Britain should intervene. Most recently, the putative agenda has been control of oil, along with the perpetuation of the arms trade.

> DANIELLE (35–44, LONDON): I do feel it is a hidden agenda sometimes in some of the wars. You feel like are we really going to war because Saddam Hussein might have some Scud missiles that have got a range of 500 kilometres or whatever, or are we going because it's sitting on huge amounts of oil resources and it would be detrimental to our economy if that was unavailable?

> FIONA (18–24, LONDON): I feel like the UK and the US are focused on oil and trade rather than the humanitarian aspect of it, and the US especially because they have such an oil dependency . . . well especially the UK as well, but to stay as a superpower the US needs the oil to have their standard of living, and their output, so I feel their view on everything is just to get the oil to remain that superpower so they can continue asserting dominance.

> MARY (35–44, DORSET): It's probably linked with economic things . . . I know everyone bangs on about it all the time but I do think we're interested in the Middle East because of oil. Therefore, it's in our interest.

> JOANNE (55–64, DORSET): If you go back to . . . Kuwait over the oil, I just feel that the interference there, or the so called help, was actually nothing to do with the people, it was to do with oil and economics. It wasn't moral.

Oil Narrative, Oil Myth

The relationship between oil and war has spawned a considerable literature attempting to establish it as the 'real' reason for Western military interventionism. Many of these texts tie a century of military history into a meta-narrative where all motives are false apart from controlling oil.[34] Tying Britain into this alongside the United States supports the *Selfish Imperialist* narrative. If postmodernism displays 'incredulity towards meta-narratives',[35] this interpretation displays 'incredulity towards humanitarianism'.

Of the 32 out of 67 interviewees (48 percent) that mentioned oil, few saw it as the sole cause of all Britain's wars. For most, it provides a heuristic to explain why Britain chooses to intervene in one conflict and not another. Britain may still be fundamentally humanitarian, but it lacks the resources to intervene in every crisis. It must therefore be selective. The need for selectivity is even more acute given how accepted the narrative of British *Material Decline* appears to be. The problem is that humanitarianism commonly implies universal concern for human beings rather than the population of one state and not another.[36] It is therefore too easy to counter humanitarian claims by asking 'why here and not somewhere else?' Access to natural resources such as oil provides a cognitive shortcut to explain selective military interventionism.[37] It therefore undermines British claims to be a *Force for Good*. Meanwhile, the plot of British military history becomes a series of selective military interventions conducted by a hypocritical, selfish power that picks and chooses where it fights.

Two prevalent examples are Rwanda in 1994 and Iraq in 2003. Rwanda, after Syria, was the second most common conflict where participants felt Britain should have intervened but did not. Despite occurring over two decades ago, people still use it to undermine claims that military interventions are humanitarian. Iraq in 2003 was by far the most opposed war, brought up by 44 out of 67 people (66 percent). Beyond these crude figures, participant responses indicate that being deceived over the real motives for the intervention has strengthened their perceptions that they are being deceived about other interventions. This impression is reinforced by Gribble et al., who found that 47 percent of sampled British citizens in 2011 thought oil was the main motive for Iraq in 2003, with only 32 percent citing the government's official 'Weapons of Mass Destruction' argument.[38]

KYLE (18–24, LONDON): . . . if we go into any country where citizens, general innocents, are being abused and killed for no reason then we should intervene and protect them. However, saying that I don't think we ever have done that for the right reason, really, because we never went into Rwanda. There was no resources we could have there, funnily enough. We never went in when genocide was happening there yet we're more than happy to go into Middle Eastern countries where there's something to be earned from it. So it's all about the reason we go in.

MARK (65+, BIRMINGHAM): I know we can't prove it was for oil in Iraq, but I think that a large majority of the country felt it was, because you've got tyrants in Africa such as Mugabe, but no one seems to bother about him killing thousands of his own people. So that makes you think all the more that had there been oil there they might have stepped in on him. It always seems to be the countries where there's oil.

Proponents of the 'oil narrative' look to debunk humanitarian narratives as 'myth', in the colloquial sense of being an 'erroneous belief' or 'popular misconception'.[39] In reality both are *mythological* by the definition used here, in that their central premises are often taken as common sense and are held with a conviction that transcends the need for factual evidence.[40] Whether a country possesses notable oil reserves is often irrelevant. They are merely seen as transit routes for future pipelines. In this way the Kosovo intervention in 1999 has been incorporated into the oil narrative despite possessing no known reserves whatsoever.[41] Oil, it seems, can be read as a motive into almost any conflict.

To illustrate this point, oil is the commonsense motive for Britain's potential intervention *and* nonintervention in Syria in the following two examples.

IRENE (55–64, WORCESTERSHIRE): I think when the Syria conflict started, there was that kind of feeling that we ought to do something because this is terrible. But I do think we should have put a lot more effort into negotiation and persuasion and sanctions. . . . I think it's very sad when Syrians were asking for help and they believed we would help. And of course there is the thing that had there been a lot of oil involved we probably would have helped.

FIONA (18–24, LONDON): I remember thinking I definitely thought it would not be a good idea to go [into Syria]. And I remember there was a TV show on BBC Three about it, saying how . . . it wasn't Britain's place to intervene because it wasn't a direct threat to Britain. And by intervening it would just show that we only care about oil, because I know there's a lot of oil in that area. I just remember I was against it. I can't remember why.

These accounts contradict each other. One assumes there is lots of oil in the area, the other that there is none. Both contain an element of truth—Syria has oil reserves but they are relatively small at 2.5 billion barrels (32nd globally).[42] But both discount the humanitarian debates about the intervention for the apparently obvious explanation that oil was the major factor. Dan (45–54, Dorset) and Joanne (55–64, Dorset) do the same in their accounts of Afghanistan and Yugoslavia respectively.

> DAN: You see the whole argument for, say, Afghanistan—we'll use Afghanistan—it's [apparently] about fighting against oppression of the people in that country . . . when we all know the routes for oil through Afghanistan are crucial for the West.
>
> JOANNE: I felt that when the whole Yugoslav thing kicked off, all I kept saying was 'why won't they go and help them? I know why they won't go and help them, they've got no oil'. And it was only public pressure in the end that forced governments to do anything.

These accounts demonstrate the flexibility of the oil narrative to explain British intervention, nonintervention, and delayed intervention, despite minimal evidence. Dan's idea that Afghan oil pipelines are 'crucial' for the West is highly doubtful, not least because they still do not exist. His statement that 'we all know' this reflects his assumption that his view is commonly held. Interestingly it is not reflected in opinion polls, with only 24 percent of the British public seeing oil as the motive for Afghanistan in 2011.[43] But given this was never an official motive for the intervention, that almost a quarter of the sample believe it shows the power of the oil myth to gain traction regardless of the evidence.

There is some evidence to support Joanne's recollection of the Bosnian War, with the international community criticised for being catastrophically slow to act and indecisive when it did so.[44] Meanwhile opinion polls at the time showed that in April 1993, a year after the war began, 52 percent of the British public felt the government was not doing enough.[45] More significantly, Joanne's statement implies that she intuitively 'knew' that delayed intervention in an immensely complex conflict was due to the absence of oil. This once more shows how obvious the explanation is to her. Her response is also illuminating because rather than seeing Britain as an exploitative power in general, she separates a self-interested political elite from an honest and charitable public. In this interpretation of the *Selfish Imperialist* narrative, the government is the villain but the British public remain the heroes.

Arms Trades and International Conspiracies

The idea that British politicians are a cynical, self-interested elite dragging an honest and charitable British public to war forms the central assumption of claims that war is motivated by the arms trade. The British people are inherently good from this perspective; their leaders are the selfish capitalists, colluding with arms manufacturers in what Dan (45–54, Dorset) describes as 'the biggest business in the world'. Such comments echo Smedley Butler's famous statement that 'War is a Racket. It always has been. It is possibly the oldest, easily the most profitable, surely the most vicious'.[46] As Irene (55–64, Worcestershire) claims about politicians, 'various of them have interest in the arms trade after all, so it's not going to benefit them if we have world peace'.

> NICHOLAS (35–44, LANCASHIRE): I've always thought it's very unhealthy to have your morality driven by economics rather than the other way round.... It probably is just a continuation of our imperial past because that's what we did. We produce arms, we don't use them anymore, but we've got to keep the industries going and sell them to somewhere else. So ... it then becomes conflict driven by ... you sometimes strangely feel that the conflict is driven by the need to maintain the machine.

This explanation that vested interests in the arms trade drive Britain's wars reinforces the *Selfish Imperialist* narrative by providing another ulterior motive for war. Ideologically this might be associated with Marxist thinking, with a villainous global capitalist elite spreading conflict at the expense of the masses. However, suspicion of war being perpetuated by the arms trade was also found among nationalist sentiment. Vincent (65+, Lancashire), a self-identifying nationalist and 'little Englander',[47] demonstrates this when reflecting on why at the time the West had not yet defeated Islamic State militarily:

VINCENT: Well, I'm fully well aware that Islamic State is a different kettle of fish to whatever previous movements have been in the Middle East. But are you telling me that it's beyond the wit of the West that we can't destroy them totally, militarily? When you're getting satellites, surveillance planes, drones all over the place and they can pick out a golf ball on a golf course from 50,000 feet, and they can't find out where groups of insurgents are? I find this beggars belief. I sometimes wonder whether or not, being cynical, the massive arms industry in the West, and particularly in the United States, I think it's within their interests to keep conflicts going.

As one of the strongest proponents of the militaristic, nationalist *Vanishing Force* narrative, Vincent's reasons for suspecting an arms conspiracy differ from those who see Britain as a *Selfish Imperialist*. Vincent expresses immense pride in the military as 'the one institution that works'. Meanwhile he distrusts politicians as 'bloody fools' with their own interests at heart. With such a superior military, logically it should be easy for the West to destroy Islamic State. That it hasn't come close to doing so must therefore be explained by other factors. Military strategists might emphasise that overwhelming dominance in conventional military means is of limited effect when identifying insurgents among a civilian population. But to Vincent, observing Western technological dominance, maintaining international arms sales provides a more intuitive explanation.

In the most extreme cases, the assumption that Western interventions are always fought for ulterior motives leads to what many would consider conspiracy theories. Dan (45–54, Dorset) takes the economic motive to such an extreme that he suggests that Islamic State were created by the West to justify its control of the Middle East.

DAN: If we actually look in detail and you study hard about the Taliban, and who funded them, it was the West. It was the West that funded them. But then they didn't play ball. We look at Saddam, who put him there? Who funded him, who put him in that position? It was the West. They wanted control of the Middle East. You could argue strongly that with Israel . . . okay there's some historical stuff going on there but you could argue strongly with Israel that the West want Israel in the middle of the Middle East. But then it all comes back again to money. Why do they want the Middle East? Well there's an awful lot of bloody oil, you know. No one talks about it but who's funding Islamic State? Who's funded them? You know, where did they get all these arms from? It most clearly came from the West, but they're not playing the game now. Or are they playing the game and that's what the West want so they can go in there and control what's going on with the Syrian leadership?

Dan's account represents the most extreme example across the sample of Britain as a *Force for Ill*. At no point does he suggest that motives for British military intervention are in any way humanitarian or altruistic. Instead, so pernicious is the Western conspiracy of which Britain is a part, that it funds terrorist groups that are putatively its enemies, for profit. There are grains of truth that make the narrative appear plausible, such as the Western support of the mujahideen in Afghanistan and Islamic State's possession of Western arms, albeit for reasons different from those he suggests.[48] Dan clearly has a broad knowledge of a range of political actors across the Middle East over several decades. More important though is the overarching idea he uses to tie decades of Middle Eastern history together: that Western and therefore British military intervention has always been about oppression and profit, and never about people.

The Significance of These Narratives

This controversial final narrative suggests the satisfactory fulfilment of a central aim of this study—to map out the broadest possible range of interpretations of Britain's role in war. Earlier on, Britain was cast as a *Force for Good*, the protector of the liberal order, the 'last, best hope for mankind'.[49] At the other extreme, it has become a *Force for Ill*, an 'evil empire' participating in a global conspiracy that is 'ruining the world'.[50] Considering that these views are extremely broad, as well as being derived from a highly diverse sample interviewed beyond the point of data saturation, it can be said with reasonable confidence that these genres incorporate an extremely broad range of views on Britain's wars. This suggests that while statistical generalisation to the broader population is impossible due to the study's sample size, 'representational generalisation' can occur. In other words, it can be reasonably inferred that the genres identified would be *present* in the broader population. It is their relative prevalence that would require further research.[51]

The validity of these narratives can also be demonstrated through their 'transferability' to different contexts.[52] In other words, if these genres accurately reflect those used by British citizens to interpret war, then it should be easy to fit new conflicts into these general patterns. As Bruner explains, genres enable people to make sense of the particulars of unfamiliar events by providing a familiar framework into which they can be embedded.[53] The first major shift in Britain's military posture after data collection ended came almost a year later, when parliament voted to extend British airstrikes against Islamic State into Syria in December 2015. Supported by 397 MPs and opposed by 223, the decision engaged the public in a prolonged and emotional debate on whether the country should expand its existing operations.[54] The debate illustrates well how readily new interventions can be incorporated into existing public narratives of war.

The Syria intervention reflected both the *Continuous War* and *Material Decline* narratives particularly well. The opposition's formal questions during the ten-hour parliamentary debate focused almost solely on the efficacy of the intervention rather than the principle of military intervention itself. Questions asked included whether intervention would 'make a significant military impact'; 'be successful without ground forces'; lead to 'mission creep'; or increase the 'threat of terrorist attacks in the UK'.[55] The general principle of whether Britain should use military force to achieve political objectives was not questioned. The debate thus reflected continuity in military force being a legitimate and natural policy instrument. The smaller size of the intervention compared to past wars also strongly reflected the *Material Decline* narrative.

The government's justification for extending airstrikes contained strong echoes of the *Punching Above Its Weight* narrative. It specifically emphasised that Britain's allies had requested Britain's help because it possessed the Brimstone missile system, which is apparently technologically superior to their own. Cameron emphasised that the precision of the missile system was a capability 'even the US do not possess'.[56] He described Britain's intelligence and surveillance as 'second to none'. Together these would give Britain an 'important and distinct role' in coalition efforts against Islamic State.[57]

The other pillar of Cameron's argument was Britain's moral obligation to support its allies, particularly in the wake of the Paris terrorist attacks in November 2015.[58] By playing the role of 'reliable ally' there was also continuity in Britain being willing to step in when others might lack the same self-sacrificing attitude.[59] Taken together, the government's arguments emphasised Britain's superior military technique and moral fortitude in being willing and able to help others. In other words, it was *Punching Above Its Weight*.

The rhetorical trick in this narrative was that in focusing on Britain's supposed technological superiority, it obscured the tiny material contribution Britain actually made. After a month of the operation, only four sorties had been flown in Syria by British forces, and one of those was an unmanned drone strike.[60] Two months in, Britain's 'unique' Brimstone missiles had not killed a single fighter.[61] This suggests that the intervention was more about making Britain appear to be a heroic central character as the drama unfolded rather than achieving meaningful strategic results.

Consequently, the Syria intervention also fits the *Vanishing Force* narrative. It seems an obvious example of a country disappearing further from the world stage that can only send a derisory force to a conflict upon which it has no real influence. Moreover, it is evidence of the duplicity of politicians whose claims that Britain punches above its weight are empty rhetoric. It is unsurprising then that, along with Britain recently sending military advisors to Iraq and Ukraine, commentators have dismissed such small-scale contributions as desperate attempts to appear relevant by a state that risks becoming little more than 'Belgium with nukes'.[62]

The smaller scale and more cautious targeting in the Syrian air campaign could also fit into the *Learning from Its Mistakes* narrative. From this perspective the use of more accurate Brimstone missiles and the limited scope of British military action showed Britain becoming more discriminate in the use of military force and more cautious about civilian casualties. Again, the impression that Britain is more concerned about this than other issues further reinforces British moral exceptionalism.

The Syria intervention could also be framed to fit the Britain *Led Astray* narrative. For once more Britain was following the United States into a conflict in the Middle East with no long-term political objective, or at least no explicit roadmap for a political solution, and with the clear potential for mission creep. The intervention could be seen to fit both of these liberal interpretations simultaneously. Britain could be perceived as *Learning from Its Mistakes* in minimising civilian casualties, but despite this it was still being *Led Astray* into wars it should have kept out of.

Finally, the Syrian intervention also fits the *Selfish Imperialist* narrative. Through this interpretive lens, Syria was just another example of a Middle Eastern country that either has oil, or is next to Iraq that does, and so Britain's involvement was just a continuation of Western attempts to control resources. Moreover, the government's emphasis on Brimstone could be interpreted as reflecting the desire to perpetuate the arms trade. Whether these interpretations correspond to reality is irrelevant; the idea that war is 'fought for oil' has become sufficiently common sense and provides an intuitive explanation for Britain's involvement whether notable resources are at stake or not.

This analysis of Britain's extended intervention against Islamic State into Syria demonstrates how readily each genre can make sense of subsequent conflicts. However, it is not claimed that the typology is applicable to all wars Britain has ever fought and will ever fight. That said, cultural change tends to be slow and, as multiple researchers attest, national identity narratives rarely shift dramatically.[63] A key reason for this is the reassurance identity groups derive from seeing the world, and their role within it, as 'pretty much the same from one day to the next'.[64] Because of this desire for ontological security, it is far more likely that new events are incorporated into existing narratives rather than new stories being created from scratch.[65] 'It is always possible to add another twist to the plot or even another chapter', but narratives are rarely discarded altogether.[66]

By implication, there is good reason to anticipate that these genres have enduring value beyond the moment of their telling. The *Punching Above Its Weight* and *Selfish Imperialist* narratives are based on transhistorical generalisations that can readily be used to frame new conflicts. Even the most minuscule military intervention can fit the story of Britain *Punching Above Its Weight* because it is doing more than those that do nothing. It is also hard to prove that there are no ulterior economic motives for war, which makes the *Selfish Imperialist* narrative likely to persist as long as Britain's warring does. Ultimately, though, how the narratives British citizens use to interpret war will change in the future is an empirical question that only subsequent research will answer.

Having revealed a typology of general patterns citizens use to summarise Britain's role in war, a vital question that remains concerns how participants deal with wars, or episodes within them, that contradict their narrative identity claims. Generalising that the overall pattern of British military history is one of progress does not mean that one cannot identify setbacks too. To construct a coherent story, a narrator must process both supporting and contradictory events in some way. To understand more fully how citizens do this, the book moves from the macro-level to the micro-level to examine how citizens emplot individual events to create the general pattern of their stories. Examining this will reveal in detail how citizens try to persuade the audience that their interpretation of war is the right one.

CHAPTER 6

Is Britain a Force for Good?

Emplotment and Narrative Coherence

SHAUN (55–64, DORSET): To be honest, I can't think of a time when we have gone hell-bent to war because we wanted to. I might be wrong, but I can't think of a time.

History rarely unfolds as smoothly as the stories we tell about it.[1] To construct a narrative that generalises that the past is characterised by progress, continuity, decline, or some combination of these, the narrator must deal with a range of events, some of which may contradict their overall claim. How do people try to do this convincingly? Through emplotment: the way they select and link events temporally and causally to create the overall pattern of their stories. Memory provides the resources to do this, since the only source of information to explain the present is the past. In an active process—even though narrators may not be consciously aware of it—people choose to bring up some events and not others, emphasising some aspects while downplaying others.[2] The more coherent the resulting plot is, the more convincing the overall narrative is likely to be.

This process applies to narratives about war and national identity as much as any other social phenomenon. The foreign policy literature has addressed some aspects of how political actors narrate their histories selectively, highlighting past military glories and silencing atrocities to portray themselves more favourably.[3] Nevertheless, the process of combining multiple emplotment mechanisms to create an overall narrative has not been systematically analysed in foreign policy, and not using the war stories told by ordinary citizens.

To address this void, this chapter moves to the micro-level, examining how citizens selectively emplot their memories of British military history to try and construct more coherent narratives about Britain's international identity. This is achieved through novel use of a framework that examines how individuals combine multiple emplotment mechanisms to make their narratives more compelling. Doing this addresses the question of how the complex emplotment process can be systematically analysed, using a method applicable to narrative analysis of any social phenomenon. Here the focus of analysis concerns how individuals use Britain's past wars to support or oppose a central claim of British defence policy: that it is a *Force for Good* in the world.[4]

Analysing Selective Emplotment

Emplotment was examined by augmenting a framework originally used in Spector-Mersel's work on biographical narratives and identity formation.[5] A framework of seven mechanisms was used to assess how individuals support or challenge the identity claim that Britain has always been a morally exceptional *Force for Good* in the world. The seven mechanisms are as follows:

Inclusion: selecting facts that fit the identity claim being made.
Example: selecting wars to support the overall claim that Britain's military intervenes for the good of humanity.
Linking: establishing a temporal, causal, or spatial relationship between events.
Example: causally linking victory in the First World War to the allied naval blockade rather than America joining the war.
Sharpening: emphasising specific aspects of events that fit the identity claim being made.
Example: an embedded story emphasising atrocities conducted during a particular war as part of a story portraying Britain's wars as morally wrong.
Clarifying: explaining what an event was 'really all about', as opposed to alternative, commonly assumed meanings.
Example: arguing that a war was not about natural resources but actually about defending democracy.
Omission: not including events that are *irrelevant* to the point of the story.
Example: excluding wars where Britain was not obviously trying to help others in a story about British humanitarian interventions.

Silencing: not including events that *contradict* the point of the story.

Example: highlighting Britain's moral leadership in abolishing the slave trade but silencing the fact that it had transported more slaves than any other state.

Flattening: selecting but telling little of events that may contradict the point of the narrative. These events may be condensed and receive minimal focus. Alternatively they may be mentioned to assert their insignificance.

Example: bringing up British imperial violence to explain it away because Britain was comparatively more benevolent than other colonial powers.

Identifying how citizens combine these emplotment mechanisms is more than a descriptive exercise. If the overall point of a story is not explicitly stated, as is often the case, the framework can be used to infer it inductively.[6] In this way it provides a grounded method to determine how similarly people construct identity claims about the nation. However, the framework can also be used as a structural guide for how to use emplotment to argue. A policymaker may want to make a claim about Britain's military role in the world, and the framework indicates different elements to consider when constructing a narrative to support it. It is potentially a detailed process; the complexity of emplotment has led quantitative analysts of 'policy narratives' to avoid studying it.[7] But if plot is what distinguishes narrative from other modes of discourse, and effective strategic communication rests on coherent storytelling, then being able to analyse the emplotment process comprehensively seems vital.

To demonstrate, the remainder of the chapter examines how citizens emplot their narratives to support or challenge the view that Britain's military is a *Force for Good* in the world. This seminal claim of British defence policy was supported in some form in 58 out of 67 interviews (87 percent).[8] It is implicit in the *Punching Above Its Weight*, *Vanishing Force*, *Learning from Its Mistakes* and *Led Astray* narratives, at least in terms of Britain's intentions when it goes to war, although each varies on the extent to which it has been the case throughout history. In contrast, underpinning the *Selfish Imperialist* narrative (9 out of 67 interviews—13 percent) is the idea that Britain has always been a *Force for Ill*, fighting for the remorseless, selfish pursuit of territory and resources. Both sides of this narrative battle have the same wars to use as building blocks for their stories. Consequently, micro-analysis of emplotment can reveal how citizens try and make their interpretation more convincing.

Force for Good

An obvious way of portraying Britain as a *Force for Good* is to tell a story that focuses on the positives of its military interventions while omitting any negatives. Denise (25–34, Birmingham) provides a typical example, telling a somewhat romantic tale of a morally exceptional nation always trying to use its military to 'make the world a better place':

> DENISE: I think it's always been with good intentions. First and foremost, they've always had such good intentions. We've tried to help people. Initially going back all those years, with Germany, it was good intentions to help other countries with the immense problems that they had. You know, we didn't have to. We didn't have to go and do any of that, but we chose to. It's like with Iraq. We didn't have to go. We've never had to go as a country to do any of it, but we've always gone and supported and tried to make the world a better place. But that's always what it seemed to be about, is wanting to make it a happy world, liveable and safe for everybody. It seems that's what the country's tried to do. Unfortunately a lot of souls have been lost along the way.
>
> RESEARCHER: Do you think Britain's succeeded?
>
> DENISE: . . . I think it has been successful. I mean obviously with the First World War and the Second World War, that was successful going back all that time. That was successful. Iraq, that seems to have helped the people. You know, obviously there are still conflicts underlying and things do still happen. It's like with Afghanistan. We've given them the tools to learn how to police themselves properly, how to . . . food, water, how to do all of that. So I do think it has been successful.

Denise's account portrays Britain as a *Force for Good* in several ways. It focuses almost exclusively on the positive aspects of Britain's wars. No explicit negative consequences are mentioned. She *includes* several events, such as the First and Second World Wars, Afghanistan, and Iraq. These events are causally *linked* by Britain's desire to help others. A specific link is also drawn between two events, with war against Germany said to be 'like Iraq' in that Britain did not have to go and help other countries in either situation. Afghanistan is *sharpened* as she goes into more detail, explaining the specific benefits Britain's intervention has supposedly brought to locals, such as food, water, and policing. This may or may not be factually accurate and could be interpreted as somewhat Orientalist in implying the local population could not do these things already. More importantly, though, Denise's interpretation is that Britain fights to help those perceived as disadvantaged. In an example of *clarifying*, she explains that Iraq 'seems to have helped', but by acknowledging that 'obviously there are still conflicts underlying', she suggests her understanding that others may interpret the Iraq War as one where Britain's involvement failed to prevent ongoing conflict. There is an element of *flattening* in this statement, which gives no indication of who might be responsible for the 'conflicts underlying'. In a further example of *flattening*, she admits that it is 'unfortunate that a lot of souls have been lost along the way', but without providing any more detail. The use of the passive voice here also leaves vague who is culpable for the 'souls' that 'have been lost'; the active statement that 'Britain killed soldiers and civilians along the way' would not fit the *Force for Good* narrative.

Another noteworthy aspect of Denise's narrative is the absence of reference to the wars of the British Empire. For most participants, 'empire' was the overwhelming focus when considering Britain's past. Whether this is a product of *omission* through lack of knowledge or deliberate *silencing* is a matter of interpretation. Both are possible. Empire has often been conspicuously absent from British history curricula in recent years.[9] Consequently, many younger citizens may have little knowledge of it, good or bad. In contrast, older participants such as Leonard (55–64, Wales) and Neil (65+, Worcestershire) both cite proud moments at school of being shown the map of the world with 'all the areas of pink' Britain controlled. Denise only discusses the empire once asked about it later in her interview. So while she did show knowledge of it, it is hard to assert definitively that she *silenced* it to make it easier to uphold her *Force for Good* narrative. Generally, *flattening* is a more concrete form of evidence, because it involves explicitly naming events before their significance is minimised or explained away. This was a recurrent feature of citizens' attempts to justify imperial violence when framing Britain as a *Force for Good*.

Empire: The Elephant in the Room

To portray Britain as a *Force for Good* or *Force for Ill* throughout history, narrators must address the British Empire in some way. As Dawson observes, 'the history of Empire continues to maintain a determining influence over cultural and political life in modern Britain'.[10] As the country's greatest achievement or greatest tyranny, depending on perspective, its size is only matched by the controversy over its purported costs and benefits. Since success in war was essential in its establishment and maintenance, to evaluate it is to evaluate the violence required to sustain it.

The need to explain empire was particularly prominent for those arguing that Britain has been a *Force for Good*. Citizens used selective emplotment to legitimise the British Empire in multiple ways. They emphasised its apparent liberalism and benevolence, while justifying its wars as defensive, innocently adventurous, civilising, and based on good intentions even if people suffered as a result. These ideas reflect what Marshall describes as the 'liberal lie', in that they downplay the brutality often used by the military to pacify colonial populations.[11] But since humans generally 'want to have an acceptable view of who we are, there is always a temptation . . . to ignore colonialism and imperialism while praising one's cosmopolitanism and philanthropy'.[12]

Empire: Omission through Start Point and Periodisation

Telling a story of a continuous state of affairs throughout history gives the narrator considerable flexibility to emplot different events. If it is taken for granted that Britain is always a *Force for Good*, any event can theoretically be *included* and the positive aspects of it *sharpened*. Meanwhile the imperial violence that might contradict the *Force for Good* narrative can be *silenced*. However, this can also be complemented by judicious choice of start point. The narrator can begin after events that are more obviously aggressive or exploitative. Periodisation can then be used to focus on times when Britain allegedly went to war for the right reasons while other conflicts can be ignored. This process was facilitated by open-ended questioning, since people could begin and end their stories at any point in history. Denise has already demonstrated this by focusing only on the world wars and after. An even more telling illustration is provided by Paul's (55–64, Worcestershire) response to being asked to 'tell the story of Britain's historical role in war and conflict':

> PAUL: Interesting question . . . if you limit the past to the 1900s rather than going back any further, we have a distinguished history of standing up for what was right and sacrificing ourselves as we should. From the 2000s onwards I'm not so sure.

RESEARCHER: What about before 1900?

PAUL: Well before then we were doing things like fighting Napoleon. We had a long history of defending England against nasty foreigners . . . Spain, France. It was more about religion, it was a different sort of war . . . not right or wrong but to persuade people to go to a different church. It was not a good use of religion. The Boer War . . . that was questionable.

Even in a few lines, Paul's brief response reveals several ways Britain is portrayed as a *Force for Good*. He first attempts to do so by starting his narrative in the 1900s. Thereafter he uses the twentieth century as a convenient framework to generalise that Britain has a 'distinguished history of standing up for what was right'. He *sharpens* focus on this, although he speaks in generalities rather than naming specific wars. Meanwhile he *silences* what happens before 1900 since he implies it contradicts the point of his story. Only when prompted does he discuss it. And despite implying that British history may be less distinguished before 1900, he frames Britain's role as 'defensive' (defending 'England') and thus legitimate. Empire or colonialism are not mentioned. Instead he *clarifies* that these earlier wars were about religion. Nevertheless, his final sentence indicates his awareness of the morally dubious nature of some of Britain's wars in his description of the Boer War as 'questionable'. This may be a way to appear more balanced in acknowledging that Britain has not always been ethically exemplary. However, it is also a *flattening* statement, since it minimises discussion of the 'questionable' issues themselves. These may have invalidated his central claim. Overall, the combination of start point, periodisation, and selective emplotment portrays Britain's history as morally right and minimises attention to any other evidence. Britain is a *Force for Good*, a shining light in a destructive era famously described by Isaiah Berlin as 'the worst century there has ever been'.[13]

Framing Empire Positively

While some omitted the empire, most recognised that the violence involved could undermine claims that Britain has always been a *Force for Good*. Acknowledging this, they deliberately brought it up to *sharpen* focus on its positive effects and explain away violence and atrocity. Participants praised Britain for bringing parliamentary democracy, language, and civilisation to the world. Typically they *clarified* that imperial wars were really only defensive and about trade. Meanwhile they *silenced* or *flattened* illiberal, violent aspects of imperial rule as just 'the way things were back then' or as being less violent than other imperial powers. Having provided significant detail about the positives of Britain's imperial past, they downplayed any negatives. Even those who see the empire as immoral tended to avoid naming specifics. Instead they alluded to imperial atrocities using vaguer descriptions of Britain as having 'not handled it very well', 'not exactly bathed ourselves in glory', or with the military being 'used in ways nowadays we probably wouldn't want'. Combining these discursive tactics deflects from imperialism's fundamentally discriminatory and illiberal nature by framing it as comparatively benevolent.[14]

Defensive Imperialism

Framing imperial wars as defensive was one of the strongest ways the sampled participants supported the *Force for Good* claim. Defending liberal democracy is a common theme underpinning British military interventionism. With the empire, according to this perspective, Britain was defending itself against other nations seeking to undermine its preeminence. More extreme viewpoints lead to the somewhat contradictory idea of 'defensive imperialism', and even the denial that Britain ever voluntarily took over another country. This is not a new idea. Comparing the British Empire to the Roman Empire, some historians have claimed that both were established 'accidentally' or 'reluctantly' for security reasons rather than the drive to colonise.[15] Unsurprisingly, this stance is criticised for being an apologist justification of aggressive expansionism.[16] But, as the following narratives show, it persists among some citizens today.

> VINCENT (65+, LANCASHIRE): I'd tell as a result of the conflict and the spread of . . . British influence, which we have done throughout the world whether we like it or not, commerce, scientific discourse all being done in English, which we took to the world. We started off with trade, and to defend those trading stations we used military force . . . to protect them. I think we've been a tremendous influence on the world. Our political thinking, our method of democracy. God knows how many countries use the sorts of parliaments that we have now. They might be slightly different in various ways, but it's English democracy that sort of started it, and people look towards us as a democracy. And that's what we've

spread, and that's been our influence. That and the language. I know we've done terrible things, but then you know, that's sort of . . . we used to hang little boys for stealing apples and things like that. That's the way history is. You can't go back on it, you can't apologise for things you've done.

Vincent attempts to frame the British Empire as morally justifiable in several ways. Most of his account addresses positive aspects of colonial rule. First, he *clarifies* that the empire was really about trade. He then *links* military force with trade, but trade comes first. This temporal ordering frames Britain's wars as defensive and therefore justifiable, caused by the need to protect trade routes from others. He *sharpens* focus on the positive aspects of British imperial rule, by focusing most of the story on its 'tremendous influence' on the world—'our political thinking, our method of democracy'—reflecting the traditional idea of England as the 'mother of parliaments'.[17] Then, rather than *silencing* the 'terrible things' Britain has done as an imperial power, Vincent consciously brings them up, albeit briefly, to *flatten* them, by claiming that Britain's more oppressive imperial conduct—such as 'hang[ing] little boys for stealing apples'—was simply 'the way history is'. This imputes a logic onto imperial violence as justified and natural at the time. In his example, Britain may have been strict, but it was still ultimately disciplining criminals. As a result, it should not detract from all the positives of British colonial rule.

Harry (35–44, Birmingham) goes even further in his claim that Britain's wars have only ever been defensive:

HARRY: Well I think that a lot of what they've done through history is because they've <u>had</u> to do it. It's not necessarily going out there . . . we've never been over there and said 'well right, we're taking over your country'. We've just defended what we've had to defend. I don't think we've ruled the world with an iron hand. I think we just do . . . I know we had quite a big . . . we were sort of widespread throughout the whole world, colonised places. But more of that was to do with trade and stuff. Whereas England has always been invaded by every single person who's ever lived, throughout history. You know, I don't think England's necessarily gone out there to say 'right, we're going to take over this country. We don't believe what you're doing'.

Harry's account is general and he does not *include* any specific wars. But as with Vincent, the key point of the story is to *clarify* that Britain's wars have only ever been defensive. The story does not contain a clear temporal sequence of events. However, there is a clear causal chain throughout, a continuous plotline in which Britain repeatedly defends itself against attackers. Even taking colonies is incorporated into this defensive logic. This is despite clear contradictions in his story. He initially claims that Britain has never said 'well right, we're taking over your country', and yet admits later that Britain 'colonised places'. This undermines narrative coherence. Like Vincent he attempts to resolve the contradiction by claiming that this was only about trade. He appears to take for granted that trade is a legitimate and benign activity, which suggests the influence of neoliberal ideology. Claims that the empire was a benevolent trading enterprise administered by Britain, a fundamentally 'honest broker',[18] ignore the fact that much of this trade was mercantilist and exploitative, with the military far more than mere protectors. Negative consequences of Britain's wars have been entirely *omitted*. Harry does not necessarily seek to characterise Britain as a hero, but he does attempt to dismiss claims that it is a villain. Indeed by describing Britain hyperbolically as having 'always been invaded by every single person who's ever lived', he paints it as a victim who has only colonised others 'defensively', something of an oxymoron.

The claim that the British Empire began as an innocent trading enterprise and any military action was defensive arguably rests more on myth than the historical record. Ferguson, even as he maintains that the empire was a 'good thing' overall, acknowledges that it began based on piracy and theft of existing empires of the Spanish, Dutch, and Portuguese.[19] This does not appear widely known though. Instead the assumption that the empire began in order to safeguard trade obscures the often violent process through which Britain acquired territories to 'defend'. But as Vincent and Harry's stories demonstrate, these contradictions are subsumed within the overall logic that Britain's actions have always been just. Some historians support this stance too. Roberts judges Britain's wars as generally defensive. Furthermore, any 'harsh measures' Britain 'occasionally adopted' were only because they had to defend themselves and the world against the repeated assaults of Prussian militarism, fascist aggression, Soviet communism, and now Islamic fundamentalism.[20]

In addition to the defensive justification, others look to portray Britain as a *Force for Good* through emphasising the benevolence of the British Empire compared to other powers.

SHAUN (55–64, DORSET): I'm not against the fact that we had the British Empire. I think people are too quick to criticise the British Empire and have <u>totally</u> forgotten all the good it did. But there was corruption in it. But I mean what we did for India, Pakistan, some of the African countries, the West Indies, you name it. I mean . . . it sounds terrible to say we brought civilisation to them . . . I don't think we necessarily brought civilisation to them, but . . . would they have been better had they been left alone? Who knows? But if it hadn't have been us it would have been somebody else, and I think the other empires of the time probably were worse than us. I mean the one blot on our copy book is slavery, but that's the same for everybody. But yeah, I think looking over the years, I think the conflicts we've got involved in we had no choice. I'm not saying it was right, or the way it was done was right. But it's living proof that we do need a military force, if history's anything to go by.

It is noteworthy that when asked to tell a story about any aspect of Britain's military past, Shaun only chooses to discuss what he sees as misperceptions of the empire. This is despite him showing knowledge of many other wars during the interview. It can be inferred that of all the stories that could be told, the one that matters most to him is ensuring the empire is framed positively. This was typical of the participants who saw British history through the lens of the nostalgic *Vanishing Force* narrative (see chapter 4).

Shaun's response demonstrates numerous ways in which the depredations of the British Empire can be presented more favourably. First, he *sharpens* focus on 'all the good' the empire did, *including* examples in South Asia and Africa. He *links* conflicts together with the general statement that Britain had no choice but to participate, but also the implication that Britain's colonisation may have had subsequent civilising effects. Clearly aware that his views could be seen as controversial, he then seeks to explain them away, acknowledging that 'it sounds terrible to say we brought civilisation to them', and claims that he is not trying to say that. Though having explicitly emphasised 'all the good' it did, he had already implied that he may actually support this position. He does ask rhetorically 'would they have been better had they been left alone?', but certainly doesn't question whether they would have been worse off.

Shaun's account is replete with examples of *flattening* that explain away common criticisms of the empire. He admits that 'there was corruption' but *omits* evidence or examples. It is unclear who is corrupt, and it is certainly not clear that Britain acted negatively. In a further example of *flattening*, he brings up Britain's participation in slavery but then diminishes its moral significance by using the excuse that it was 'the same for everybody'. In this way, he justifies an illiberal aspect of the British Empire by insisting on Britain's moral equivalence to other powers. He also *flattens* the significance of colonisation by arguing that other powers were 'probably worse than us'. The overall effect of these points is to *clarify* that colonialism was an unavoidable but positive experience for the colonised, thanks to the comparative beneficence of British rulers. The claim that Britain 'had no choice', without further evidence, implies that the British were almost obliged to colonise to protect natives from other more vicious imperial powers. Britain's military has by implication been a *Force for Good* throughout history.

Empire as Adventure

Another way a few participants sought to justify imperialism was through the idea of exploration. Both imperialism and war have long been associated with adventure in British culture. Particularly in fiction, authors such as Defoe, Stevenson, and Kipling wrote heroic tales of brave, innocent explorers spreading the civilising virtues of England. Beyond Victorian times, real-life characters such as T. E. Lawrence further embodied adventurous, military virtues such as strength, courage, and endurance.[21] Postcolonial thinkers have criticised such works as Eurocentric, sometimes racist, as well as silencing the voices of those subjugated by British rule.[22] Nonetheless, a handful of participants also legitimised imperialists as innocent adventurers. As Denise (25–34, Birmingham) explains about the British Empire:

> DENISE: I think it was what worked at the time, it was the thing at the time. They'd got the ships, they decided 'let's go conquer'. People might not necessarily have wanted to be conquered and (*talking while laughing*) were quite happy doing their own thing, but I think it was obviously [that] we've built all these ships, let's go and find the world, and they went and found it, didn't they. You can't blame them for it.

Denise's story justifies imperialism by describing it as the done thing, a positive and natural act if one has the necessary resources. The views of the people being colonised are *silenced*, while the colonisers cannot be blamed for something so apparently normal at the time. Admiration for the adventurer is also found in Kate's (35–44, Dorset) response to being prompted about the empire having mentioned it earlier in the interview. Her response, however, also reveals an emotional tension between the adventurism of imperialism and the violence involved.

> RESEARCHER: So how important do you think the empire is to British culture, Britishness?
> KATE: Definitely, you know, it is a key thread to I think a sense of identity. Yeah, . . . it's bizarre isn't it, because there's this barbaric edge which is [that] we were this people that were just going to . . . we were so arrogant and up ourselves that we were just going to have everything and have as much as we could, and we were going to go and get it and shoot it and take it. So that whole personality that we could just have everything that we wanted, and we were going to get it. And it's almost two sides, a despicable, nasty bit, and on the other side there's kind of a pride as well. I think there's part of us that is kind of like (*affects masculine voice*) 'yes, come on. How amazing that we had the balls to go and do that'.

Kate later describes this dualism as a combination of 'pride and shame'. She was then asked which was more significant to her:

> KATE: Yeah, more shame, definitely. But I suppose maybe there is an element of . . . I just like the adventurer. You have to identify with that sense of wanting to adventure and explore and yeah, there is something amazing about that. But that is more about the human spirit rather than a Britishness, just the general human craziness to just go out and see what's over there.

The following narrative from Nathan (45–54, Dorset) ties together many of these ideas in his justification of the empire. He does not overtly characterise Britain as a *Force for Good*. However, his account is remarkable for the lack of even a minor acknowledgment that some might see the opposite as the case.

> NATHAN: I think we've always been ready, outward looking. We're a small island, we're an island nation, we've been outward looking, and we've

had the curiosity and the technology at the time to go and look. And having looked we saw it was good. And so we'll have a bit of this, and we used religion, the fact that there was nobody else there at the time that there might have been to have that bit, and went on from there. And it probably builds an arrogance within us as a country, but that's 150 years before I was born so I don't know. But it probably did, where we just thought it was brilliant, and as we expanded we needed more and more soldiers, and lots of people didn't have jobs, and subsistence farming was a dull thing to do. You could actually get some wages if you went into the military. You could get a gun. And we kind of built the army on the back of that, and the whole jingoistic thing kicked off, really in Victorian times I guess, and we have a hangover from that today.

As with the previous extracts, this one frames imperialism as a positive and natural response for a nation that is inherently 'outward looking' and 'curious' about the world. Nathan *includes* no specific events from British history, but his story contains a clear beginning, middle, and end. Actions follow one another, and the narrative appears to be coherent as a result. It starts with a small, curious, and technologically advanced nation, which decided to discover the world. Having seen that 'it was good'—a phrase with biblical overtones[23]—Britain proceeded to expand, aided by the absence of rivals and driven by the positive benefits the empire brought to British citizens. It ends with a rather abrupt jump from Victorian jingoism to Britain's imperial 'hangover' today. He *sharpens* focus on British colonisers, characterising them as innocently seeking employment and a better way of life. He does acknowledge that arrogant Britain 'used religion', although the choice of 'used' without specifying how suggests his *flattening* of any sense that Britain imposed its beliefs on others. Instead his story appears to *clarify* that the spread of the empire had nothing to do with the will to power. The causal logic is that it developed due simply to innocent citizens' desires for work and adventure. The statement that there was 'nobody else there at the time' may refer to other colonial powers or indigenous populations. Either way, it too has a *flattening* effect, since it justifies conquest while minimising the violence and displacement involved.

Overall, the most notable feature of Nathan's account is the complete absence of reference to the colonised. Each of the narratives so far has used a variety of emplotment mechanisms and many different wars to cast Britain as a *Force for Good*; but they all have in common the *flattening* and *silencing* of the negative consequences of Britain's wars for others. This contrasts starkly with the following narratives, which seek to characterise Britain as a *Force for Ill*.

Force for Ill: Opposing Narratives, Identical Tactics

Those portraying Britain as a *Force for Ill* use the same emplotment mechanisms as those who see Britain as a *Force for Good*, but in reverse. *Force for Good* advocates *clarify* that Britain's wars are humanitarian, *sharpen* positives, and *silence* atrocity and oppression. Conversely those who see Britain as a *Force for Ill clarify* that Britain's wars are really about economic gain, emphasise atrocities, and *omit* or *silence* any supposed benefits.

One difference in how they emplot events is that those that see Britain as a *Force for Ill* attempt to disrupt the continuity of the *Force for Good* narrative. Rather than simply including atrocities and wars they deem unjust, they *link* together contrasting wars where Britain intervened in one but not the other. They do this to show that Britain's military interventionism is selective and therefore any claims to be humanitarian are hypocritical at best, disingenuous at worst. This is then used to support the claim that Britain's interventions are driven by ulterior motives, such as economic gain. Comparisons drawn are diverse and vary depending on individual knowledge. Examples include Britain's intervention in Libya but not Syria, Iraq but not Rwanda, even Afghanistan but not North Korea or Zimbabwe. The wars do not necessarily temporally coincide.

The overall effect is to undermine the continuity of the *Force for Good* narrative and impose a different continuity: that throughout history, all Britain's wars have been driven by exploitative motives such as 'where there's oil' (Mark 65+, Birmingham). Emplotment is used to support an argument about the 'real' reason Britain is continuously at war.

The following responses from Dan (45–54, Dorset) illustrate these emplotment mechanisms particularly well. Extracts from them have already been presented as exemplars of the *Selfish Imperialist* narrative, but they are also insightful at this more forensic level of analysis.

DAN: If we go back to Richard the Lionheart, we were over there imposing on the Middle East. Now clearly there was no oil there at that time, but we wanted to impose our system on them. We look at the British Empire, when we went around the world and imposed our rule everywhere, and imposed our religion everywhere, and we imposed things on countries. We have oppressed, we have oppressed many, many times. . . . We go back to the British Empire and we went around the world and we routed places, and stole their mineral wealth and all good things from them, and then buggered off. And I think it's very similar today. It's about cash.

Perhaps the most interesting aspect of Dan's narrative is his attempt to make imperial exploitation appear transhistorical. Just as national identity groups have often sought to strengthen competing territorial claims by going further and further back in history,[24] Dan tries to strengthen his claim by suggesting that British control of the Middle East has been a relentless, thousand-year pursuit. He does this by *linking* the Crusades to intervention in the Middle East today, a link thought to have backfired spectacularly on George W. Bush in instigating the War on Terror by inspiring resistance to Western intervention.[25] Dan then *sharpens* focus on the empire and the imposition, oppression, and theft involved. He then jumps straight to the present day, *omitting* any other wars. These choices support his *clarification* that Britain's wars are really all about 'cash' and always have been.

In this relatively short account, it is unclear how he evaluates other wars Britain has fought. However, elsewhere in the interview a far longer response provides greater insight into how those who see Britain as a *Force for Ill* use emplotment to support their claims:

DAN: In the old days, First World War, Second World War, military intervention was about defence, defending your country or defending your group of countries against tyrannical invasion. Today, I very much feel that that's not what it's about. There are too many paradoxes there. You take for example the situations with the Middle East, with Weapons of Mass Destruction, Afghanistan, all of these places. When you actually look at the detail of it, it's about controlling situations in terms of oil, mineral resources, etcetera, etcetera. You see the whole argument for, say, Afghanistan—we'll use Afghanistan—it's about fighting against oppression of the people who are controlling that country. But there are too many other examples around the world where the West doesn't intervene because there's too much to lose. You take the situation in Israel, or Palestine, as I'd like to call it, it's a big prime example. And I find it very testing, I find it testing. It's just you think 'no, that's just not the truth'. You have the situation just recently where Obama was given the Nobel Peace Prize, and you've got a situation where he's slapping the wrist of Israel saying 'you mustn't be like this', but continuing to sell arms to Israel. There is, you know, the oppression of people, the thing in Afghanistan, when we all know the routes for oil through Afghanistan are crucial for the West. And is it about the oil itself or the money that can be made from the oil? We look at China, and we look at the oppression of the people of China. . . . The West does nothing about China, but then China has power over the West, primarily America, in terms of its debt to them. China could pull the plug tomorrow on America and that would be it, it would be bankrupt. So yes, this idea that military intervention is all about freedom, it's not. It's not in my mind.

In this longer narrative, Dan does not refer explicitly to Britain but instead considers it part of the West, alongside America. He initially *includes* the First and Second World Wars as part of a former era when wars were justified on defensive grounds. Since these were not included in his previous account it can be inferred that he *silenced* them as they would have challenged the continuity he tried to establish in British imperialism since the Crusades. All the events included are *linked* together in their demonstration of Western neo-imperial exploitation, oppression, or hypocrisy. Dan *sharpens* focus on Afghanistan and *clarifies* that it was not actually about 'fighting against oppression' but really about oil. This is in stark contrast to Denise earlier in the chapter, who chose to focus on Afghanistan to show how the British military helped improve the lives of Afghans through food, water, and policing. Dan then *sharpens* focus on Israel, or 'Palestine, as I'd like to call it', to show Western hypocrisy in condemning aspects of Israeli foreign policy while selling them arms. He also considers hypocritical the failure to respond to the 'oppression of the people in China' since it apparently shows that the West does not intervene in powerful countries. Almost the entire response focuses on the negative aspects and ulterior motives for military intervention, just as *Force for Good* narratives focus overwhelmingly on the positives. The overall point is an emphatic assertion that Britain's wars are not about freedom or justice; if they were, such responses would not be selective. Selective humanitarianism is seen as an oxymoron, even if some may argue that economic constraints render it inevitable.

The following exchange with Bethany (18–24, London) provides further evidence of how people use selective emplotment to depict Britain as a *Force for Ill*. Her responses also reveal the challenges involved in analysing narratives in spoken discourse. Up to this point, many of the stories analysed have been discrete responses to a single question, containing a clear series of emplotted events. This exchange contains these elements but they emerge haphazardly in interaction and therefore need to be interpreted, extracted, and reordered. Nevertheless, examining the emplotment mechanisms Bethany uses makes it possible to infer the plotline of the story and the identity claim behind it: that Britain is a hypocrite, as shown by a continuous stream of selective, duplicitous, and economically driven military interventions.

The interaction begins with Bethany being asked if she can think of any times when she disagreed with the decision to intervene militarily in a conflict. She immediately names Iraq, which was by far the most common response to this question.[26] She describes the war as immoral, hypocritical, and 'really problematic given our support for Saddam Hussein in the years moving up to [the conflict]'. When prompted about any other conflicts she could recall opposing, her response was particularly revealing:

BETHANY: Erm . . . I think in Libya, same thing. We go in, we do some kind of half-arsed military invasion thing to make us feel like we're doing something, and then we leave when the problem's still there. But we should never have been there in the first place. And also why did we support Qaddafi in the first place? Did we not foresee this, you know? It seems that British foreign policy, and I guess this is true of a lot of . . . because I guess you've got to be realistic, we turn a blind eye, we make friends with dictators and human rights abusers because it suits us, and because it's easier for us, and it protects our interests in those areas, particularly <u>economic</u> interests. But actually we also spout about being in favour of democracy and human rights. It's just completely at odds with one another.

RESEARCHER: When you mentioned this—I can't remember your precise words—Britain needing to be seen to be doing something, what's that all about?

BETHANY: I think again it is this kind of 'white man saviour' image that we have of ourselves, and I think it's also because historically, and the way that we're taught about Britain's involvement in these countries, is that we did good. And whether that's true or not doesn't seem to matter because that's how we see ourselves. And we've been on the right side of history. And I don't feel it's necessarily true. In fact I think it's false on a lot of occasions.

Extracting the overall narrative from the exchange, Bethany's main point is that Britain's wars are primarily economically motivated. Just like Dan, she deliberately brings up the claim that interventions are humanitarian to *clarify* that she sees this as hypocritical. Having already discussed Iraq, she *sharpens* focus on Libya to support her claim that Britain 'turn[s] a blind eye' to 'dictators and human rights abusers'. A secondary causal logic is that Britain's wars stem from the desire to 'feel like we're doing something'. This can be read as a criticism of the *Punching Above Its Weight* narrative for encouraging military intervention based on the desire to seem influential rather than genuine humanitarian need. Meanwhile the claim that Britain actually 'did good' in its wars is later *flattened* as being due to false consciousness, a product of British citizens being erroneously taught that their interventions have had positive effects. Overall she dismisses as delusion the idea that Britain's military is a *Force for Good*.

A third example of a typical *Force for Ill* narrative is provided by Lily (18–24, London) in response to being asked to tell the story of Britain's historical role in war. Once again her chosen account focuses exclusively on the damage caused by Britain's wars:

> LILY: I think the role we've played historically is like a kind of dim-witted giant just stomping around. You know, being very indelicate and crass and doing these things which are very ill-thought out. India would be a prime example of that. I read somewhere recently that Kashmir is the most heavily militarised zone of any country of the world . . . country . . . whatever you would call it. The ratio of citizens to soldiers is the highest of anywhere in the world, and we're responsible for that, pretty much. I'd think about it like that, that there's just been a series of . . . generously you could call them blunders. If you were being ungenerous you could say that they were kind of manipulations or calculated disruptions. In the same way, I don't know a huge amount about African conflicts, but the bit I do know, obviously we had a huge role there as well. I read a book recently about conflict in Sudan, and the history of that. The role we played in that conflict is also shameful. So we've got a

lot to answer for I think, but none of it particularly good. And then I suppose there is . . . I've given a very negative view. If you didn't know anything about it, the impression of it I've given is very negative. I suppose there are some positive things, and I think like what are the things we can take credit for? The Irish conflict? But then that was caused by us in the first place, so I don't know.

Lily's story is informative for several reasons. The emplotment mechanisms she uses are typical of other *Force for Ill* narratives. She *includes* and *sharpens* focus on the damage caused by Britain's wars. She overwhelmingly focuses on the British Empire, specifically on conflicts such as in Kashmir that emerged out of decolonisation. The story contains no positive evaluations of Britain's wars. As with Dan, she *omits* the world wars. Since she admits earlier in the interview that the Second World War may have been justified as it was defensive, its *omission* could be interpreted as deliberate since it does not fit the overall story about the 'shameful' consequences of Britain's wars.

However, the last few lines of her story throw this interpretation into doubt. They also provide valuable insights into the challenges in interpreting omissions and silences in people's narratives.

Lily is unusual in being openly reflexive about her own story. While many will do this in their head, she verbalises her thought process, as evidenced by her acknowledgment that she had 'given a very negative view'. She then attempts to balance this by thinking of some positives of Britain's military past. Why she does this is open to interpretation. As a student being interviewed by an academic, she might have assumed that good academic practice is to provide a balanced response. Alternatively, her ontological security as a British citizen may have been threatened by the idea of being part of a nation that uses war in a deliberate, calculated way. Framing Britain as 'dim-witted', 'indelicate', and 'crass' softens criticism of Britain's character since the destructive side-effects of its wars are just unintentional 'blunders'. It leaves open the possibility that Britain intends to be a *Force for Good*, even if it has not always succeeded.

Speculation aside, Lily's open attempt to find positives reveals concrete insights about the analysis of omissions and silences in people's narratives. She cannot think of any positives on the spur of the moment. She attempts to *sharpen* focus on 'the Irish conflict' but then recalls her perception that it was caused by Britain. But had she not verbalised this process, it could easily be inferred that she had deliberately *omitted* or *silenced* wars where Britain could 'take credit' for doing good. This inference would be wrong though. She seems genuinely unable to think of any at the time, which is different from deliberately omitting contradictory evidence. This reveals the value of qualitatively analysing what is not included in a narrative, but also the difficulty in doing so.

Perhaps the most significant aspect of Lily's narrative is her demonstration that individuals can be aware of different interpretations of Britain's military past. Lily's depiction of Britain as a 'dim-witted giant stomping around' implies that the damage it has wrought reflects incompetence and ignorance rather than ill-intent. Later though she suggests that one could instead interpret Britain's past wars as 'calculated manipulations'. She therefore presents two different causal logics through which events in her narrative can be *linked*, be it as the result of a malevolent actor seeking to profit from conflict or a country trying to help that consistently does more harm than good. Lily is uncertain which is most apt, but because both are present in the account it becomes less coherent, resulting in a story that ends abruptly and uncertainly with 'I don't know' rather than a clear conclusion. It is evident that Lily sees Britain as a *Force for Ill* but it is unclear whether this is deliberate or unintentional. She is knowledgeable and articulate, but this does not necessarily mean that she has a fixed narrative understanding of Britain's wars. The 'shameful' consequences she describes produce contrasting claims about Britain's international identity, depending on how its intentions are evaluated.

This provides an important reminder about the hybridity and contestation at the heart of citizens' narrative understandings of war. Seeing Britain as a *Force for Good* or a *Force for Ill* throughout history oversimplifies a far more complex historical record. Some citizens held more nuanced positions, noting that the amount of 'good' that has come from British military interventions varies from one war to the next. As Grace (55–64, Worcestershire) summarises, Britain has 'done a certain amount of good in the world and a certain amount of harm', sometimes being the aggressor, sometimes not. Unpicking these nuances requires probing beyond general statements and patterns to the complex layers of understanding beneath. This demonstrates the additional depth of analysis that can be achieved when viewing narratives through the dual lenses of genre and emplotment.

Next Steps: Interpreting Silence

To conclude, narrative research in the foreign policy literature has focused more on the general pattern of a story (genre) rather than the selective process through which this is created (emplotment). Instead this chapter has sought to provide a method through which the emplotment process can be systematically analysed. Adapting and extending a framework originally used in biographical narrative research, it has tried to provide a nuanced picture of how citizens marshal their knowledge of Britain's past wars to support or oppose the claim that Britain's military is a *Force for Good* in the world. Those looking to portray Britain as a *Force for Good* typically *include* and *sharpen* focus on humanitarian episodes, *clarify* that colonisation was really benevolent or only defensive, *link* supposedly positive aspects of Britain's wars together while *omitting, silencing,* and *flattening* atrocity and exploitation. *Force for Ill* advocates largely do the opposite, although their narratives tend to explicitly *link* wars where Britain intervened in one conflict and not another to highlight hypocrisy and imply exploitative intent. Combining these emplotment mechanisms enables individuals with vastly different knowledge to make similar identity claims with their narratives, and do so more coherently. They can also be used by the researcher to infer the overall point of a story if it is not explicitly stated.[27]

Many of these selection mechanisms are neither new nor unique to narrative; most discourse is selective rather than a total stream of consciousness. However, what differentiates this analysis is in seeing how these mechanisms combine to construct a story as a whole, in contrast to discourse and content analyses that tend to isolate specific features or segments of text.[28] This is important because it is the overall impression created by plot that is central to how narratives persuade differently from other modes of discourse. Theoretically, narratives persuade differently from argument by presenting a sequential account of how selected events transpire rather than a cost-benefit analysis of a given course of action.[29] Emplotment achieves this by presenting a temporal and causal logic that ties events together, even though contingencies and contradictions may be omitted.[30] In other words, narratives are rendered persuasive through a combination of what is included *and* what is silenced.

This raises an issue with analysing emplotment that warrants further scrutiny: how one determines whether a given event is deliberately silenced, unwittingly forgotten, or the narrator has simply never heard of it. Determining why something is unsaid is always a matter of interpretation. Many factors can influence event selection and exclusion, including how recently an event took place, its salience due to media coverage, knowledge and education, ideological influences, and a narrator's assumptions about what the audience already knows.

Despite these challenges, excluded events are particularly interesting if one expects them to be commonplace. This invites the researcher to revisit their own assumptions about which events they expect people to recall and why. However, a puzzle emerges when exceptionally memorable events are not mentioned by multiple individuals even though the researcher has reasonable confidence that such events are both familiar to participants and relevant to the topic under discussion. One such puzzle is the subject of the next chapter: the surprising absence of 9/11 in people's stories about the War on Terror. Investigating this conundrum will reveal novel insights about the relationship between strategic narrative, collective memory, and forgetting, challenging commonly held assumptions about how people think about contemporary international relations.

CHAPTER 7

Forgetting 9/11

Narrative and Collective Memory

SUSAN (55–64, OXFORDSHIRE): Well like everybody else I know exactly
where I was on 9/11 . . . It's one of those happenings in one's life that
you'll never, ever forget.

Memory and forgetting are two sides of the same coin. Both are shaped by narratives, whether they are constructed by historians, governments, or their citizens.[1] The events societies collectively remember are politically influenced, as
politicians and the media tell stories that include certain events while silencing
others.[2] Exalting victories, silencing atrocities, exaggerating successes, and
blaming others for failures enable nations to maintain favourable views of who
they are.[3] Amidst this process, a small number of occurrences appear so inherently shocking that it is assumed they could never be forgotten. Yet just because
people recall what happened or how they felt when an event occurred does not
mean they recall its causes and effects identically over time. Memory is notoriously unreliable.[4] Political actors and historiographers can offer alternative interpretations, and perspectives can shift because of subsequent events. Causes
that initially seemed obvious can be forgotten.

This chapter drills down even further into British citizens' narrative understandings of war. The preceding analysis has shown how individuals emplot
Britain's wars using the mechanisms of *inclusion, linking, sharpening, clarifying,
omission, silencing,* and *flattening* to try and make more coherent claims about
Britain's international identity. The aim here is to deepen understanding of the
role of memory in the emplotment process by considering a central interpretive
challenge: determining whether an event that narrators do not include has been

deliberately silenced or merely forgotten. Addressing this challenge, the chapter shows how narrative analysis can be used to identify a process of 'collective forgetting', using a particular event that is surprisingly absent from British citizens' war stories: the 9/11 terrorist attacks of 11 September 2001.

Despite occurring on American soil, 9/11 was a highly significant event in British military history. The spectacular attack was immediately framed as an iconic moment that 'changed the world'.[5] Even though its perpetrator, Al Qaida, had attacked American targets before,[6] it was proclaimed a watershed marking the beginning of a new global 'War on Terror'.[7] It also produced a global counterterrorist response on an unprecedented scale in which Britain has been a leading participant.[8] It directly precipitated war in Afghanistan, and the perceived threat of Al Qaida was used to justify the 2003 invasion of Iraq.[9] Britain's military is still active in both theatres. Moreover, while the term 'War on Terror' is no longer in vogue, British policy is still heavily influenced by the perceived terrorist threat from Islamist extremists.[10] Consequently, 9/11 seems a vital event in understanding recent British military interventions.

Despite this, remarkably few participants (11 out of 67—16 percent) included it in their narratives. More puzzlingly, on further questioning some participants could not even remember that the attack was the basis for war in Afghanistan. Cawkwell, writing about British strategic communication, claims that 'it is obvious that the Afghan campaign began as a response to the terrorist attacks of September 11'.[11] If so, why have some British citizens apparently forgotten this?

This surprising observation emerged inductively during the interview process. This chapter aims to determine the most plausible explanation for it. Rather than testing hypotheses about this, it employs abductive reasoning, which seeks to infer the most likely explanation of an emergent phenomenon.[12] It is a mode of thought crucial in the development of new theory.[13] A variety of evidence is used to support the process, including narrative and content analysis of citizens' stories, the academic literature, government statements, policy documents, and opinion polls.

The starting assumption is that the more frequently events are emplotted in stories, the more likely they are to be remembered, whereas repeatedly excluded events are more likely to be forgotten.[14] Having established this, the chapter then considers a variety of reasons why some participants appear to have 'forgotten 9/11' in their accounts of war in Afghanistan. These include the notion that the event was never particularly significant in the United Kingdom, that terrorist attacks are not readily associated with war, or that the study's methodology is responsible.

After rejecting these possibilities for various reasons, I contend that an alternative explanation is more convincing: that the original motive for Afghanistan is being steadily forgotten because of changes in the narration of the conflict over time. Initially, Afghanistan was explained as a just response to a destructive terrorist attack. However, it now appears to be understood by many as part of an *Iraqistan* narrative. In this story, Iraq and Afghanistan are conflated as one generic, never-ending quagmire within a failing War on Terror. They seem to have been 'going on forever'. This narrative shift is partly because the conflicts overlapped, but also because Western governments deliberately united them as fronts in the War on Terror. However, the War on Terror was partially discredited due to the perceived illegitimacy of the Iraq War, and since people increasingly conflated the two, this sense of illegitimacy transferred to Afghanistan. Consequently, seeing Afghanistan through this Iraqistan narrative has progressively inhibited recall that the original motive was widely accepted and considered legally just.[15] This, combined with the government's oscillation between different justifications for Afghanistan—be it counterterrorism, stabilisation, countering narcotics, or promoting female education—has eroded memories of the intervention's original purpose.[16] Inadvertently, strategic narration has helped sever the temporal and causal link between the war and its original justification. Consequently, when remembering Afghanistan, some British citizens have forgotten 9/11.

Narrative, Collective Memory, and Forgetting

The relationship between memory and narrative is integral to how similarly British citizens narrate stories about war. To tell similar stories, citizens must remember Britain's military history in similar ways. When people select the same events, start points, and turning points and frame them similarly, this can be taken as evidence of collective memory. Some authors limit their definitions of collective memory to the deliberate 'acts of remembrance' that groups perform, be it through constructing monuments, visiting museums, or ritual commemorations such as Armistice Day.[17] Here though collective memories are defined as 'representations of the past shared by members of a group'.[18] In this case the group of interest is the British nation.

Collective memory is a continuous social process realised through narrative emplotment.[19] In other words, the meaning of an event is a function of its relationship to other events.[20] The way past events are shared socially will also affect how the individual remembers them. Emplotting an event in a narrative makes it more likely to be remembered; repeatedly excluding events makes them more likely to be forgotten.[21] In this way, 'narratives become a critical filter through which our memories evolve'.[22] In the process, people can add emotions, beliefs, and knowledge obtained since the event.[23] Since any occurrence can only be viewed with hindsight, present perspectives can introduce bias to interpretations of the past.

Forgetting and memory are inextricably related; indeed memory is 'in large measure not forgetting'.[24] Failing to remember an event can be a product of deliberate attempts to shape collective memory. To preserve their ontological security, nations can select aspects of their history to portray themselves positively while deliberately silencing or denying unsavoury episodes.[25] They also fight a 'struggle against forgetting' by deliberately commemorating or designing education curricula to include events deemed important to promote a given national image.[26]

The importance of forgetting to memory in British military history is illustrated powerfully by the historiography of the Second World War. Critics lambast Prime Minister Neville Chamberlain for naively appeasing Hitler by accepting his annexation of the Sudetenland in the Munich Agreement of 1938. However, it is routinely forgotten that Chamberlain received great praise at the time for delivering civilisation from destruction, at a time when citizens were desperately digging air raid shelters and armed forces were on full alert.[27] Conversely, the speeches of his successor, Winston Churchill, are commonly regarded as crucial in inspiring the British people to stand firm against Germany in 1940.[28] Yet it is widely forgotten that the reception of the speeches at the time was mixed at best.[29] Enshrining Chamberlain's folly and Churchill's heroism into collective memory through repeated narration causes alternative interpretations to be forgotten.

Such memory shifts are not instantaneous; they occur as war stories are told and retold over time. Similarly, it is suggested here that the phenomenon of participants appearing to 'forget 9/11' should be seen as part of a broader process in which collective memory of war in Afghanistan is shifting. Doubtless the process is far from complete. What is particularly fascinating is that the event in question is considered so cataclysmic that it seems unimaginable that someone would forget it.[30] As Coman et al. state, to forget 9/11 is to 'forget the unforgettable.'[31]

Initial Evidence

To clarify, it is not claimed that British people are starting to forget 9/11 per se. The assertion is that they are starting to forget that it led to the invasion of Afghanistan. This is surprising given how clear the causal link originally was. Of all the participants in which this was observed, the accounts of Bill (35–44, Yorkshire) and Bridget (25–34, London) provide particularly explicit examples. Both showed significant knowledge of Britain's wars, bringing up seven and ten wars in their respective interviews, often discussing them in reasonable depth. Yet despite this knowledge, they cannot recall how Afghanistan started:

> BILL: . . . I've never really understood . . . I've not been close enough to understand why we ended up in Afghanistan. I can't go as far as to say I vehemently disagree with it, but I never really understood it. And I have trouble in my head distinguishing Iraq as a conflict from Afghanistan. But I can distinguish Kuwait from those, so I've got that in my head as 'somebody invaded Kuwait and we said that's not on'. But then we've started going into other sovereign states.
>
> RESEARCHER: What can you remember about your views at the start of Afghanistan?
>
> BILL: I can't even remember it starting, this is my thing. I can't remember where Iraq ended and Afghanistan started. I can't remember a time when . . . since Kuwait, when British military's most popular dress code wasn't the sort of khaki desert colour.
>
> RESEARCHER: It's very common . . . this sense that it's always been there for years, this Afghanistan conflict, rumbling on.
>
> BILL: Yeah, but I don't know if it has been Afghanistan that's been rumbling on, or was it Iraq that came before it? The two kind of merge together in people's heads, and therefore it's decades of people in sandy places chasing people that there's no obvious front line of 'bad guys this side, us the other side, are we making progress or not'.

Bridget also cannot remember what caused war in Afghanistan, as indicated by her response when probed about when it started:

BRIDGET: I suppose it's one that's always baffled me. I had a friend in the Foreign Office and she went out to live out there, and also in Pakistan as well and Iraq. And to this day I kind of have a loose understanding of what she was doing in Iraq, but to this day I haven't really understood what she was doing in Afghanistan. I know there was a huge amount of unrest. Has it been resolved? I didn't even think it had come to any conclusion. It's strange that isn't it. Everything we've talked about so far I know a little bit about, but I don't know anything about Afghanistan.

(. . .)

For me it never feels like it had a start and it doesn't feel like it's had a finish. I don't really know where it began and what the . . . turning point was, what happened. Because like I say I can go back to World War Two and say 'they invaded Poland'. I have a vague recollection of someone being shot in Austria prior to that. You know, so that's when the tensions pick up, and Iraq the reasons, it sounds like they were wrong but they were the turning point. But for me, do I know what happened in Afghanistan? It may be something really obvious. I just don't know, myself. I don't know.

These are just the first two examples of a broader trend in which a variety of citizens failed to link the invasion of Afghanistan to 9/11. Only 11 out of 67 (16 percent) mentioned 9/11 at all, and only four of these explicitly linked it to Afghanistan.[32] While there were 226 mentions of Afghanistan throughout the interview corpus, 9/11 was mentioned only 21 times. It is particularly fascinating that both Bill and Bridget can remember the triggers of other conflicts. Bridget can recall that the Second World War began because 'they invaded Poland'. Bill can recall that the first Gulf War began because 'somebody invaded Kuwait and we said that's not on'. But neither can recall that Afghanistan started because 'somebody flew planes into the Twin Towers and we said that's not on'. Participants such as Bill and Bridget appear to have forgotten the unforgettable, or at least its consequences. The question is, why?

Their accounts are also important because they challenge an obvious explanation for why people don't name 9/11: that they assume its importance is common knowledge and thus need not be said. If a narrator deems it obvious that Afghanistan began because of 9/11, they may not see the need to mention it. In some cases this may well explain why 9/11 is not brought up, but Bill and Bridget confound this explanation as they explicitly state that they cannot recall how Afghanistan began.

While these are but two exemplars of a broader phenomenon, they provide intriguing clues about why some may have forgotten that war in Afghanistan started because of 9/11. Bill's statements that he 'can't remember when Iraq ended and Afghanistan started' and later that 'the two kind of merge together in people's heads' suggest that conflating the two has undermined his recall of the unique circumstances of Afghanistan. Similarly, Bridget's statement that 'it never feels like it had a start and it doesn't feel like it's had a finish' suggests that the prolonged nature of the conflict may have shaped her memory of it. As will be shown, a range of other participants echo these sentiments in the stories they tell about these conflicts.

Alternative Explanations

To strengthen the claim that the most plausible explanation for participants 'forgetting 9/11' is because of changes in how war in Afghanistan has been narrated over time, it must be shown why alternative explanations are less convincing. The first possibility is that 9/11 was never actually particularly significant to the British people or the individuals in this study, despite prevailing assumptions about its iconicity. Forgetting would therefore be unsurprising. The second is that the absence of references to 9/11 is a product of the study's open-ended methodology. People may think terrorist acts are irrelevant in an interview about war, or alternatively they may deem the significance of 9/11 so obvious that it need not be stated. In this case, my expectations as a researcher should be interrogated.

The Significance of 9/11 to the British People

While it is possible that few British people mentioned 9/11 as a cause of Afghanistan because it is not particularly memorable to them, multiple sources of evidence suggest this is not the case. Both theoretical and empirical research indicates that 9/11 remains a highly influential event in the United Kingdom. In precipitating Afghanistan and initiating the War on Terror, it strongly shaped Britain's domestic and foreign policy. British political discourse on war in Afghanistan has also persistently linked the two.

The Iconicity of 9/11

Literature in memory studies, psychology, sociology, and International Relations all support the significance of 9/11 to the British people. Authors such as Leavy, Bolt, and Hansen assert that 9/11 was an 'iconic' event, images of which are instantly recognisable throughout the world.[33] As Hansen explains, images of the Twin Towers do not just provide a snapshot of what happened; they are a symbol that crystallises the meaning of the global War on Terror.[34] For psychologists, 9/11 is one of few events of sufficient magnitude to trigger 'flashbulb memories', when people remember exactly what they were doing at the time.[35] Certainly events that trigger flashbulb memories will vary from culture to culture. While Pearl Harbor and the Challenger explosion are more frequently cited in the United States, the death of Princess Diana is cited more frequently in Britain.[36] But 9/11 is considered so significant that it has spawned countless flashbulb memory studies.[37] This vast research assumes that the public are like Susan (55–64, Oxfordshire), who explained in the chapter's opening quotation that 'like everybody else I know exactly where I was on 9/11'.

Empirical findings also support the claim that 9/11 was highly significant in Britain. A BBC survey in 2006 found that 9/11 was the most common public flashbulb memory.[38] Proximity to the event makes this less surprising. Still, Scott and Zac found that British and American publics remember historical events in 'strikingly similar' ways.[39]

However, 9/11 is particularly significant for British citizens for several more reasons. According to psychologists, events are more memorable if they are unique, evoke strong emotions, are actively rehearsed, and are associated with subsequent behaviour and belief change.[40] 9/11 fits each of these criteria. The fear provoked by the event is likely felt by people not only when it is commemorated in the United States but every time global citizens go through airport security. Additionally, while the attack took place on American soil, 9/11 can also be read as a symbolic attack on the Western liberal order, of which Britain is a leading member. Sixty-seven British citizens were also killed in the attacks, lending further weight to the suggestion that Britain was under attack too.[41] As Prime Minister Tony Blair noted, 'it was not America alone who was the target, but all of us who shared the same values'.[42] Later, Britain also experienced Islamist terrorist attacks in London in 2005. Even the name given to these attacks, '7/7', demonstrates a symbolic link through the idea that they were 'Britain's 9/11'.

Linking 9/11 and Afghanistan in British Political Discourse

Another reason why it seems unlikely that the link between 9/11 and Afghanistan was never strong in Britain was how extensively the two have been linked in political discourse. The British press immediately framed the September 11 attacks as acts of war, using headlines such as 'We are at War',[43] 'War on the World',[44] and 'A Declaration of War'.[45] An explicit link between Britain and the United States was established immediately, as Blair emphasised on the evening of September 11:

> This is not a battle between the United States of America and terrorism, but between the free and democratic world and terrorism. We, therefore, here in Britain stand shoulder to shoulder with our American friends in this hour of tragedy, and we, like them, will not rest until this evil is driven from our world.[46]

As well as linking Britain and America together in a liberal democratic cause against international terrorism, Blair sharpened focus on the British victims. As he explained at the outset of the air campaign in Afghanistan (Operation Enduring Freedom) on 7 October 2001:

> First, let us not forget that the attacks of September 11 represented the worst terrorist outrage against British citizens in our history. The murder of British citizens, whether it happened overseas or not, is an attack upon Britain. But even if no British citizen had died, we would be right to act. This atrocity was an attack on us all, on people of all faiths and people of none.[47]

The link between 9/11 and Afghanistan was even clearer later in the same statement:

> We made clear following the attacks upon the US on September 11 that we would take action once it was clear who was responsible. There is no doubt in my mind . . . that these attacks were carried out by the Al Qaida network headed by Osama Bin Laden. Equally, it is clear that they are harboured and supported by the Taliban regime inside Afghanistan.[48]

The strong link between 9/11 and Afghanistan is also reflected in extensive public support for the initial military intervention. Theories of framing, agenda setting, and priming assert that the way issues are presented by politicians and the media will affect how citizens interpret them.[49] That polling so strongly supported British involvement in initial operations suggests wide acceptance of the idea that terrorists based in Afghanistan posed a profound security threat to Britain too. According to an ICM poll shortly after intervention began, 74 percent of the public supported British military intervention in Afghanistan, and there was almost total consensus among political elites.[50] Public support for war rose to 85 percent if Britain was subsequently attacked in retaliation for supporting the United States.[51]

Despite this initial support, Blair appeared concerned even after the first month of the campaign that 'the memory of 9/11 was fading'.[52] As he explained to the Welsh Assembly:

> It is important that we never forget why we are doing this; never forget how we felt watching the planes fly into the trade towers; never forget those answerphone messages. Never forget how we felt imagining how mothers told children they were about to die.[53]

So not only was the link between 9/11 and Afghanistan explicit at the time, the government sought to foster ongoing public memory of 9/11 to sustain support for intervention. This continued throughout the conflict, although other justifications were added. Even the coalition government in 2013 sought to ensure people still remembered 9/11:

> The UK is in Afghanistan because the country had become a base for terrorists that threatened our country and the rest of the world. The Taliban government gave Al Qaida safe haven in Afghanistan and this allowed terrorists to plan and carry out attacks around the world, most notably the 9/11 atrocities in 2001.[54]

Taken together, this evidence strongly demonstrates that 9/11 was a highly memorable event for British citizens and the clear *casus belli* for British intervention in Afghanistan. Moreover, the link between the two has been repeatedly made in subsequent political discourse on the conflict. A more convincing explanation is therefore needed for why citizens in this study have apparently forgotten what was profoundly obvious in late 2001.

Methodological Explanations

This study's methodology provides another possible explanation why few participants mentioned 9/11 and why still fewer linked it to war in Afghanistan. Employing open-ended questioning meant that it could not be established definitively whether a person was familiar with an event or not. The purpose of open-ended questioning was to identify the wars that were more significant to individuals rather than the researcher assuming these beforehand. This creates opportunities as well as challenges. The only way to have identified that people do not bring up 9/11 was by not asking about it in the first place. However, it is always difficult to infer why a particular event is not mentioned. Participants may have been familiar with Afghanistan or 9/11 but chose to discuss other conflicts that were more significant to them. They may have considered the link between Afghanistan and 9/11 so obvious that it need not be mentioned. Alternatively, they may simply perceive a terrorist attack such as 9/11 to be irrelevant in an interview about war. Each of these reasons could affect whether they emplot the event in their narratives.

Empirical evidence counters each of these explanations though. Participants did not just omit 9/11 from their stories; they explicitly stated that they could not remember how Afghanistan began. The idea that 9/11 might be seen as irrelevant in an interview about Britain's wars is similarly doubtful. From the outset, it was portrayed as an act of war.[55] Britain's wars in Iraq and Afghanistan have been repeatedly framed as different 'fronts' in the wider War on Terror, or 'acts' in 'the global drama triggered by 9/11'.[56] The War on Terror discourse represents the dominant interpretive lens through which the ongoing conflict is understood.

Still, observing far fewer mentions of 9/11 than expected suggests the need to question my assumptions about why I anticipated that it would appear more frequently. This reflexivity is important in enhancing the validity of narrative research.[57] Reflecting on this, I realised that I assumed that because 9/11 is so commonly portrayed as a day the world changed and the War on Terror began, I anticipated that it would be a common turning point in participants' stories. As a researcher in international affairs, I exist within a social field in which 'the idea that September 11 "changed everything"' is commonplace.[58] The notion of a post-9/11 world is but one way of periodising British history, alongside its colonial wars, the world wars, the Cold War, wars of decolonization, and post-Cold War humanitarian interventions. But just because academics might periodise history this way does not mean that citizens experience real life this way. On terrorism for example, a vast literature defines 9/11 as part of an era of 'new terrorism'.[59] Yet for British citizens it may be that decades of terrorist threats from variations of the Irish Republican Army (IRA) mean that 9/11 and 7/7 reflect continuity rather than change. Investigating this fell beyond the scope of this study, but it cannot be dismissed, despite the weight of evidence of the iconicity of 9/11 to the British people.

My age may also have also shaped my perception of the significance of 9/11. Numerous researchers have found that events occurring in the 'formative years of adolescence and emerging adulthood' are more memorable.[60] I was aged 18 when 9/11 took place. Then again, Bill and Bridget, who have already been shown to have 'forgotten 9/11', were in their early twenties and late teens respectively when it occurred. Theoretically they were at precisely the age at which 9/11 should have been particularly memorable. This suggests the need for caution in assuming that aggregate findings are applicable to specific individuals. However, it also suggests that some other social process might be taking place that explains the unexpected absence of 9/11 in citizens' accounts of Britain's recent wars.

The Iraqistan Narrative

Returning to the study's empirical data, arguably the most compelling explanation for British participants 'forgetting 9/11' is that the narrative of the Afghanistan war has evolved over time. Having begun as a straightforward response to 9/11, it has since become part of an Iraqistan narrative in which the original motive for the intervention has been lost. Content analysis of the entire interview corpus revealed that after 'and' and 'the', by far the most frequent word linked with Afghanistan is Iraq.[61] They overlapped considerably, so it is understandable that people narrate them together. Crucially, this appears to be shaping how each war is individually remembered.

The major distinguishing feature of the Iraqistan narrative is that it lacks the conventional narrative features of a clear beginning, middle, and end. Prolonged, seemingly intractable conflicts in Iraq and Afghanistan have created the impression of never-ending war. Rather than having a clear cause, subsequent action, and resolution, they have melded together into a continuous stream of distant violence. This is despite a three-year hiatus between the 2011 withdrawal of British ground troops from Iraq and the 2014 initiation of the air campaign against Islamic State. The wars are framed as unjustified and unnecessarily costly operations that were poorly planned and executed, based on flawed premises and without an 'exit strategy'. In the words of Felicity (45–54, Dorset) and Grace (55–64, Worcestershire), Britain was 'going in all guns blazing with no backup plan' to 'get rid of what's there' but without 'bother[ing to] think about what we're going to put in its place'.

In the resultant quagmire, the specifics of each war are obscured. This explains why people have forgotten that Afghanistan started because of 9/11. Consider the evidence from Bill's response earlier. He 'can't even remember' Afghanistan starting, or even whether Iraq or Afghanistan came first. He also cannot recall 'when [the] British military's most popular dress code wasn't the sort of khaki desert colour'. All he perceives is 'decades of people in sandy places' fighting 'strange skirmishes in far-flung lands for no obvious reason' in which 'there's no obvious front line'. He cannot recall that this all started after arguably the biggest terrorist attack the world has ever known.

Other participants also tell an Iraqistan narrative that conflates Afghanistan and Iraq. None recalls 9/11 as the original cause.

RESEARCHER: You mentioned Afghanistan and Iraq. What can you recall of your views of those conflicts, maybe when they started or over time?

RAY (45–54, BIRMINGHAM): Well with that one I don't think we should have got too much involved. We lost a lot of soldiers. I know that was more to do with oil. I suppose they needed to go over, but I don't think they should have put so many . . . it cost a lot of money as well, which I don't think we should have been doing at the time. I think we maybe should have held back, maybe put a bit in to help, but not put as many soldiers in.

MABEL (55–64, SCOTLAND): As far as combat is concerned, yes I am very proud of what the British military do, but . . . I'm removed from it because I don't know enough about it. So yes . . . Iraq and Afghanistan I was not happy about us becoming involved in that. That's a lack of knowledge in a way though, because of not knowing about those countries and what made them tick at the time. So it was ignorance really, made me not quite as patriotic. Not that I wasn't patriotic about it, I was just wondering why is Britain having to go there and having to do this, and watching all these young people. . . . And I didn't like the fact that Tony Blair got us embroiled in that, I have to say.

Both Ray and Mabel discuss Iraq and Afghanistan as if they are a single war. For Ray, the Iraqistan conflict is one in which Britain has overcommitted men and materiel. Meanwhile, Mabel wonders generally why Britain has to 'go there and do this' at all. As Kate (35–44, Dorset) suggests, 'it feels kind of [like] a hopeless, sad cycle of bad decisions'. Yet as polls indicate, Afghanistan did not seem like a bad decision at the time.[62]

Conflating the two conflicts into a single Iraqistan narrative also leads people to confuse them:

> FELICITY (45–54, DORSET): I think we need to back off a bit because . . . our politicians keep committing us to things that are not necessarily in the national interest, and they're certainly not in the interests of the people they chuck out there to do the work.
>
> RESEARCHER: Any particular conflicts, incidents that come to mind?
>
> FELICITY: Yeah there was one, what was it, the one when Tony Blair committed us to? I can't remember now whether it was Iraq or Afghanistan. I get the two muddled up.
>
> RESEARCHER: Can you think of any times when you disagreed with a decision to use military force?
>
> HENRY (35–44, LONDON): I think that would be, well, the Iraqi conflicts . . . Afghanistan I'm not so sure about either way. I don't feel I know enough about the background on that, and that's because I've not been paying attention.
>
> RESEARCHER: What can you remember of the origins?
>
> HENRY: I'm not sure I can really separate out in my mind without, you know going back and reading about it. But there's been various bits about axes of evil. Saddam Hussein, clearly not a nice chap, but did we actually need to go and, you know, invade without actually having a clear plan of what was going to happen afterwards.

So far the evidence has focused on people who do not name 9/11 as a cause of Afghanistan. However, the power of the Iraqistan narrative to sever the link between the two can even be shown in people that can recall 9/11 but not which conflict it led to.

> NIGEL (35–44, YORKSHIRE): Well I guess when September 11 happened, and I can remember George Bush saying whatever he said, 'we're going to

find them, we're going to kick somebody's arse' or whatever he said. And I was like 'yeah, yeah, yeah'. And at that time I was like, somebody has to be responsible for this. There has to be some kind of payback. But that . . . I was a lot younger then, and was probably not as . . . informed as I am now. But still, there was still a need to do something I think. There was still a need to show that the West as such would not tolerate that kind of behaviour. But actually pinpointing who was responsible . . . so I agree that something had to happen, but I'm not quite sure if we did the right thing or not. I don't know. In the end what was the outcome? I can't remember, it's been blurred. Did we go to Afghanistan or did we go to Iraq? I can't remember.

Taken together, these examples show how the conflation of Iraq and Afghanistan into a single Iraqistan conflict has eroded memories of how Afghanistan originally began. People may not have forgotten that 9/11 occurred, but the narrative shift has altered their collective memory of what it led to. The question is, what caused the narrative of the Afghanistan war to shift over time?

Explaining the Narrative Shift

The reasons for the narrative shift are partly unintentional and partly a product of human agency. Communicators can shape perceptions of a conflict through projecting their own strategic narratives. However, they are powerfully constrained by the prevailing narratives in which they are embedded as well as by events on the ground.[63] They are also limited by the 'discourse traps' they have already set themselves, where past terms used to conceptualise war restrict how it can be described in the present.[64]

Unintended Consequences

Part of the reason for the strength of the Iraqistan narrative is simply the power of hindsight. 'We tend to remember wars—and to story them—based on how they turned out' rather than how they began.[65] Iraq and Afghanistan turned into costly quagmires in which at times there was no obvious progress or end in sight.[66] The wars have thrown doubts on the efficacy of Western military intervention and, after the outcry over deceptions involved in the justifications for Iraq, have seemed increasingly illegitimate. Observing this, some people appear to have read the present into the past. This results in retrospective claims that they had always opposed Afghanistan and Iraq when they are likely to have supported the former at the time. Opinion polls reflect this distortion. The 2011 British Social Attitudes Survey found that 48 percent of the population agreed that it was wrong to intervene in Afghanistan, compared to 74 percent support a decade earlier.[67] Similarly, YouGov found that while 54 percent of the British public supported Iraq between April and December 2003, only 37 percent recall originally supporting it a decade later.[68] The effect of hindsight is unsurprising, for individual and collective memories are selective, malleable, and often unreliable.[69] What is surprising is that the effect is sufficiently powerful to cause people to 'forget the unforgettable' in the form of 9/11.

The Iraqistan narrative is also an unintended consequence of the conflicts' similarities. They occurred simultaneously and both were justified using a combination of liberal democratic and counterterrorist rhetoric, although 9/11 made the counterterrorism arguments for Afghanistan far more convincing. The military story of each conflict was also broadly similar for those without knowledge of the nuances of military strategy. Rapid initial successes in conventional war were followed by prolonged counterinsurgencies. These similarities made it harder for strategic communicators to separate the two conflicts convincingly.

Media Bombardment

The impression of a continuous Iraqistan conflict appears to have been enhanced by media coverage of the two wars. Images of soldiers in desert landscapes could easily be from either conflict. Only paying closer attention would reveal whether dead soldiers' coffins draped in Union flags were from one war rather than the other. These effects are also compounded by the impression that, as Danielle (35–44, London) observes, 'war is covered so heavily on the news all the time'. As the following participants suggest, bombardment with images of war leads some to disengage from the specifics of each theatre. Replicated more broadly, this desensitisation would further explain why the conflicts become even more blurred in citizens' minds.

ROBERT (35–44, DORSET): Well, the average working person probably becomes a bit bored of it, you know what I mean? They get a little bit
overloaded by it. It's an everyday thing. And I don't think it affects many
people these days, unless you've got someone in the army or in the
forces, which maybe 50 years ago [when] most people would have had
a family member. But now I think it's sort of ignored to a certain extent.
People have got a bit bored of it all. It's a constant flow of either Afghanistan or Iraq. There's a constant flow of Guantanamo Bay or this or
that, you know. There's a constant flow of information. And I think
there's too much media almost. You're flooded with it 24 hours a day. . . .
I find people become a bit detached, until it affects you directly, which
the average person it doesn't, does it.

OLIVE (65+, OXFORDSHIRE): I think that the first time you see the news bul-
letin it shocks you. But the more and more you see it, I think you become desensitised in a way, because you know what's coming and it
doesn't have the shock value.

MARY (35–44, DORSET): A massive part of our culture is worrying about the
Islamic terror. That's the latest thing that we're all worrying about. I'm
not saying we shouldn't be worrying about it and it's not a real threat,
but for me going about my day-to-day business I'm not sure how much
time I should be spending thinking about it because I can't really do
anything about it. But it's very difficult to avoid it because you're constantly bombarded with it in all forms of media all the time. . . . So in the
paper, on the radio, or on the BBC news, pretty much every day there
will be something about the War on Terror. And so yeah, I've kind of got
a little bit to saturation point with it actually.

As well as desensitisation from the volume of news coverage, the tone of
coverage may also have weakened the link between Afghanistan and 9/11. Research reveals that as Afghanistan became more prolonged and citizens increasingly questioned its purpose, the media increasingly portrayed British
soldiers as victims, fighting for a questionable cause without sufficient material
support.[70] Saturation with such coverage makes it understandably harder to
associate the war with the justness of its original cause.

The Discourse Trap of the War on Terror

The pervasiveness of the Iraqistan narrative is not just because of the inherent similarities between the conflicts or public inattention to their specifics. It is also a product of the strategic narration of political actors. Specifically, the decision to justify Iraq as a new front in the global War on Terror primed people to conflate the two. This association may have strengthened the link between Afghanistan, Iraq, and 9/11 in the short term, but in the long term it appears to have weakened it.

This may be because of what Michaels describes as 'blowback', a discourse trap whereby a rhetorical concept can end up undermining the cause for which it was created.[71] In this case, the discrediting of the Iraq War undermined the War on Terror, which came to be associated with ill-considered, illegitimate military interventions.[72] Afghanistan was undermined by association, because the Iraqistan narrative merged the conflicts in people's minds. Trapped in the ongoing discourse of the War on Terror exaggerated people's sense of being in the middle of a single, never-ending story. As Bridget explained, 'it never feels like it had a start and it doesn't feel like it's had a finish. I don't really know where it began'. Unintentionally, therefore, blowback from the discredited War on Terror discourse has contributed to some forgetting that Afghanistan began because of 9/11.

Chronically, the War on Terror was undermined by the failures of military operations in Iraq and Afghanistan to establish security, stability, and democracy. Acutely, it was fatally undermined by the tenuous initial justification for the Iraq War. The link between Saddam Hussein's alleged weapons of mass destruction (WMD) and the fear that they could be given to Al Qaida was calculated to generate fear of an attack worse than 9/11. However, it came to be regarded as based on erroneous intelligence, once no weapons were found.[73] The British government's spurious claim that Iraq could deploy WMD in 45 minutes was condemned as a crude propaganda attempt to manipulate the public.[74] This fostered suspicion that there were ulterior motives at play, the most intuitive being the control of oil.[75]

Suspicions about whether Britain was complicit in a US attempt to control Iraqi oil long predated the conflict. Some argue that Middle Eastern oil has been an American foreign policy preoccupation since the Second World War.[76] After 9/11 there was cross-party consensus in Britain in support of intervention in Afghanistan, but not before the invasion of Iraq. In the absence of explicit

UN authorisation, the Liberal Democrats adopted a strictly antiwar position; a third of Labour MPs voted against their own government, and Blair's former foreign minister, Robin Cook, resigned.[77] Elite dissensus was reflected in media coverage, which included a plethora of articles questioning the intervention's motives.[78] Until a rally-round-the-flag effect boosted public support just after intervention began, public opposition had been extensive too.[79] In this climate, the administration fielded several allegations that Iraq was really about oil. Blair himself sought to counter the 'conspiracy theory' in parliament by arguing that were that so, it would have been 'infinitely simpler to cut a deal with Saddam, who, I am sure, would be delighted to give us access to as much oil as we wanted if he could carry on building weapons of mass destruction.'[80]

Despite government efforts, by 2011 oil had become by far the most common perceived motive for the war according to the British Social Attitudes Survey.[81] Every year, new media articles emerge around the anniversary of the conflict making the same claim about oil.[82] It has retrospectively become the dominant narrative for the original invasion of Iraq, by providing a compelling, commonsense explanation for why the government might concoct intelligence to deceive citizens into supporting the war. It also discredited the broader War on Terror, since it had been used to justify what was widely perceived as an illegitimate war.

The claim here is that negative perceptions of the War on Terror due to Iraq have been transferred to Afghanistan over time due to the Iraqistan narrative. As the wars turned into lengthy counterinsurgencies, they became indistinguishable to casual observers. Seeing them as one generic conflict enabled memories of the illegitimacy of Iraq to transfer to Afghanistan, making them both appear 'so very ill-advised.'[83]

This 'contagion effect' went in the opposite direction to the government's intention; it had hoped to use fears of another 9/11-style attack to persuade people to support Iraq.[84] Instead citizens' narratives suggest that the Iraqistan narrative has undermined memory of the original motive for Afghanistan and the almost universal support for it. Indeed the Labour government recognised the damaging effect of Iraq on Afghanistan. Foreign Secretary David Milliband expressed the hope that

> we can move to a situation where we don't have Iraq and Afghanistan in the same breath . . . they are different conflicts with different dynamics. I think the situation in Afghanistan is a central aspect of national security. If you think about 9/11.[85]

Despite such attempts to separate Afghanistan and Iraq, evidence here has shown that many citizens still conflate the two. Furthermore, Gribble et al. provide corroboratory evidence that this transfer from Iraq has shaped collective memories of the purpose of Afghanistan. Their 2011 survey found that controlling oil had become the third most cited perceived motive for Afghanistan by British citizens, after countering terrorism and stabilising the country, despite its scarcity in the initial discourse on the conflict.[86] This shows how blowback from using the War on Terror to justify Iraq inadvertently undermined Afghanistan, despite government efforts to reverse the trend. It no longer appeared to be an unequivocally just response to 9/11. The temporal and causal link between the two was weakened and, for some, severed entirely.

Inconsistent Government Strategic Narratives

The final factor explaining why some people have forgotten that Afghanistan started because of 9/11 is the British government's oscillation between different narratives to explain the conflict. No war is ever fought for just one reason. Debates invariably centre on the most significant motive among many. Wars, and the reasons they are fought, also evolve over time. The problem is that presenting multiple motives for intervention generates confusion, contradiction, and ambiguity about an intervention's actual purpose.[87] As Bolt puts it, 'to nuance and adjust is considered appropriate as unforeseen events unfold . . . but to U-turn, repeatedly ripping up the text, seems to reveal a lack of strategic vision'.[88]

Since the initial invasion, the British government has consistently failed to provide a simple answer to the question of 'why are we in Afghanistan?'[89] This is despite its own strategic communications policy emphasising that 'the best strategic narratives are short, succinct and simple to explain'.[90] Instead it has provided a range of contradictory explanations, which has eroded public support. Opinion polls in 2012 showed that up to 46 percent of citizens were unsure why Britain was in the country.[91]

The result of this inconsistent strategic communication has not just been wavering public support. Evidence here suggests that these competing narratives have shaped collective memories of the conflict, leading people to forget the 'unforgettable' reason it began. This is because every time a justification for war is chosen, others are excluded. Justifications that are reinforced less frequently are more likely to be forgotten.[92]

Cawkwell illustrates comprehensively how the British government vacillated between different strategic narratives in its ongoing attempts to 'sell Afghanistan'. According to him, the government has at different times justified Afghanistan primarily as a mission based on counterterrorism, stabilisation, and democratisation, or on counternarcotics.[93] Each narrative was present from the start: indeed shortly before intervention began Blair emphasised that 'the humanitarian coalition to help the people of Afghanistan is as vital as the military action itself'.[94] The problem, Cawkwell suggests, is that the arguments exhibit 'almost total incompatibility'.[95] For example, the stabilisation narrative was premised on the notion that a purely counterterrorism mission was insufficient to make Afghanistan a secure and prosperous state. Meanwhile the counterterrorism narrative implied the need to downplay stabilisation efforts as these were damaging the unity of the ISAF alliance.[96] Meanwhile public confusion developed over whether the mission was one of peacekeeping or warfighting.[97] As shown by the following responses, these multiple reasons appear to have fostered public uncertainty about the mission's purpose, which had been clear immediately after 9/11.

Nathan (45–54, Dorset) explains how he supported Afghanistan initially but opposed it in retrospect. He recalls that the original motive was about the Taliban, and particularly their treatment of women.

> NATHAN: Well I think Afghanistan is a case in point. I agreed with it in the first place, because of women being beheaded and not being allowed . . . being repressed and everything else. You think let's go and sort them out, and the Taliban are doing nasty things. Go in and sort them out. And again it was easy to win the main battle. We can go in there and get them out of the capital, but then it was always going to come back and bite us, so now you think has it really made a difference? There's this girl at Birmingham University who's won the Nobel Peace Prize for being shot in the head by the Taliban aged 14. I can't remember her name now. . . . And you kind of think we went to war to stop that, but obviously we didn't, because we've been there ten years and she was still shot in the head by the Taliban. . . . So the waters [have] become muddied. At the time I thought it was a good thing but, I don't know.

Ray (45–54, Birmingham) cannot recall the precise reason for Afghanistan, although he suggests like Megan (65+, Oxfordshire) that the original motive was for counternarcotics purposes, 'to destroy the opium'.

RAY: I'm not really a hundred percent sure about Afghanistan. . . . Yeah no,
I'm not sure on Afghanistan. That weren't really nothing to do with . . .
there's no oil over there or anything.

. . .

RAY: I know there's a lot of drugs over there, there's fields of that. So then
they wouldn't get involved . . . they do a lot of opium farming . . . is it
poppies and stuff? So . . . I mean they just really went in to help America, because America went in. Where America tends to go, we tend to.

Once more neither Nathan nor Ray appears to recall that the dominant
initial motive for Afghanistan was to respond to 9/11. Instead the specific motives they remember are the Taliban's treatment of women and to counter the
drugs trade, justifications that were far more prominent in subsequent years.
Ray struggles to recall the intervention's original purpose. He appears to rely on
commonsense ideas about British defence policy such as the tendency to follow
the United States, the relevance of oil to war, and generally that 'there's a lot of
drugs over there'. His uncertain response is more insightful than it appears.
Several authors consider maintaining Britain's special relationship with the
United States the 'real' reason for ongoing British intervention in Afghanistan,
but this was too unpalatable to be openly stated.[98] On that basis, Ray's intuitive
assessment that Britain went in 'because America went in' is sound.

These reasons for the original intervention in Afghanistan are not erroneous; following the United States and the Afghan drug trade did feature periph-
erally in initial government rhetoric. But by far the most prominent *casus belli*
was the counterterrorist response to 9/11. Efforts in counternarcotics and female education were more prominent in the middle years of the conflict between 2003 and 2009 as the government sought further moral justifications for
an increasingly costly counterinsurgency.[99] Nonetheless, references to both had
virtually 'disappeared' by 2011, due to perceptions that these arguments were
too weak to sustain public support.[100] Instead, particularly from 2008 onward,
the government reverted to narrower counterterrorism arguments. It hoped to
sustain flagging support by emphasising the need to prevent Afghanistan once
more becoming a terrorist haven from which future 9/11s or 7/7s could be
launched.[101]

However, this change appears to have come too late to avoid shaping collective memories of the conflict for a variety of citizens. The government's strategic
narrative shifts have contributed to public confusion over Afghanistan. This
confusion undermines narrative coherence. 'Terrorists attacked the World

Trade Center, so we are in Afghanistan to ensure more females are educated'
makes less narrative sense than the original counterterrorist justification.
Rather than an understandable response to a horrific attack, it is underpinned
by far more abstract logic about how education brings development, stability,
and therefore reduces the risk of terrorism. Creating more inclusive regimes
that respect human rights certainly fit within liberal internationalist ideas of
ethical military intervention that were prevalent in the Blair administration.[102]
Crucially, though, the importance of 9/11 as the initial event in the story is reduced. Since it is less prominent over time, it is more likely to be forgotten *in the
context of the war*. Factoring in these mixed motives alongside the appeal of the
Iraqistan narrative, over a conflict lasting twice as long as the Second World
War, helps explain how some citizens appear to have forgotten how it all began.

To conclude, in his memoirs Blair reflects on Britain's war in Afghanistan as
follows:

> We look back now, almost a decade later when we are still at war ... and we can
> scarcely recall how we ever came to be in this position. But on that bright New
> York morning, not a cloud disturbing the bluest of blue skies, we knew exactly
> what was happening and why.[103]

The events on that 'bright New York morning' are considered unforgettable.
Yet for various reasons, a diverse range of British citizens can 'scarcely recall'
that Afghanistan was precipitated by the most spectacularly destructive terrorist attack in history. The most plausible explanation offered here is not that this
is due to individual ignorance or methodological artefact, but because of
changes in how the conflict has been narrated over time. Simultaneous war in
Iraq and Afghanistan, and the development of both into prolonged counterinsurgencies, fostered an Iraqistan narrative, merging them into a seemingly endless struggle. Seeing both as one enabled Iraq's perceived illegitimacy as part of
the War on Terror to transfer to Afghanistan, despite government attempts to
extricate itself from the discourse trap it had created. The government added to
the confusion by using different primary motivations for Afghanistan over
time, be it terrorism, drugs, women, democratisation, stability, or maintaining
the 'special relationship' with the United States. Together these factors have
ruptured the temporal and causal link between 9/11 and Afghanistan, altering
for some the plot of the story of Britain's Afghanistan War.

This novel finding raises important points about how narrative emplotment can both shape and reflect collective memory. If asked directly about 9/11, it is likely that the vast majority of British citizens would be familiar with the attacks. In that sense 9/11 is memorable as an isolated event. However, this does not mean that they recall its causes and effects in the same way over time. In other words, the meaning of events such as 9/11 is a product of the narratives into which they are incorporated. If the story changes, the meaning of the event changes. Consequently, determining how wars are collectively remembered or forgotten requires an understanding not just of the conflicts themselves but the narratives into which they are emplotted at different points in time. In the discourse on the War on Terror, the one thing that seemed clear was its start point. Over time, though, the story appears to be shifting. Even an event as iconic as 9/11 does not contain its own meaning; it derives from the narratives into which it is incorporated.[104] The meaning of an event is not complete after a single speech-act; it is an ongoing process of production, reproduction, interpretation, and reinterpretation.[105] If the overall plot shifts, the meaning of the events within it shifts too. This affects how events are remembered and forgotten in relation to one another.

By revealing the unintended consequences of strategic communication, this case has also shown the constraints governments face trying to respond to the interpretive shifts caused by subsequent events. The similarities of Iraq and Afghanistan made it difficult for policymakers to separate the two wars in people's minds. Layers of hindsight sew new linkages between events, just as the threads linking previous conflicts degrade. Understanding this process necessitates studying not just the narratives projected by politicians and the media but those by ordinary people too. Policymakers may seek to frame concurrent wars as separate entities. Academics periodise history in ways that designate certain events as turning points. But that does not mean that ordinary citizens perceive these differences so clearly.

CHAPTER 8

Looking to the Future

NIGEL (35–44, YORKSHIRE): In the future . . . we just need to make sure that when we do go to war, it's for the right reasons.

In August 2013, images emerged of Syrian civilians of all ages gasping, convulsing, and frothing at the mouth in Ghouta, a suburb of Damascus, from a suspected chemical attack. Hundreds died. UN inspectors later found clear evidence that this was the result of the Syrian government using sarin gas against its own citizens. Having been declared a 'red line' by then US President Barack Obama, this violation of international law led to calls for military intervention against the Assad regime. In Britain, war weary from the prolonged conflicts in Iraq and Afghanistan, Prime Minister David Cameron put intervention to a parliamentary vote on 29 August. Parliament voted 'No'.

For many in Britain, a country with a proud tradition of military interventionism and an identity forged through standing up to dictators and tyrants, failing to act was a profound shock. As Chancellor George Osborne lamented, there would now be 'national soul searching about our role in the world'.[1] This outpouring of anxiety demonstrated the perception of a close link between the British people's sense of self—their ontological security—and military interventionism.

One conclusion drawn from this 'soul searching' was that Britain lacked a coherent strategic narrative to explain its international role. As a House of Lords Select Committee concluded in 2014:

> In a now almost totally transformed international scene, full of unfamiliar and bewildering new aspects, it is vital that the UK maintain its sense of purpose and direction: the British need to feel confident in knowing who we are

and what our role is in a transformed and turbulent world. The Government must present, and keep updating, a strong narrative about the UK's changing position; a story about what values the UK stands for and where it should be heading.[2]

If the world looked 'turbulent', 'unfamiliar', and 'bewildering' in 2014, this was magnified exponentially in June 2016, when Britain voted to leave the European Union. The uncertainty that has followed as people try to come to terms with the complexity of the contested 'Brexit' process makes the House of Lords Select Committee's conclusion particularly prescient. Commentators have pored over the causes and consequences of the decision to leave, citing causal variables such as age, education, socioeconomic status, geography, attitudes to immigration, and resistance to globalisation.[3] Whichever combination of these best explains the vote, the Brexit debate also represents a narrative contest between competing interpretations of Britain's past, present, and future identity and role in the world.

If anything Brexit has brought to the fore what commentators have long suspected when invoking US Secretary of State Dean Acheson's comment in 1962 that Britain has 'lost an empire and not yet found a role': that British society is riven with profound cleavages over who Britain is, has been, and should be.[4] The House of Lords Select Committee report was merely tapping into a prevailing assumption in foreign policy and international relations: that solutions to problems of how to think about who one is and how one should act in the world can be solved as long as one has a compelling strategic narrative. This is based on the assumption that narratives are the most natural form of human communication and the way humans construct their identities to create a stable sense of self in unfamiliar situations.

The importance of constructing a compelling narrative to explain one's purpose has becoming increasingly taken for granted in a wide range of fields, whether strategists are aiming to persuade publics to buy products or support wars. Strikingly, though, rarely is this narrative construction process informed by asking people what stories they already use to understand the world. Instead researchers and practitioners overwhelmingly turn to quantitative measures to produce indicators of aggregate attitudes and opinion rather than explore the messy ways people interpret reality. As a result, we know a fair amount about what ordinary people think about various foreign policy issues but remarkably little about how they narrate them.

This book has sought to address this by adopting a ground-up, interpretive approach to the case of how British citizens narrate their country's role in war and what these stories reveal about how they construct Britain's international identity. The aim throughout has been to provide a more nuanced perspective based on sociological research at the individual level. It has also sought to address another weakness in existing research on strategic narrative in foreign policy and IR: that despite assuming that narratives possess unique persuasive properties, few researchers are methodologically clear on how they separate narratives from other forms of discourse. One cannot realistically sustain the claim that narratives are uniquely persuasive if one treats all political discourse as narrative. Any assessment of the power of narrative can only come from first separating it from other modes of communication, and doing so clearly and consistently.

Since a core rationale was the importance of directly investigating the stories ordinary people tell, no prior assumptions were made about their exact content and form. Instead analysis proceeded inductively, focusing primarily on plot, based on the argument that this represents the key distinction between narrative and other modes of discourse. Breadth and depth of analysis were enhanced by adopting a two-level analytical framework, examining *genre*—the general pattern of citizens' stories—and *emplotment*—the process of selecting and linking events to create these overall patterns. This combination of the general and the particular made it possible to analyse broad accounts of Britain's history as well as the minutiae of how an individual event is remembered or forgotten.

This process revealed that there is a limited range of narratives British people tell about wars. At the level of genre, two storylines quickly emerged on which there was widespread agreement: a narrative of Britain's *Continuous War* and one of its simultaneous *Material Decline*. Citizens' judgments of Britain's international identity are based on the assumptions that Britain always seems to be at war, but its ability to do so is diminishing.

The *Continuous War* narrative is particularly striking because it reveals how routine Britain's participation in war appears to be for such a wide variety of people. Certainly many disagreed with specific military interventions and generally hoped that all other means to resolve conflict would be exhausted first. Nevertheless, British citizens across the board see military interventionism as an expected and legitimate policy option, something that Britain has always done throughout history. Partly this is a product of the historical record, since

Britain has been at war pretty much constantly for centuries. However, the stories here also suggest that war is an integral aspect of what it means to be British for a wide range of citizens. For others it is a normal, everyday, background occurrence, as has been evident recently, with Britain using air power, special forces, and military advisors in the war against Islamic State with apparently minimal public concern.[5] People may distrust government motives or question the effectiveness of military intervention, but Britain's ongoing military operations provide a continuous reminder of the assumed superior capability, will, and integrity of the British soldier. In this way Britain's wars do not just engender outpourings of nationalism as conflicts begin. They continually reproduce a form of 'banal nationalism' that reinforces the commonsense assumption that Britain's military is a *Force for Good* compared to others.[6]

While military intervention seems remarkably normal, similarly taken for granted is that *Material Decline* has made Britain less capable of intervening effectively. Since the peak of its imperial power, the story of Britain's material strength is emplotted as a crudely linear economic decline that has weakened its international position relative to others. In response, some participants and political elites have given the impression that Britain's persistent interventionism is a defensive response akin to 'small island syndrome', a way of compensating for Britain's diminished material position. For others, Britain's reduced ability to conduct independent global military operations undermines an essential aspect of 'what Britain is all about'—in other words, its ontological security.

While the *Continuous War* and *Material Decline* narratives can be considered genres in their own right, their assumptions were typically subsumed within more complex narratives that also included contrasting moral judgments about Britain's wars. Analysing how these strands are woven together revealed a typology of five distinct narratives citizens used to summarise Britain's past, present, and future role in war. Each constructs Britain's identity differently. The *Punching Above Its Weight* narrative is commonplace in elite defence policy discourse and is a story of continuity in which Britain has always achieved disproportionate influence relative to its size. It has been more willing than others to step in to uphold international peace and security, and its qualitatively superior military is a *Force for Good*. In contrast, the *Vanishing Force* narrative casts Britain far less heroically. Starting from Britain's imperial heyday, subsequent years have seen nothing but material and moral decline. This nostalgic interpretation assumes that Britain should be a world leader as it once was, but its advantages have been squandered by inept leadership, societal malaise, and, for some, dilution of British greatness through excessive immigration. Britain is inherently a *Force for Good* compared to others but is incapable of acting upon this unless massive military reinvestment occurs. With the additional 'clout' that would result, Britain could be great again, returning to its purported former position as the defender of the liberal order.

In the third and marginally most common narrative, Britain is cast as *Learning from Its Mistakes*. This liberal interpretation emphasises progress toward a more peaceful, civilised world, ideally without the need for war. The plot takes Britain from using its military to perpetrate misguided imperial atrocities to using it for more humanitarian purposes. Britain is learning to use its military for good. Ideally its future would be as a mediator of world conflict rather than a direct participant, but war is an accepted necessity in a world of dictators and tyrants. The fourth narrative initially follows the same progressive trajectory, but Britain's progress is interrupted by following the United States into illegitimate, destructive conflicts. Britain's intentions have always been good when participating in war, but it has recently been *Led Astray*. Returning to the path of progress will be contingent on whether it relies on its own superior moral judgment and historical experience compared to its gung-ho Atlantic ally. The final narrative casts Britain as a *Selfish Imperialist*. Imbued with Marxist undertones, British military history is a tale of continuous economic exploitation, be it for territory, money, or resources. Unlike the previous narratives, this explicitly antiwar interpretation sees Britain as a *Force for Ill*.

The relative prevalence of these narratives could not be statistically generalised to the broader population. However, they are a product of a research process that ensured the widest possible range of perspectives on British wars, from unequivocal support to universal opposition, conducted until beyond the point of data saturation. This ensured that these narratives represent a comprehensive range of public interpretations of Britain's wars, although there is significant hybridity when people narrate them. Still an obvious area of future research concerns how demographic factors such as age, gender, ethnicity, and education affect who tells which story. More interesting still would be to compare how English, Welsh, Scottish, and Northern Irish citizens interpret Britain's wars. Given recent calls for Scottish independence and schisms over the Brexit vote, it may be interesting to investigate how individual citizens narrate a military history in which Britain has fought united since the eighteenth century, from the perspective of a disunited present.

Useful insights into cross-cultural narrative understandings of war might

also be gained through comparing British public narratives with other countries. Stories are always likely to be culture-specific and topic-specific in terms
of the events and analogies people choose. Nevertheless, their general patterns,
and the meta-narratives underpinning them, such as liberalism, Marxism, or
nationalism, lend themselves to certain narrative trajectories more than others.
Echoes of Donald Trump's call to 'Make America Great Again' can be found in
Mao's call to end China's 'century of humiliation', as well as the desire of Brexit
supporters to 'put the "Great" back in Great Britain'.

The extent to which the same plot is applicable in different situations is
important in considering the utility of these narratives beyond the topic and
period of this study. It is widely recognised that national narratives rarely shift
dramatically, and that people tend to make sense of new events by incorporat-
ing them into old stories rather than creating new ones.[7] This suggests that
these genres may be visible in future articulations of Britain's international role.
However, as ontological security theorists suggest, crisis moments can provide
ruptures from which new narratives can emerge.[8] Brexit provides an obvious
example. This raises the question of how this book's stories of Britain's past,
present, and future relate to citizens' narrative understandings of Brexit and the
role of defence in contested visions of Britain's international future. Assessing
events ongoing at the time of writing is always fraught: the analysis that follows
therefore reflects primarily on the decision to vote for Brexit itself rather than
the ongoing negotiations. Nonetheless, since both Britain's role in war and its
relationship with Europe are fundamentally about contested ideas of who Britain is and how it should act in relation to others, the narratives identified here
may provide useful insights.

Brexit, Britain, and Future War

When analysing the British public's narrow decision to withdraw from the EU
from a narrative perspective, caution is needed in assuming that there was a
single 'Leave' narrative as understood by British citizens, a single 'Remain' narrative, and in a battle of the narratives, one side won.[9] Such thinking has been
common in the literature on strategic narrative and wars, which tend to be
framed in Manichean terms between good and evil. Such simplification obscures significant variation in how people interpret complex political issues. It
is easy to stereotype Leave voters as nostalgic old nationalists longing for a re-

turn of the British Empire, as Liberal Democrat leader Vince Cable did after the vote, for example, but people voted for and against Brexit for a variety of reasons.[10] Factors cited immediately included demographic variables such as age, education, and socioeconomic status, alongside differing attitudes to immigration and globalisation.[11]

This does not mean interpretations are infinite; there tend to be a limited range of narratives available within public discourse through which people view new events.[12] Considering the genres identified in this book about Britain's role in the world, the recent Brexit debate reveals some of these complexities.

The narrative most closely aligned with pro-Brexit discourse is the *Vanishing Force* narrative, whereby people explicitly blame the EU for dragging Britain's economy and society down, hoping that leaving will enable Britain to become great again. This narrative assumes Britain's inherent greatness and that its military is a force for good in the world, and something that needs significant reinvestment to give Britain the hard power it used to have.

However, others voted to leave the EU out of a sense of dislocation and detachment from a self-serving political elite perceived as indifferent to the needs of ordinary citizens.[13] Plausibly therefore, Brexit might also be appealing to opponents of Britain's wars who narrate its past through the lens of the *Selfish Imperialist* narrative, which blames the exact same self-interested political elite who ignore public opinion in decisions on military intervention, such as on Iraq in 2003. The point is that people with diametrically opposed views of Britain's international identity might vote for the same policy. Once one examines national identity narratives at the level of the ordinary citizen, things appear far more complex than a binary narrative battle.

In spite of these complexities, in practice the Brexit debate was between two sides, and one side won. What is clear from this binary perspective is that the Remain side had a clear disadvantage when it comes to narrative, be it in terms of myth, character, or plot. The mythology underpinning the contemporary EU is based on having forged a sustainable peace on a continent previously riven by war and eventually genocide. However, the notion that this peace stems from increasing integration contrasts with centuries of British nationalist myth based on its distinction from Europe. According to Marcussen et al., independent British parliamentary sovereignty symbolises freedom from Catholic Rome, and freedom from Europe, going back arguably to at least the Battle of Hastings in 1066.[14] The French, like the British, have long held a sense of exceptionalism derived largely from their imperial past. However, they managed to reframe their sense of national exceptionalism after decolonisation by emphasising their role in shaping Europe.[15] With an identity built largely on difference from Europe, Britain never managed to do this.

The Leave side of the narrative debate arguably had the advantage in terms of character construction, both in terms of Britain's character and specific historical figures they could deploy in their stories. Narratives of Britain's exceptionalism compared to Europe can be populated with many of the most recognisably heroic figures from British history. Brexit advocates could invoke the spirit of Churchill, calling forth brave heroes who stood strong to protect Britain and the world from tyrants, many of which emerged from Europe. Britain in these epic moments was master of its destiny, intervening in conflicts when it chose to, or standing alone to save Europe when its existence was threatened.[16] In contrast, the character Britain has played as a member of the EU has never really been clearly determined. It isn't obviously the hero, having been an awkward partner on so many issues.[17] At best it has perhaps been one of many actors working together for mutual benefit, although steadily improving peace and prosperity is both undramatic and hard to pin on a particular heroic individual with whom people can emotionally identify.

The plot of the story of Britain's membership of the EU is also unclear. Its beginning was portrayed more as a reluctant 'slide into Europe' rather than a positive decision to integrate.[18] Thereafter, the plot seems to consist mostly of a series of difficult conflicts and negotiations, which appear to be largely unmemorable to much of the public. Incidents of apparent EU dictation over seemingly trivial and bizarre matters seem far more memorable and acquire mythological status whether true or false, be it apparent edicts on the straightness of bananas or power limits on vacuum cleaners.[19]

This is not to say that the Remain campaign only had weak narrative resources to draw upon. The mythology of progressive, liberal peace as embodied by post-World War II Europe is also deeply embedded in British culture. This is demonstrated by the most common narrative in this study being the *Learning from Its Mistakes* narrative, which constructs Britain's ideal postimperial role as working with others to make the world more peaceful and democratic. This is part of the reason why the Brexit vote was so contentious; it pitted deeply embedded myths of Britain's identity and role in the world against each other. Significantly, though, the *Learning from Its Mistakes* narrative is not predicated on Britain doing this as one of 28 countries; it is based on Britain playing a leading role as 'the world's peacemaker' or 'mediator' of global conflict. So again, the Remain camp was at a narrative disadvantage when facing the heroic, independent image many British people have of their country, perceived by many as under threat from the homogenising forces of globalisation and integration.

In the absence of a clear sense of Britain's character in the European story or a positive narrative about Britain's role in European integration, Remain narratives possessed less coherence and instead focused on countering the Leave campaign with narrow, economic logic, persuading more through argument than narrative. This was not necessarily ineffective; research suggests that the difference in persuasiveness of narrative and argument is far less than is commonly assumed.[20] However, it clearly wasn't effective enough. At the time of writing, fear of economic collapse in the event of Brexit remains rife, with some calling for a second referendum to vote on whether Brexit should take place at all. Fear of negative economic consequences no doubt motivated many to support Remain, and clearly a large proportion of the population see Britain as better off in Europe and, indeed, identify as European too. Still the Remain campaign never convincingly answered the question of 'Remain *Whom?*' in relation to Europe, if indeed this has ever been convincingly articulated. In a contest of identity narratives, this placed them at a distinct disadvantage.

Defence and war were peripheral issues in debates leading up to Brexit, which focused far more on immigration, sovereignty, and the economy.[21] In the wake of the vote, however, defence emerged as both a source of concern and optimism. Concern was based on the approximately 15 percent reduction in the value of the pound against the dollar, which raised the defence budget overnight, since it involves extensive procurement from the United States.[22] Optimism centred on the idea that Britain's superior military strength, investment, and leading role in European security were sources of leverage during exit negotiations but also areas where cooperation would continue for pragmatic reasons.[23] That said, ongoing concerns about the creation of an 'EU army' were voiced before and after the referendum, as once more the idea of Britain subordinating its security to Europe stands in contrast to a military history in which Britain's ability to intervene selectively in Europe was integral to its way of war.[24] Just being one of the 28 clashes with the historical notion of independent British military capability. As Edgerton suggests, in British defence circles, 'the idea of Britain being like Holland, Belgium, Germany, Italy, or even France . . . is viewed with deep hostility'.[25]

The narratives in this book suggest that pride in British exceptionalism makes it unlikely that people on either side of the Brexit debate will be comfortable with Britain taking on a diminished international role.[26] Of course, declining influence in Europe would be an inevitable outcome of leaving the EU, whether Britain likes it or not. For this reason, it is highly likely that of all the narratives uncovered here, the *Punching Above Its Weight* narrative is the most likely source of continuity in Britain's sense of self, no matter how Brexit proceeds. Since there are always likely to be others doing relatively less well than Britain, and because of the assumed superiority of the average British soldier, diplomat, businessman, or artisan, it is a claim with enduring rhetorical appeal. It may therefore provide a bridge between pre- and post-Brexit that maintains British ontological security even if the process is traumatic.[27]

That said, the *Punching Above Its Weight* narrative has received ongoing criticism in the defence debate, as the gap continues to grow between Britain's material capabilities and its ambitions.[28] Likely defence cutbacks due to the devaluation of the pound will make the gap between exceptionalist rhetoric and ordinary reality even greater. As King suggests, Britain may no longer be able to punch above its weight; it just maintains its sense of identity by talking above it, however unsound this may be for strategic purists seeking a strict congruence between material means and political ends.[29] There will still therefore be those who suggest that Britain will become even more of a *Vanishing Force*, and they are likely to continue to blame politicians for it.

At what point the disparity between Britain's intent and capabilities undermines the *Punching Above Its Weight* narrative completely remains to be seen. At that point, one might anticipate an increase in military activism to demonstrate that in military matters at least, Britain is still more ready and willing to use force for righteous causes than others. The scale of interventions may remain small: sending military advisors, special forces, and selected air power resources assumed to be superior to other countries' capabilities means that Britain's ontological security as still *Punching Above Its Weight* can be maintained at comparatively little cost. Whatever happens, with British citizens still viewing the military as a primary source of global influence,[30] it is likely to remain a key character in the identity narratives British people construct about their international future.

The unpredictable nature of President Trump's foreign policy raises interesting questions for future defence policy in the wake of the Brexit vote. Initially, the intuitive answer to stepping away from Europe was for Britain to move closer to Washington. However, Trump's election and his provocative and inconsistent foreign policy made this less palatable, especially given widespread antipathy toward him among the British public.[31] But from a narrative point of view, far from reflecting change, Trump's unpredictable and seemingly erratic behaviour reinforces the ideas underpinning the *Led Astray* narrative: that Britain might not be as powerful as America, but it is a more intelligent and considered international actor. Much is made of how Trump's approach to foreign policy and diplomacy differs markedly (and dangerously) from what has come before. However, from the perspective of British citizens, Trump's conduct actually reinforces deeply embedded ideas about Britain's superior understanding of international affairs. Ironically, Trump's behaviour may undermine Britain's physical security while reinforcing its ontological security.

What the election of Donald Trump and Brexit have in common is the association with the advance of populism and the growing sense that liberal democracy is under threat. These concerns were less viscerally apparent both when this project began and in the motivations of military interventions that preceded it. Doubt about the future of the Western liberal order stands in contrast with the unbridled confidence in the inevitability of its triumph that underpinned the American and British invasion of Iraq in 2003. There appears to have been a rediscovery that liberal democracy is far from perfect and perhaps only the least worst form of political order among others. Moreover, recent attempts to impose it by force have been extremely destructive. This suggests that policymakers may wish to reflect on the utility of the *Learning from Its Mistakes* narrative, since it may present a more honest and realistic portrayal of Britain's role in war and the promotion of liberal democratic governance in general. The ability of populist politicians in particular to gain credit for authenticity, by appearing to present honest views even if they offend, suggests the value of reflecting on whether a more honest portrayal of the imperfections of foreign policy may be preferable to repeating exceptionalist soundbites and catchphrases. Rather than seeing itself as being 'trapped in a remarkably limited discursive space' characterised by a constant need to project superiority,[32] Britain's admission that it is learning from its mistakes might enable policymakers to project more authentic foreign policy that still aspires to a leading role in the world. As shown here, it is an interpretation held by a wide range of citizens too.

Whatever narratives come to dominate discourse on Britain's international role as the Brexit process develops, the strongest impression I have gained from the war stories presented here is that international activism, military or otherwise, provides a sense of exceptionalism to British citizens across the political spectrum that they do not want to give up. Britain is portrayed as special for always *Punching Above Its Weight* compared to others, in both military technique and moral fortitude. In the *Vanishing Force* narrative, the British people are inherently superior but will only rise to greatness again if the government reinvests in hard power to give Britain the influence it and the world needs. In the *Learning from Its Mistakes* and *Led Astray* narratives, Britain has unparalleled military and diplomatic experience to resolve conflict and bring peace to the world if it chooses. In the *Selfish Imperialist* narrative, Britain's imperial achievements have caused immense damage to the world. Despite this, the country has developed other unique traits, such as being at the 'forefront of modern thinking' for its 'incredible tolerance', 'open-mindedness', and 'multiculturalism'. Even those that oppose war believe that the global security situation may mean Britain's military has an important role in forging peace, and it may be better for the world that Britain takes on that self-sacrificing role than someone else. Britain being at war is not exceptional, but it makes the British people feel exceptional.

In none of these stories was Britain seen as 'just another nation'. Across those interviewed there was a sense of 'the enormity of our military influence and what a truly awe-inspiring power, for bad and for good, our country has been right across the world'.[33] Indeed part of why Brexit is so contentious is how strongly one side believes this power is magnified by being in Europe while the other believes it is diminished by it. Either way, possessing a strong military and being willing to use it seems to be one of a dwindling number of ways British people can assure themselves that they still play a crucial international role. The costs of war may currently be unappealing; the tale of the warrior nation is likely to endure.

Emplotment, Narrative, and Memory

As well as identifying the general patterns of the stories people tell about war in relation to Britain's past, present, and future, this book has emphasised the value of examining plot construction in detail. Until now, the foreign policy literature analysing plot has mostly focused on the overall pattern of a story (genre) rather than the process through which its constituent parts are put together (emplotment). The process through which ordinary citizens construct the plot of their stories about the nation's military history has also received scant attention.

This book sought to address this by providing a method through which the emplotment process could be systematically analysed. Adapting and applying a framework originally used in biographical research to examine how people make personal identity claims through their life stories, it showed how individuals combine a range of emplotment mechanisms to portray their country positively or negatively.[34] It was shown how people try and portray Britain's military as a *Force for Good* in the world by *including* examples of humanitarianism or *sharpening* focus on wars where Britain defended others against invasion, while *clarifying* that conflicts that appeared selfish were actually defensive or altruistic. It was shown how they *link* certain wars together in sequence or alternatively select otherwise disconnected wars to show that British military history has always been ethical. It was also shown how people would *omit* or *silence* aspects that do not support their story, such as imperial exploitation or atrocities, or instead use *flattening* to play down their significance. Combining these elements enables people to construct more coherent claims about Britain's identity in the present, based on their narrative representation of its past. The framework potentially benefits narrative researchers in a range of fields because examining these elements enables them to infer the overall point of a story if it is not explicitly stated, be it in this case portraying Britain as heroic, humanitarian, inept, or imperialist. It may also inform strategic communicators looking to construct the plot of strategic narratives more coherently, since it provides a tool to understand how selected historical events can be framed to support whatever identity claim they are trying to make.

A further benefit of studying emplotment in depth is that it can illuminate intricacies in how events are collectively remembered and forgotten over time. This was demonstrated by interrogating the surprising finding that some British citizens no longer seem to recall that 9/11 caused Britain's war in Afghanistan. I argued that this unexpected finding is partly due to changes in how the conflict has been narrated over time. First, the wars in Afghanistan and Iraq were purposefully described as fronts in the broader War on Terror. But as they developed into prolonged counterinsurgencies citizens saw them as indistinguishable parts of a single *Iraqistan* narrative: the story of an unnecessary, never-ending quagmire as part of a failing War on Terror. This allowed the perceived illegitimacy of the Iraq War to pass to Afghanistan, making it seem illegitimate too rather than an understandable response to a violent attack. This, combined with the British government's multiple, conflicting narratives to justify Afghanistan over time, has led some citizens to forget the 'unforgettable' circumstances from which the war began. Strategic communication efforts in Afghanistan have been extensively criticised for their incoherence.[35] However, this research has advanced the literature by revealing how this incoherence has shaped the way citizens are collectively remembering the conflict, to the point where some are forgetting its links with the largest terrorist attack in human history.

The novel observation that some citizens have forgotten 9/11 in relation to Afghanistan has implications for the study of strategic narrative, collective memory, and research methodology more generally. By showing how this phenomenon is partly due to inconsistencies in the way the war was narrated over time, it provides a snapshot of how strategic narration can shape, both advertently and inadvertently, how individual citizens remember and forget wars and why they are fought. However, it also demonstrates the constraints policymakers face in how they frame ongoing conflicts.[36] Afghanistan and Iraq turning into overlapping counterinsurgencies thwarted government efforts to separate them discursively, particularly since they had linked them previously. This is one example of what Freedman describes as the 'possibilities and limits of strategic narratives'.[37]

The findings also have implications for the study of the collective memory of iconic events such as 9/11. As Leavy notes, events are not inherently iconic; they are made so by political actors and the media who frame them as turning points in history.[38] A turning point is a narrative concept though; it indicates a present-day shift from a past state of affairs to an alternative future. An event may retain its iconicity in isolation, but the plot into which it is temporally and causally embedded may change over time. An event may be unforgettable; its causes and effects might not be. This suggests the value of a narrative understanding of iconicity. Future research from this perspective would not just focus on whether an event is unforgettable and how it remains so; it would also consider how its meaning changes as the stories into which it is emplotted evolve.

These observations demonstrate the value of this book's ground-up, inductive methodology. Keeping questions open-ended generated a rather unpredictable and diverse corpus of data that would be inappropriate for a researcher looking to aggregate attitudes or test predetermined hypotheses regarding a specific conflict. Nonetheless, it enabled unexpected findings to emerge, potentially leading to subsequent theory generation. Also, by avoiding asking about specific conflicts until participants brought these up, it was possible to examine events that were omitted from stories as well as those that were included. When conflicts were discussed, they were those deemed most significant by the participant rather than those primed by my prior assumptions. This approach arguably gets closer to identifying the frames of reference people actually use to interpret issues such as war rather than those academics, pollsters, or policymakers assume that they use.

The findings offer a reminder of the importance of reflexivity when conducting social research. Reflexivity ensures that the process through which interpretive decisions are made is as transparent and credible as possible, but it can also raise important issues about researchers' prior assumptions. The absence of 9/11 in stories of British military history was only noticed because of my assumption that it was a logical turning point that started the War on Terror, which has shaped British military strategy ever since. This shows the importance of scholars reflecting critically on how they periodise history, rather than presuming the broader population share their assumptions. Once more this strongly justifies directly examining the stories citizens tell rather than assuming they understand the world in a certain way.

It is also important to note that methodological choices will shape researcher perceptions of their participants. Contrary to research suggesting contradictory or incoherent attitudes to war, I concur with the conclusions of Hines et al. and Towle that a wide range of British citizens possess an 'intuitive understanding of war'.[39] This is because the vast majority of participants could tell relatively coherent stories about Britain's conflicts over the years, even though their knowledge varied considerably. Furthermore, those who knew little of specific conflicts could still tell simplistic stories about war based on mythological, commonsense generalisations regarding what war is 'all about', such as oil, religion, or human nature. Even so, narratives are always likely to appear more coherent than off-the-top-of-the-head answers to closed survey questions, which may vary in design from one war or one study to the next. So while I have suggested that British people have a more advanced understanding of war than previous studies have implied, the influence of my methodology on this observation cannot be dismissed. The value of this book's alternative approach has been to deepen understanding of how citizens' perspectives are expressed through their stories, and how they try and convince others that their interpretations are valid. This approach offers the potential of providing a fresh perspective to social scientific research in a range of fields.

The Future: Post-Truth Era or Narrative Age?

One way this book has sought to encourage people to think differently about public attitudes to war is in drawing attention not to what people know or think about war but to the narratives that they use to understand it. As repeatedly shown, people hold generic understandings of war that require very little factual knowledge to support them. These mythological ideas appear to be common sense, though they are often factually suspect, or at least the narrator appears unconcerned by the need for evidence. These include the notion that all wars are caused by religion, that Britain has never been invaded, that its soldiers are indisputably superior to others, that Britain contributes far more to peacekeeping operations than other powers, and that it more likely fights alone than alongside others. These ideas support and reflect mythological narratives that explain why, in Britain, victory over Napoleon at Waterloo is proclaimed as a great British victory rather than one of an international coalition, and why according to the British the defining moment of the entire Second World War is when they stood alone when all others faltered.[40]

These interpretations are debatable, but the fact that many people appear to hold understandings of war that contradict the historical record suggests that probing questions need to be asked about the role of politicians, the media, and private communication professionals in shaping why people tell the stories they do. For as shown earlier in the case of how some British people appeared to have 'forgotten 9/11', shifts in the way events are narrated over time, whether deliberate or accidental, can alter how even the most iconic events are remembered or forgotten. These mythological understandings are less visible when using quantitative approaches to test foreign policy knowledge or, as is currently popular in 'Big Data' analytics, using psychographic profiling to match personalities with political ideologies and likely behaviour.[41]

Better understanding of public narratives and myths is particularly important because the strength with which they are held makes people vulnerable to persuasion by narratives that resonate with them, even though they may contain inaccurate information. Fears of public vulnerability to disinformation are at the heart of contemporary concerns that we are living in a 'post-truth' era, in which emotion trumps reason, myths trump facts, and 'fake news' is increasingly powerful.[42]

In many ways this is a corollary of perceptions that we are in a new 'narrative age'. When humans assess narratives, they tend not to do so on the basis of whether they are factually accurate but on whether the overall impression the story generates is *plausible*. Factual truth is certainly important in narrative persuasion, because claims that obviously contradict what the audience believes to be true are easily identified and this can instantly undermine narrative coherence and the credibility of the narrator. However, narrative persuasion occurs at a more subtle level and is more about portraying or alluding to a plausible representation of reality than a logically and factually correct one.

The plausibility of a story is also typically assessed based on how far it relates to previous stories a person has encountered rather than a critical assessment of the story's premises or factual content.[43] This can be shown by thinking about Western fears of Russian electoral interference, where it is frequently asserted that Russia has played an outsized role in events such as the election of Trump and the Brexit vote. Fearing this influence is logical if you see a world where narratives are ever-present and uniquely persuasive, because it means that others can use these attributes against you. Nonetheless, measuring this influence is exceptionally difficult given the media ecology's complexity, and it may well be far less than is popularly assumed given the historical tendency to assert propaganda's immense influence, regardless of evidence.[44] It is worth reflecting on whether the plausibility of Russian electoral interference derives less from people's critical evaluation of its measurable effects but instead from their experience of a lifetime of stories, even from early childhood, in which evil villains and masterminds possess a remarkable ability to manipulate world events. These may be fictional, such as the villains (often Russian) James Bond repeatedly faces—a series of narratives incidentally that do much to reinforce the idea that Britain plays a heroic, exceptional international role. They may also be factual, such as the oversimplification inherent in much Cold War thinking that all wars were part of a Moscow-led communist conspiracy to take over the world. Criticism that such stories blind people to the nuances and complexities of individual situations occurs precisely because such narratives are assumed to be so compelling.[45]

Asking whether a story is 'real' or 'fake' does little to help us understand why audiences find some narratives more plausible than others. A more important question to ask, I argue, is about what narratives people already use to understand the world. This is not just a methodological suggestion; it goes to the heart of how strategic communicators currently assume humans think—through narrative.

We should also treat claims that we are in a new post-truth era or narrative age cautiously. Neither of these phenomena is new: storytelling is as old as human history, and even for some the key to explaining it.[46] There is far too much we still do not know. As mentioned previously, the case for narrative over argument is much less clear-cut than many assume. Despite increasingly taking for granted that strategic narrative is the ideal mode of foreign policy communication, researchers have not yet proven definitively that foreign policy discourse is notably more persuasive when structured as narrative rather than argument, or whether some combination might be best.[47] As Krebs suggests, it may be preferable to use narrative in certain foreign policy situations and argument in others.[48] When it comes to emplotment, it is not clear whether narratives are more persuasive if more or fewer wars are included. Is recounting one powerful example more persuasive or should one present several sources of evidence, as one would look to do in an argument? Are the identity claims made by stories more convincing if events that contradict them are *silenced* or *flattened*? If we are truly interested in using narratives to persuade, we should seek to understand better how precise narrative features contribute to the process.[49] A useful way forward may be to step back from the uncritical assumption of narrative primacy and test experimentally whether narratives about foreign policy and war really are more persuasive and, if so, why.

Needless to say, such research should start with a clear distinction between what is narrative and what is not, that is then put into practice during empirical analysis. If researchers or foreign policy practitioners are to uphold the claim that narrative is a uniquely persuasive device, it should not be thought of as everything said about a topic over time.

Thereafter, efforts to construct strategic narratives that resonate with target audiences would be better informed by understanding the stories those audiences tell, be it about war or any other social phenomenon. Thinking of 'fake-news' and 'post-truth' politics metaphorically as diseases requiring inoculation may be productive if it leads to citizens engaging more critically as they interpret information. I would argue that a more crucial endeavour is to understand citizens' narratives directly, since these represent the personal filters through which people interpret the world.[50]

Emplotment may be a particularly useful aspect of narrative for policymakers to analyse because it can provide a more subtle picture of how strategic communicators try and use narratives to persuade. It allows one to look beyond outright lies to examine the way narratives are more commonly used to disinform: through combining half-truths and omissions within a coherent framework, including real events, that is congruent with narratives audiences are already familiar with.

Studying emplotment can provide a more nuanced perspective on how historical events are used to justify military interventions. So far, attention to the uses of history by foreign policymakers has primarily focused on specific analogies chosen to explain subsequent conflicts.[51] This book began with the classic example of the 'Munich Analogy', where the latest rogue leader or state is compared to Hitler and the Nazis, with the seemingly timeless lesson that dictators need to be challenged immediately rather than being appeased.

Analysing emplotment moves beyond this by considering not only the analogies people use but how they highlight some events and downplay others, and how they explain those that contradict their overall message. For as this book has repeatedly shown, in Britain at least, public knowledge of war is extremely diverse, not least because it seems to have been always at war over the centuries. Citizens of different ages have different wars as their primary frames of reference.[52] There is arguably no need to stick slavishly to the Second World War as the only possible frame of reference people understand. It might be better to think about how to use emplotment mechanisms to weave together a narrative of different conflicts that can each appeal to the different generations that experienced them. In other words, rather than thinking 'how do I sell intervention or nonintervention', policymakers might instead ask, 'of what story is this intervention a part?'

Ultimately, understanding how citizens interpret war is very much like any other social issue; it is not just about what people remember but what they forget, what they include and what they silence, the analogies they draw and the ones that no longer make sense. Understanding these issues in depth requires qualitative, interpretive approaches that can identify why people talk about some events and silence others, and explain why. This book has shown the novel findings that can emerge from such a flexible, open-ended approach. In doing so, it has attempted to reveal the significance of war in how ordinary people understand their pasts and anticipate their futures.

Appendix

Transcription Conventions

As closely as possible, participant responses were transcribed verbatim directly from audio recording. However, the text was 'cleaned' of certain aspects for presentation purposes based on the following principles:

- Alterations were only made when it was judged that they would not significantly alter the response's meaning.
- Hesitations and fillers were removed only where they were considered excessive and distracting to the meaning conveyed in the text.
- Digressions onto issues deemed irrelevant to the interview topic were omitted.
- Verbal expressions of my agreement (e.g., 'okay', 'mm-hm', etc.) *during* a response were omitted. Indications of my agreement / disagreement in between participant responses were included.
- Overlapping talk was transcribed wherever possible as if in a sequential conversation. If not, my speech was omitted.
- False starts were ignored unless deemed relevant. False starts were included if, for example, they suggested uncertainty regarding the issue at hand or conscious attempts by participants to 'choose their words carefully' regarding a particular topic.

Conventions

. or ,	Indicate breaks in speech rather than correct punctuation, except for questions. See below.
?	Indicates upward inflection at end of sentence, as if question being asked.
'inverted commas'	Indicates that participants were talking about previous speech or thought, e.g., when someone said: Well at the time I thought 'let's destroy them as quickly as possible'.
(*italics*)	Used for nonlexical features that were deemed particularly relevant, e.g., (*laughs briefly*) / (*sarcastic tone*).
<u>underlined</u>	Indicates stress placed on a particular word.
//	Indicates when either researcher or participant interrupted each other. Placed at the point where the interruption begins.
. . .	Indicates pauses between speech or false starts. Sentence ending and a pause thereafter is indicated by a full stop and then three dots, e.g., 'I supported Iraq. . . . Then again, I can't remember any other wars'.

Notes

Introduction

1. Haven, Kendall. *Story Proof: The Science Behind The Startling Power Of Story.* Westport, CT: Libraries Unlimited, 2007; Salmon, Christian. *Storytelling: Bewitching the Modern Mind.* Translated by David Macey. Brooklyn, NY: Verso, 2010.

2. Roselle, Laura, Alister Miskimmon, and Ben O'Loughlin. "Strategic Narrative: A New Means to Understand Soft Power." *Media, War and Conflict* 7, no. 1 (2014): 70–84; Vlahos, Michael. "The Long War: A Self-Fulfilling Prophecy of Protracted Conflict and Defeat." http://nationalinterest.org/commentary/the-long-war-a-self-fulfilling-proph ecy-of-protractedconflict-and-defeat-1061, accessed 20 June 2013. For the distinction between hard and soft power, see Nye Jr., Joseph. *Soft Power: The Means to Success in World Politics.* New York: Public Affairs, 2005.

3. Nye, Joseph, Jr.. "Soft Power and the UK's Influence Committee: Oral and Written Evidence—Volume 2." House of Lords Select Committee on Soft Power and the UK's Influence, 2014, http://www.parliament.uk/documents/lords-committees/soft-pow erukinfluence/SoftPowerEvVol2.pdf, accessed 2 May 2014.

4. Barthes, Roland, and Lionel Duisit. "An Introduction to the Structural Analysis of Narrative." *New Literary History* 6, no. 2 (1975): 237–72; Fisher, Walter. "Narration as a Human Communication Paradigm: The Case of Public Moral Argument." *Communication Monographs* 51, no. 1 (1984): 1–22; Polkinghorne, Donald. *Narrative Knowing and the Human Sciences.* Albany: State University of New York Press, 1988.

5. Archetti, Cristina. *Understanding Terrorism in the Age of Global Media: A Communication Approach.* New York: Palgrave Macmillan, 2013; Freedman, Lawrence. "The Transformation of Strategic Affairs." *Adelphi Papers*, No. 379. International Institute for Strategic Studies, 2006.

6. See Freedman, Lawrence. "Introduction: Strategies, Stories and Scripts." In Lawrence Freedman and Jeffrey Michaels, eds. *Scripting Middle East Leaders: The Impact of*

Leadership Perceptions on US and UK Foreign Policy. New York: Bloomsbury, 2012, 1–14; Reiermann, Christian. "Fighting Words: Schäuble Says Putin's Crimea Plans Reminiscent of Hitler", *Der Spiegel*, 31 March 2014; Rucker, Philip. "Hillary Clinton Says Putin's Actions Are Like 'what Hitler did back in the '30s'", *Washington Post*, 5 March 2014; Sylvester, Rachel, "No Appeasement—This Is All-Out War on Isis", *The Times*, 21 July 2015.

7. Miskimmon, Alister, Ben O'Loughlin, and Laura Roselle. *Forging the World: Strategic Narratives and International Relations*. Ann Arbor: University of Michigan Press, 2017, 47.

8. De Graaf, Beatrice, George Dimitriu, and Jens Ringsmose, eds. *Strategic Narratives, Public Opinion and War: Winning Domestic Support for the Afghan War*. New York: Routledge, 2015; Ringsmose, Jens, and Berit Kaja Børgesen. "Shaping Public Attitudes towards the Deployment of Military Power: NATO, Afghanistan and the Use of Strategic Narratives." *European Security* 20, no. 4 (2011): 505–28.

9. De Graaf et al., *Strategic Narratives*.

10. McCormack, Tara. "The Emerging Parliamentary Convention on British Military Action and Warfare by Remote Control." *The RUSI Journal* 161, no. 2 (2016): 22–29.

11. Forster, Anthony. *Armed Forces and Society in Europe*. New York: Palgrave Macmillan, 2005.

12. Gaskarth, Jamie. *British Foreign Policy: Crises, Conflicts and Future Challenges*. Cambridge: Polity Press, 2013.

13. See Colley, Linda. *Britons: Forging the Nation, 1707–1837*. New Haven: Yale University Press, 2009; Ferguson, Niall. *Empire: How Britain Made the Modern World*. London: Penguin, 2004; James, Lawrence. *Warrior Race: A History of the British at War*. London: Abacus, 2010.

14. Smith, Philip. *Why War? The Cultural Logic of Iraq, the Gulf War, and Suez*. Cambridge: Cambridge University Press, 2012, 19.

15. Miskimmon et al., *Forging the World*.

16. Steele, Brent J. *Ontological Security in International Relations: Self-Identity and the IR State*. New York: Routledge, 2007.

17. Delehanty, Will, and Brent Steele. "Engaging the Narrative in Ontological (in)Security Theory: Insights from Feminist IR." *Cambridge Review of International Affairs* 22, no. 3 (2009): 526; Macmillan, Alan. "Strategic Culture and National Ways in Warfare: The British Case." *The RUSI Journal* 140, no. 5 (1995): 33–38; Subotić, Jelena. "Narrative, Ontological Security, and Foreign Policy Change." *Foreign Policy Analysis* 12, no. 4 (2015): 610–27.

18. Bubandt, Nils. "Vernacular Security: The Politics of Feeling Safe in Global, National and Local Worlds." *Security Dialogue* 36, no. 3 (2005): 275–96; Croft, Stuart, and Nick Vaughan-Williams. "Fit for Purpose? Fitting Ontological Security Studies 'into' the Discipline of International Relations: Towards a Vernacular Turn." *Cooperation and Conflict* 52, no. 1 (2017): 12–30.

19. Ricoeur, Paul. *Time and Narrative, Volume 1*. Translated by Kathleen McLaughlin and David Pellauer. Chicago: University of Chicago Press, 1990; Somers, Margaret. "The Narrative Constitution of Identity: A Relational and Network Approach." *Theory and Society* 23, no. 5 (1994): 605–49.

20. See Colley, Thomas. "Is Britain a Force for Good? Investigating British Citizens' Narrative Understanding of War." *Defence Studies* 17, no. 1 (2017): 1–22.

21. Archetti, *Understanding Terrorism*; Bruner, Jerome. "Life as Narrative." *Social Research* 54, no. 1 (1987): 11–32; Hyvärinen, Matti. "Towards a Conceptual History of Narrative." *Studies across Disciplines in the Humanities and Social Sciences* 1 (2006): 20–41; Riessman, Catherine Kohler. *Narrative Methods for the Human Sciences*. London: SAGE, 2008.

22. Riessman, *Narrative Methods*, 4.

23. Salmon, *Storytelling*, 4.

24. Bal, Mieke. *Narratology: Introduction to the Theory of Narrative*. Toronto: University of Toronto Press, 2009.

25. Czarniawska, Barbara. *Narratives in Social Science Research*. London: SAGE, 2004; Selbin, Eric. *Revolution, Rebellion, Resistance: The Power of Story*. New York: Zed Books, 2010.

26. Ryan, Marie-Laure. "On the Theoretical Foundations of Transmedial Narratology." In Jan Christoph Meister, Tom Kindt, and Wilhelm Schernus, eds. *Narratology Beyond Literary Criticism: Mediality, Disciplinarity*. Berlin: Walter de Gruyter, 2005, 1–24.

27. Archetti, *Understanding Terrorism*; Halverson, Jeffry R., Steven R. Corman, and H. L. Goodall. *Master Narratives of Islamist Extremism*. New York: Palgrave Macmillan, 2011.

28. This approach is consistent with many narrative researchers. See for example Krebs, Ronald R. *Narrative and the Making of US National Security*. Cambridge: Cambridge University Press, 2015; Riessman, *Narrative Methods*; Snyder, Jack. "Dueling Security Stories: Wilson and Lodge Talk Strategy." *Security Studies* 24, no. 1 (2015): 171–97.

29. See Riessman, *Narrative Methods*, 3–7.

30. Aristotle, *Poetics*. New York: Penguin Classics, 1996; Bernardi, Daniel et al. *Narrative Landmines: Rumors, Islamist Extremism, and the Struggle for Strategic Influence*. New Brunswick, NJ: Rutgers University Press, 2012; Burke, Kenneth. *A Grammar of Motives*. Berkeley: University of California Press, 1969; Corman, Steven, et al., eds. *Narrating the Exit from Afghanistan*. Tempe, AZ: Center for Strategic Communication, 2013.

31. Frank, Arthur. *The Wounded Storyteller: Body, Illness, and Ethics*. Chicago: University of Chicago Press, 2013.

32. Miskimmon, Alister, Ben O'Loughlin, and Laura Roselle. *Strategic Narratives: Communication Power and the New World Order*. New York: Routledge, 2013; Todorov, Tzvetan. *The Poetics of Prose*. Paris: Ithaca, 1977.

33. Riessman, Catherine Kohler. "Strategic Uses of Narrative in the Presentation of Self and Illness: A Research Note." *Social Science & Medicine* 30, no. 11 (1990): 1195–1200.

34. Carranza, Isolda. "Low-Narrativity Narratives and Argumentation." *Narrative Inquiry* 8, no. 2 (1998): 287–317; De Fina, Anna. "Narratives in Interview—The Case of Accounts: For an Interactional Approach to Narrative Genres." *Narrative Inquiry* 19, no. 2 (2009): 233–58.

35. Abbott, H. Porter. *The Cambridge Introduction to Narrative.* Cambridge: Cambridge University Press, 2008.

36. This definition is strongly influenced by Miskimmon et al., *Strategic Narratives,* 5–8.

37. Freedman, "The Transformation".

38. Casebeer, William, and James Russell. "Storytelling and Terrorism: Towards a Comprehensive 'Counter-Narrative Strategy'". *Strategic Insights* 4, no. 3 (2005): 1–16; Simpson, Emile. *War from the Ground up: Twenty-First Century Combat as Politics.* London: Hurst & Co., 2012.

39. Ringsmose and Børgesen, "Shaping Public Attitudes".

40. De Graaf et al., *Strategic Narratives,* 1.

41. Ibid., 356.

42. Hodges, Adam. *The "War on Terror" Narrative: Discourse and Intertextuality in the Construction and Contestation of Sociopolitical Reality.* New York: Oxford University Press, 2011, 7.

43. Cawkwell, Thomas. *UK Communication Strategies for Afghanistan, 2001–2014.* Farnham: Ashgate Publishing, 2015, 143.

44. Jacobs, Ronald. "Narrative, Civil Society and Public Culture". In Molly Andrews et al., *Lines of Narrative.* London: Routledge, 2000, 31.

45. See for example Allen, Mike, and Raymond W. Preiss. "Comparing the Persuasiveness of Narrative and Statistical Evidence Using Meta-Analysis." *Communication Research Reports* 14, no. 2 (1997): 125–31; Feeley, Thomas, Heather M. Marshall, and Amber M. Reinhart. "Reactions to Narrative and Statistical Written Messages Promoting Organ Donation." *Communication Reports* 19, no. 2 (2006): 89–100; Frey, Kurt P., and Alice H. Eagly. "Vividness Can Undermine the Persuasiveness of Messages." *Journal of Personality and Social Psychology* 65, no. 1 (1993): 32–44.

46. Georgakopoulou, Alexandra, and Dionysis Goutsos. "Revisiting Discourse Boundaries: The Narrative and Non-Narrative Modes." *Text-Interdisciplinary Journal for the Study of Discourse* 20, no. 1 (2000): 63–82.

47. Stone, Deborah. "Causal Stories and the Formation of Policy Agendas." *Political Science Quarterly* 104, no. 2 (1989): 282; Stone, Deborah. *Policy Paradox: The Art of Political Decision Making.* New York: W. W. Norton, 2001.

48. Jacobs, "Narrative, Civil Society", 21.

49. Spector-Mersel, Gabriela. "Mechanisms of Selection in Claiming Narrative Identities: A Model for Interpreting Narratives." *Qualitative Inquiry* 17, no. 2 (2011): 172–85; Spector-Mersel, Gabriela. "Multiplicity and Commonality in Narrative Interpretation." *Narrative Works* 4, no. 1 (2014): 1–18.

50. Cronon, William. "A Place for Stories: Nature, History, and Narrative." *Journal of American History* 78, no. 4 (1992): 1347–76.

51. Davis, Joseph, ed. *Stories of Change: Narrative and Social Movements*. Albany: State University of New York Press, 2002.

52. Baynham, Mike. "Narratives in Space and Time: Beyond 'Backdrop' Accounts of Narrative Orientation." *Narrative Inquiry* 13, no. 2 (2003): 347–66; De Fina, Anna. "Crossing Borders: Time, Space, and Disorientation in Narrative." *Narrative Inquiry* 13, no. 2 (2003): 367–91.

53. Ghoshal, Raj. "Argument Forms, Frames, and Value Conflict: Persuasion in the Case of Same-Sex Marriage." *Cultural Sociology* 3, no. 1 (2009): 76–101.

54. Jones, Michael D., Elizabeth A. Shanahan, and Mark K. McBeth, eds. *The Science of Stories: Applications of the Narrative Policy Framework in Public Policy Analysis*. New York: Palgrave Macmillan, 2014.

55. Cawkwell, *UK Communication*.

56. Jones, Michael D., and Mark K. McBeth. "A Narrative Policy Framework: Clear Enough to Be Wrong?" *Policy Studies Journal* 38, no. 2 (2010): 329–53.

57. Freedman, Lawrence. *Strategy: A History*. New York: Oxford University Press, 2013, 618.

58. Miskimmon et al., *Strategic Narratives*.

59. To clarify, war, military intervention, and military force are used interchangeably in this study as general terms to indicate the participation of Britain's military forces in armed conflicts. The breadth of this definition reflects the wide range of ways British military forces are deployed, from providing military advisors, to conducting drone strikes, to total war. 'Force' in this context reflects the US Department of Defense's definition as 'an aggregation of military personnel, weapons systems, equipment', not necessarily its 'kinetic' use. See "Department of Defense Dictionary of Military and Associated Terms", Department of Defense, 2010, http://www.dtic.mil/doctrine/new_pubs/jp1_02.pdf, accessed 30 September 2016, 89.

60. Edmunds, Timothy. "Complexity, Strategy and the National Interest." *International Affairs* 90, no. 3 (2014): 531. Chatham House's most recent survey at the time of writing found that 63 percent of the public supported Britain aspiring to be a great power. See Raines, Thomas. *Internationalism or Isolationism? The Chatham House-YouGov Survey: British Attitudes Towards the UK's International Priorities*. London: Chatham House, 2015.

61. Mludzinski, Tom. "The Brits Aren't Coming: Syria and the Legacy of Iraq." *The Ipsos MORI Almanac*. London: Ipsos MORI, 2013, 96–101.

62. Rogers, Joel, and Jonathan Eyal. "Of Tails and Dogs: Public Support and Elite Opinion." In Johnson, Adrian, ed. *Wars in Peace: British Military Operations since 1991*. London: Royal United Services Institute for Defence Studies, 2014, 190.

63. Davies, Graeme, and Robert Johns. "British Public Attitudes about International Affairs". The Role of the FCO in UK Government Inquiry, 25 November 2010. http://www.esrc.ac.uk/my-esrc/grants/RES-062-23-1952/outputs/Read/4a8a5ef5-16ca-40ba-8b1b-0983464a6365, accessed 29 April 2013.

64. Johns, Robert, et al. *Foreign Policy Attitudes and Support for War among the British Public ESRC End of Award Report*. RES-062-23-1952-A. Swindon: ESRC, 2012, 2.

65. Ibid., 2.

66. Davies and Johns, "British Public Attitudes", 2.

67. This assumption is the basis of a large body of research concerning the effects of elite and media framing on public opinion regarding war. See for example Drury, A. Cooper et al. "'Pretty Prudent' or Rhetorically Responsive? The American Public's Support for Military Action." *Political Research Quarterly* 63, no. 1 (2010): 83–96; Entman, Robert. *Projections of Power: Framing News, Public Opinion, and US Foreign Policy*. Chicago: University of Chicago Press, 2004.

68. For classic exponents see Almond, Gabriel. *The American People and Foreign Policy*. New York: Praeger, 1950; Bernays, Edward. *Propaganda*. New York: Ig Publishing, 1928; Rosenau, James. *Public Opinion and Foreign Policy: An Operational Formulation*. New York: Random House, 1961.

69. Hines, Lindsey et al. "Are the Armed Forces Understood and Supported by the Public? A View from the United Kingdom." *Armed Forces & Society* 41, no. 4 (2014): 18.

70. Towle, Philip. *Going to War: British Debates from Wilberforce to Blair*. Basingstoke: Palgrave Macmillan, 2010.

71. For example see Jentleson, Bruce. "The Pretty Prudent Public: Post-Vietnam American Opinion on the Use of Military Force." *International Studies Quarterly* 36, no. 1 (1992): 49–73; Nincic, Miroslav. "A Sensible Public: New Perspectives on Popular Opinion and Foreign Policy." *Journal of Conflict Resolution* 36, no. 4 (1992): 772–89; Page, Benjamin, and Robert Shapiro. *The Rational Public: Fifty Years of Trends in Americans' Policy Preferences*. Chicago: University of Chicago Press, 2010.

72. Herbst, Susan. *Reading Public Opinion: How Political Actors View the Democratic Process*. London: University of Chicago Press, 1998.

73. Ibid.

74. Kull, Steven, and Irving Destler. *Misreading the Public: The Myth of a New Isolationism*. Washington, DC: Brookings Institution Press, 1999.

75. The one exception to this was the penultimate question that asked about ongoing conflicts in Ukraine and against ISIS, in the hope that these might draw out analogies with previous conflicts.

76. For similar approaches, see Mishler, Elliot. *Research Interviewing: Context and Narrative*. Cambridge, MA: Harvard University Press, 1986; Riessman, *Narrative Methods*.

77. 'Nonmilitary families' refers to families without an active member of the armed forces.

78. Ritchie, Jane et al. *Qualitative Research Practice: A Guide for Social Science Students and Researchers.* 2nd ed. Thousand Oaks, CA: SAGE, 2013.

79. Bryman, Alan. *Social Research Methods.* 4th ed. New York: Oxford University Press, 2012; Maxwell, Joseph. *Qualitative Research Design: An Interactive Approach.* 3rd ed. Thousand Oaks, CA: SAGE, 2012; Miles, Matthew, and Michael Huberman. *Qualitative Data Analysis: An Expanded Sourcebook.* 2nd ed. Thousand Oaks, CA: SAGE, 1994; Teddlie, Charles, and Fen Yu. "Mixed Methods Sampling a Typology with Examples." *Journal of Mixed Methods Research* 1, no. 1 (2007): 77–100.

80. Charmaz, Kathy. *Constructing Grounded Theory: A Practical Guide through Qualitative Analysis.* London: SAGE, 2006; Glaser, Barney, and Anselm Strauss. *The Discovery of Grounded Theory: Strategies for Qualitative Research.* New Brunswick, NJ: Transaction, 1967.

81. Andrews, Molly, Corinne Squire, and Maria Tamboukou. *Doing Narrative Research.* London: SAGE, 2008.

82. This was done using *NVivo* software (Version 10.0.638.0 SP6 32-bit) [Software], QSR International Pty Ltd, 2012.

83. Riessman, *Narrative Methods*; Spector-Mersel, "Multiplicity".

84. This follows the approach of researchers such as Finnemore and Ruggie. See Finnemore, Martha. *The Purpose of Intervention: Changing Beliefs about the Use of Force.* Ithaca: Cornell University Press, 2004; Ruggie, John. *Constructing the World Polity: Essays on International Institutionalisation.* London: Routledge, 1998.

85. This chapter's argument and empirical analysis features extensively in Colley, "Is Britain a Force for Good?".

Chapter 1

1. Riessman, *Narrative Methods*, 4.

2. For a small sample see Brown, Andrew D. "A Narrative Approach to Collective Identities." *Journal of Management Studies* 43, no. 4 (2006): 731–53; Davis, *Stories of Change*; De Fina, Anna, and Alexandra Georgakopoulou. *Analyzing Narrative: Discourse and Sociolinguistic Perspectives.* Cambridge: Cambridge University Press, 2012; Epstein, Charlotte. "Who Speaks? Discourse, the Subject and the Study of Identity in International Politics." *European Journal of International Relations* 17, no. 2 (2011): 327–50; Ringmar, Erik. "On the Ontological Status of the State." *European Journal of International Relations* 2, no. 4 (1996): 439–66; Somers, "The Narrative Constitution".

3. Steele, *Ontological Security.*

4. Davis, *Stories of Change.*

5. Ibid.

6. Cronon, "A Place for Stories".

7. Gergen, Kenneth, and Mary Gergen. "Narratives of the Self." In Theodore Sarbin and Karl Scheibe, eds. *Studies in Social Identity*. New York: Praeger, 1983, 255.

8. Ibid.

9. Taleb, Nassim Nicholas. *The Black Swan: The Impact of the Highly Improbable*. London: Penguin, 2008.

10. Rosenthal, Gabriele. "Reconstruction of Life Stories: Principles of Selection in Generating Stories for Narrative Biographical Interviews." *The Narrative Study of Lives* 1 (1993): 59–91.

11. Fivush, Robyn. "Speaking Silence: The Social Construction of Silence in Autobiographical and Cultural Narratives." *Memory* 18, no. 2 (2010): 88–98.

12. See for example Archetti, *Understanding Terrorism*; Somers, "The Narrative Constitution"; Tilly, Charles. *Stories, Identities, and Political Change*. Oxford: Rowman & Littlefield, 2002.

13. Patterson, Molly, and Kristen Monroe. "Narrative in Political Science." *Annual Review of Political Science* 1, no. 1 (1998): 315–31; Ricoeur, *Time and Narrative*; Venn, C. "Narrative Identity, Subject Formation and the Transfiguration of Subjects." In Wendy Patterson, ed. *Strategic Narrative*, 29–50.

14. Brown, "A Narrative Approach"; Ricoeur, *Time and Narrative*; Somers, "The Narrative Constitution"; Tilly, *Stories*.

15. Miskimmon et al., *Strategic Narratives*.

16. Halbwachs, Maurice. *On Collective Memory*. Chicago: University of Chicago Press, 1992; Zerubavel, Eviatar. "Social Memories: Steps to a Sociology of the Past." *Qualitative Sociology* 19, no. 3 (1996): 283–99.

17. Wertsch, James. "The Narrative Organization of Collective Memory." *Ethos* 36, no. 1 (2008): 120.

18. Sangar, Eric. "'Regimes of Historicity' in Media Discourses on Wars and Interventions: The Missing Link between Collective Memory and Foreign Policy Identity?" Paper presented at 57th Annual Convention of the International Studies Association, Atlanta, United States, 16–19 March 2016.

19. Wertsch, "The Narrative Organization", 120; Zerubavel, Eviatar. "Historical Narratives and Collective Memory". In Corman et al., *Narrating the Exit*, 100.

20. Giddens, Anthony. *Modernity and Self-Identity: Self and Society in the Late Modern Age*. Cambridge: Polity Press, 1991.

21. Berenskoetter, Felix. "Parameters of a National Biography." *European Journal of International Relations* 20, no. 1 (2014): 262–88; Kinnvall, Catarina. "Globalization and Religious Nationalism: Self, Identity, and the Search for Ontological Security." *Political Psychology* 25, no. 5 (2004): 741–67; Steele, *Ontological Security*.

22. Subotić, "Narrative, Ontological Security".

23. Bubandt, "Vernacular Security"; Croft and Vaughan-Williams, "Fit for Purpose?".

24. This approach to different levels of narrative is strongly influenced by Somers. See Somers, "The Narrative Constitution".

25. Bamberg, Michael, and Molly Andrews. *Considering Counter-Narratives: Narrating, Resisting, Making Sense.* Amsterdam: John Benjamins, 2004; Foucault, Michel. "Orders of Discourse." *Social Science Information* 10, no. 2 (1971): 7–30; Halverson et al., *Master Narratives*; Somers, "The Narrative Constitution".

26. Somers, "The Narrative Constitution", 619.

27. Gregory, Derek. *The Colonial Present: Afghanistan, Palestine, Iraq.* Oxford: Blackwell, 2004. See also Huntington, Samuel P. *The Clash of Civilizations and the Remaking of World Order.* New York: Simon & Schuster, 1996.

28. Sangar, Eric. "'Regimes of Historicity'".

29. Berenskoetter, "Parameters".

30. MacMillan, Margaret. *The Uses and Abuses of History.* London: Profile Books, 2009. For the concept of 'imagined communities', see Anderson, Benedict. *Imagined Communities: Reflections on the Origin and Spread of Nationalism.* London: Verso Books, 2006.

31. Colley, *Britons*; James, *Warrior Race*; Mallinson, Allan. *The Making of the British Army.* London: Transworld Publishers, 2011.

32. Gaskarth, Jamie. *British Foreign Policy.*

33. Ringmar, "On the Ontological", 455.

34. McCourt, David M. *Britain and World Power since 1945: Constructing a Nation's Role in International Politics.* Ann Arbor: University of Michigan Press, 2014.

35. Ibid.

36. Bevir, Mark, Oliver Daddow, and Ian Hall. "Introduction: Interpreting British Foreign Policy." *The British Journal of Politics & International Relations* 15, no. 2 (2013): 168–69; Hart, Liddell. *Strategy: The Indirect Approach.* London: Faber and Faber, 1967.

37. Archetti, *Understanding Terrorism*; Asari, Eva-Maria, Daphne Halikiopoulou, and Steven Mock. "British National Identity and the Dilemmas of Multiculturalism." *Nationalism and Ethnic Politics* 14, no. 1 (2008): 1–28.

38. Kenny, Michael. *The Politics of English Nationhood.* Oxford: Oxford University Press, 2014.

39. Cruz, Consuelo. "Identity and Persuasion: How Nations Remember Their Pasts and Make Their Futures." *World Politics* 52, no. 3 (2000): 277.

40. Linde, Charlotte. "Private Stories in Public Discourse: Narrative Analysis in the Social Sciences." *Poetics* 15, no. 1–2 (1986): 199.

41. Subotić, "Narrative, Ontological Security".

42. Cruz, "Identity and Persuasion", 280.

43. Riessman, *Narrative Methods.*

44. Bruner, Jerome. "The Narrative Construction of Reality." *Critical Inquiry* 18, no. 1 (1991): 1–21.

45. Bruner, Jerome. *Actual Minds, Possible Worlds.* Cambridge, MA: Harvard University Press, 1986, 11.

46. Bruner, *Actual Minds*; Georgakopoulou and Goutsos, "Revisiting Discourse".

47. Krebs, *Narrative*.

48. "Argue", http://www.oxforddictionaries.com/definition/english/argue, accessed 30 August 2016.

49. Patterson, *Strategic Narrative*, 4.

50. See Ghoshal, "Argument Forms"; White, Hayden. *Metahistory: The Historical Imagination in Nineteenth-Century Europe*. London: JHU Press, 1975.

51. Knight, Lynn, and Kieran Sweeney. "Revealing Implicit Understanding through Enthymemes: A Rhetorical Method for the Analysis of Talk." *Medical Education* 41, no. 3 (2007): 227; Krebs, *Narrative*.

52. Knight and Sweeney, "Revealing Implicit Understanding"; Snyder, "Dueling Security".

53. Feldman, Martha et al. "Making Sense of Stories: A Rhetorical Approach to Narrative Analysis." *Journal of Public Administration Research and Theory* 14, no. 2 (2004): 152.

54. Snyder, "Dueling Security".

55. Feldman, "Making Sense".

56. McCourt, *Britain and World Power*.

57. Davis, *Stories of Change*.

58. Petty, Richard, and John T. Cacioppo. *Communication and Persuasion: Central and Peripheral Routes to Attitude Change*. New York: Springer, 2011; Slater, Michael D., and Donna Rouner. "Entertainment—Education and Elaboration Likelihood: Understanding the Processing of Narrative Persuasion." *Communication Theory* 12, no. 2 (2002): 173–91.

59. De Graaf, Anneke et al. "Identification as a Mechanism of Narrative Persuasion." *Communication Research* 39, no. 6 (2012): 802–23; Green, Melanie C., and Timothy C. Brock. "The Role of Transportation in the Persuasiveness of Public Narratives." *Journal of Personality and Social Psychology* 79, no. 5 (2000): 701–21; Mazzocco, Philip J. et al. "This Story Is Not for Everyone: Transportability and Narrative Persuasion." *Social Psychological and Personality Science* 1, no. 4 (2010): 361–68.

60. Slater and Rouner, "Entertainment—Education".

61. Gergen and Gergen, "Narratives".

62. Ibid.

63. Ibid.

64. Haven, *Story Proof*; Jacobs, Ronald N., and Sarah Sobieraj. "Narrative and Legitimacy: U.S. Congressional Debates about the Nonprofit Sector." *Sociological Theory* 25, no. 1 (2007): 1–25.

65. Propp, Vladimir. *Morphology of the Folktale*. 2nd ed. Austin: University of Texas Press, 2010.

66. Gray, Garry, and Michael D. Jones. "A Qualitative Narrative Policy Framework? Examining the Policy Narratives of US Campaign Finance Regulatory Reform." *Public Policy and Administration* 31, no. 3 (2016): 197.

67. Bruner, "The Narrative Construction".

68. Zerubavel, "Historical Narratives".

69. Richardson, Laurel. *Writing Strategies: Reaching Diverse Audiences*. Newbury Park: SAGE, 1990, 20; Zerubavel, "Historical Narratives", 103.

70. Wertsch, "The Narrative Organization"; Zerubavel, Eviatar. *Time Maps: Collective Memory and the Social Shape of the Past*. Chicago: University of Chicago Press, 2012.

71. De Fina, "Narratives in Interview"; Georgakopoulou and Goutsos, "Revisiting Discourse"; Richardson, *Writing Strategies*.

72. Gergen and Gergen, "Narratives".

73. Frye's ideas about the four poetic genres are themselves strongly influenced by Aristotle. See Aristotle, *Poetics*; Frye, Northrup. *Anatomy of Criticism: Four Essays*. Princeton: Princeton University Press, 2000; White, *Metahistory*.

74. Booker, Christopher. *The Seven Basic Plots: Why We Tell Stories*. London: Continuum, 2004; Tobias, Ronald B. *20 Master Plots: And How to Build Them*. Cincinnati: Writer's Digest Books, 2012.

75. Arguably Zerubavel's 'cyclical' narrative where history is 'the same thing over and over again' could be interpreted as continuity too. See Zerubavel, *Time Maps*.

76. Ibid.

77. Andrews, Molly. *Shaping History: Narratives of Political Change*. Cambridge: Cambridge University Press, 2007.

78. Toynbee, Arnold. *A Study of History*. New York: Oxford University Press, 1972.

79. Wertsch, "The Narrative Organization".

80. Ibid., 124.

81. Ibid., 124.

82. Ibid.

83. Gergen and Gergen, "Narratives".

84. Somers, "The Narrative Constitution".

85. Colley, Thomas. "What's in It for Us." *The RUSI Journal* 160, no. 4 (2015): 60–69; Corman et al., *Narrating the Exit*; Miskimmon et al., *Strategic Narratives*.

86. Ó'Tuathail, Gearóid. "Theorizing Practical Geopolitical Reasoning: The Case of the United States' Response to the War in Bosnia." *Political Geography* 21, no. 5 (2002): 601–28.

87. See Entman, *Projections of Power*.

88. Baumeister, R., and S. Hastings. "Distortions of Collective Memory: How Groups Flatter and Deceive Themselves." In J. Pennebaker, D. Paez, and B. Rime, eds. *Collective Memory of Political Events: Social Psychological Perspectives*. Hoboken: Taylor and Francis, 2013, 277–94; MacMillan, *The Uses*.

89. Pierce, Jonathan, Aaron Smith-Walter, and Holly Peterson. "Research Design and the Narrative Policy Framework." In Michael D. Jones, Elizabeth A. Shanahan, and Mark K. McBeth, eds. *The Science of Stories: Applications of the Narrative Policy Framework in Public Policy Analysis*. New York: Palgrave Macmillan, 2014, 27–44.

90. See Khong, Yuen Foong. *Analogies at War: Korea, Munich, Dien Bien Phu, and the Vietnam Decisions of 1965*. Princeton: Princeton University Press, 1992; Neustadt, Richard E., and Ernest R. May. *Thinking in Time: The Uses of History for Decision-Makers*. New York: Free Press, 1988.

91. Spector-Mersel, Gabriela. "'I Was . . . Until . . . Since Then . . .': Exploring the Mechanisms of Selection in a Tragic Narrative." *Narrative Works* 4, no. 1 (2014): 19–48; Spector-Mersel, "Mechanisms of Selection".

92. In Spector-Mersel's original framework, 'clarifying' was termed 'appropriate meaning attribution'. The adjustment is purely for stylistic purposes.

93. Davis, *Stories of Change*.

94. See Patterson and Monroe, "Narrative", 316.

95. Marks, Michael. *Metaphors in International Relations Theory*. New York: Palgrave Macmillan, 2011.

96. Khong, *Analogies at War*; Neustadt and May, *Thinking in Time*.

97. Wilkinson, Benedict. "The Narrative Delusion: Strategic Scripts and Violent Islamism in Egypt, Saudi Arabia and Yemen." PhD diss., King's College London, 2013.

98. Entman, *Projections of Power*, 5.

99. Benford, Robert D., and David A. Snow. "Framing Processes and Social Movements: An Overview and Assessment." *Annual Review of Sociology* 26 (2000), 611–39; Gamson, William A. et al. "Media Images and the Social Construction of Reality." *Annual Review of Sociology* 18 (1992): 373–93.

100. Miskimmon et al., *Strategic Narratives*.

101. Davis, *Stories of Change*, 12.

102. Miskimmon et al., *Strategic Narratives*.

103. Bruner, "The Narrative Construction", 4.

104. Fivush, "Speaking Silence".

105. Fiske, Susan, and Shelley Taylor. *Social Cognition*. 2nd ed. New York: McGraw-Hill, 1991.

106. Bamberg and Andrews, *Considering Counter-Narratives*; Elliott, Jane. *Using Narrative in Social Research: Qualitative and Quantitative Approaches*. London: SAGE, 2005.

107. Potter, Jonathan, and Margaret Wetherell. *Discourse and Social Psychology: Beyond Attitudes and Behaviour*. London: SAGE, 1987; Spector-Mersel, "Mechanisms of Selection".

108. Gergen and Gergen, "Narratives"; Linde, "Private Stories"; Riessman, "Strategic Uses".

109. The extent to which Britain is a 'moral' or 'ethical' actor is a frequent theme throughout this study. However, since citizens tend to use them interchangeably, no distinction is drawn between their meaning here.

110. Fiske and Taylor, *Social Cognition*, 463; Chaiken, S. "Attitude Formation: Function and Structure." In Neil Smeler and Paul Baltes, eds. *International Encyclopedia of the Social & Behavioral Sciences*. Oxford: Pergamon, 2001, 899–905.

111. Carranza, "Low-Narrativity".

112. Ibid.

Chapter 2

1. Edmunds, "Complexity"; House of Lords Select Committee on Soft Power and the UK's Influence. *Persuasion and Power in the Modern World*. London: The Stationery Office, 2014.

2. MacMillan, "Strategic Culture"; McCourt, *Britain and World Power*; Ritchie, Nick. "A Citizen's View of 'National Interest.'" In Timothy Edmunds, Jamie Gaskarth, and Robin Porter, eds. *British Foreign Policy and the National Interest: Identity, Strategy and Security*. Basingstoke: Palgrave Macmillan, 2014, 85–101.

3. See Barber, James. "Britain's Place in the World." *Review of International Studies* 6, no. 2 (1980): 93; Cohen, Robin. "Fuzzy Frontiers of Identity: The British Case." *Social Identities* 1, no. 1 (1995): 35–62.

4. Vincent, 65+, Lancashire.

5. Dan, 45–54, Dorset.

6. McCartney, Helen. "Hero, Victim or Villain? The Public Image of the British Soldier and Its Implications for Defense Policy." *Defense & Security Analysis* 27, no. 1 (2011): 49.

7. H.M. Government. *The National Security Strategy of the United Kingdom; Security in an Interdependent World*. Cm 7291. London: The Stationery Office, 2008; H.M. Government. *A Strong Britain in an Age of Uncertainty: The National Security Strategy*. Cm 7953. London: The Stationery Office, 2010.

8. Gaskarth, *British Foreign Policy*, 124.

9. Dudziak, Mary L. *War Time: An Idea, Its History, Its Consequences*. Oxford: Oxford University Press, 2013.

10. "Britain's 100 Years of Conflict", *Guardian*, 11 February 2014, http://www.theguardian.com/uk-news/ng-interactive/2014/feb/11/britain-100-years-of-conflict, accessed 8 September 2015.

11. The Ebola crisis beginning in 2014 does not fit the definition of military intervention here, though this does not interfere with the overall point of Dennis's explanation of the expectation that Britain should always be involved in major world events.

12. Carranza, "Low-Narrativity".

13. Riessman, "Strategic Uses".

14. O'Shaughnessy, Nicholas. *Politics and Propaganda: Weapons of Mass Seduction*. Manchester: Manchester University Press, 2000, 88–89.

15. Cavanaugh, William T. *The Myth of Religious Violence: Secular Ideology and the Roots of Modern Conflict*. Oxford: Oxford University Press, 2009.

16. Gaskarth, *British Foreign Policy*; Krahmann, Elke. "United Kingdom: Punching Above its Weight." In Emil Kirchner and James Sperling, eds. *Global Security Gover-*

nance: Competing Perceptions of Security in the Twenty-First Century. New York: Routledge, 2007, 93–112.

17. Edmunds, Timothy. "The Defence Dilemma in Britain." *International Affairs* 86, no. 2 (2010): 382.

18. Edmunds, "Complexity", 526.

19. Rogers and Eyal, "Of Tails", 190.

20. De Waal, James. "Is the UK's Expeditionary Posture Both Necessary and Sustainable?" *The RUSI Journal* 159, no. 6 (2014): 21.

21. Paris, Michael. *Warrior Nation: Images of War in British Popular Culture, 1850–2000*. London: Reaktion Books, 2002, 8.

22. Sanders, David. *Losing an Empire, Finding a Role: British Foreign Policy since 1945*. Basingstoke: Palgrave Macmillan, 1990.

23. "The Blair Doctrine", http://www.pbs.org/newshour/bb/international-jan-june99-blair_doctrine4-23/, accessed 9 November 2016.

24. Gaskarth, *British Foreign Policy*, 126.

25. Ritchie, "A Citizen's View".

26. Hodges, The "War on Terror".

27. Dudziak, *War Time*; Tsoukala, Anastassia. "Defining the Terrorist Threat in the Post-September 11 Era." In Didier Bigo and Anastassia Tsoukala, eds. *Terror, Insecurity and Liberty: Illiberal Practices of Liberal Regimes after 9/11*. London: Routledge, 2008, 49–99.

28. Hodges, The "War on Terror".

29. Paris, *Warrior Nation*.

30. Gokay, Bulent. "Oil, War and Geopolitics from Kosovo to Afghanistan." *Journal of Southern Europe and the Balkans Online* 4, no. 1 (2002): 5–13.

31. Kertzer, Joshua D., and Kathleen M. McGraw. "Folk Realism: Testing the Microfoundations of Realism in Ordinary Citizens." *International Studies Quarterly* 56, no. 2 (2012): 245–58.

32. Evans, Michael. "From Kadesh to Kandahar: Military Theory and the Future of War." *Naval War College Review* 56, no. 3 (2003): 141.

33. Ritchie, "A Citizen's View".

34. Cavanaugh, *The Myth*.

35. Cavanaugh, *The Myth*, 4.

36. Swidler, Ann. "Culture in Action: Symbols and Strategies." *American Sociological Review* 51, no. 2 (1986): 273–86.

37. White, *Metahistory*.

38. Hoggart, Richard. *The Uses of Literacy: Aspects of Working-Class Life*. London: Penguin Classics, 2009, 86.

39. Jacobs and Sobieraj, "Narrative and Legitimacy".

40. See Ritchie, Nick. "Trident and British Identity: Letting Go of Nuclear Weapons." *Bradford Disarmament Research Centre*, September 2008; Strachan, Hew. "The Strategic Gap in British Defence Policy." *Survival* 51, no. 4 (2009): 49–70.

41. Kinnvall, "Globalization", 763.

42. Leuprecht, Christian. "The West's Last War? Neo-interventionism, Strategic Surprise, and the Waning Appetite for Playing the Away Game." In Gerhard Kümmel and Bastian Giegerich, eds. *The Armed Forces: Towards a Post-Interventionist Era?* Dordrecht: Springer, 2013, 63–72.

43. The annual Chatham House-YouGov Survey on British foreign policy attitudes routinely polls people about their views of 16 preselected states inside Europe and 19 states outside. Switzerland is not included. Here, though, out of approximately 200 countries that could be chosen for comparison, 9 out of 67 (13%) participants chose Switzerland, making the comparison worth investigating. See Knight, Jonathan, Robin Niblett, and Thomas Raines. *Hard Choices Ahead: The Chatham House–YouGov Survey 2012: British Attitudes Towards the UK's International Priorities*. Chatham House, July 2012; Raines, *Internationalism*.

44. Knight et al., *Hard Choices*; Raines, *Internationalism*.

45. Hannan, Daniel. *Inventing Freedom: How the English-Speaking Peoples Made the Modern World*. New York: Harper Collins, 2014; Marcussen, Martin et al. "Constructing Europe? The Evolution of French, British and German Nation State Identities." *Journal of European Public Policy* 6, no. 4 (1999): 614–33.

46. McDonald, Karl. "David Davis: We Coped with World War Two, We Can Cope with Brexit," *Independent*, 18 January 2017. https://inews.co.uk/essentials/news/politics/david-davis-we-coped-with-world-war-two-we-can-cope-with-brexit, accessed 31 October 2017; Foster, Peter. "Bluff, Fold, Check, or Raise? Britain's Brexit Options Explained", *Telegraph*, 18 October 2017, http://www.telegraph.co.uk/news/2017/10/18/bluff-fold-check-raise-britains-brexit-options-explained, accessed 31 October 2017.

47. See for example Henley, Jon. "Why Vote Leave's £350m Weekly EU Cost Claim Is Wrong", *Guardian*, 10 June 2016, https://www.theguardian.com/politics/reality-check/2016/may/23/does-the-eu-really-cost-the-uk-350m-a-week, accessed 31 October 2017.

48. Los, Bart, Philip McCann, John Springford, and Mark Thissen. "The Mismatch between Local Voting and the Local Economic Consequences of Brexit." *Regional Studies* 51, no. 5 (2017): 786–99.

49. "The UK and United Nations Peace Operations", *United Nations Association*, March 2016, https://www.una.org.uk/sites/default/files/UNA-UK%20briefing%20on%20the%20UK%20and%20UN%20peace%20operations%2016%20March%202016.pdf, accessed 20 September 2016.

50. Ryan, Missy, and Karen DeYoung. "Obama Alters Afghanistan Exit Plan Once More, Will Leave 8,400 Troops", *Washington Post*, 6 July 2016, https://www.washingtonpost.com/world/national-security/obama-alters-afghanistan-exit-plan-once-more/2016/07/06/466c54f2-4380-11e6-88d0-6adee48be8bc_story.html, accessed 20 September 2016.

51. Wallace, William. "A Liberal Democrat View of UK Defence Policy." Royal United Services Institute, London, April 20, 2015.

52. Ibid.

53. Steele, Brent J. "Ontological Security and the Power of Self-Identity: British Neutrality and the American Civil War." *Review of International Studies* 31, no. 3 (2005): 519–40.

54. Subotić, "Narrative, Ontological Security".

55. Linde, "Private Stories".

56. Ibid., 200.

57. For the 'shame' generated by a political actor when they behave incongruently with their sense of self-identity, see Steele, "Ontological Security", 526–27.

58. De Waal, "Is the UK's".

59. Dennis, 55–64, Worcestershire.

60. Mitzen, Jennifer. "Ontological Security in World Politics: State Identity and the Security Dilemma." *European Journal of International Relations* 12, no. 3 (2006): 341–70.

61. Tsoukala, "Defining the Terrorist".

62. Billig, Michael. *Banal Nationalism*. London: SAGE, 1995.

63. Ritchie, "A Citizen's View", 97.

64. De Waal, "Is the UK's", 22.

Chapter 3

1. Lindley-French, Julian. *Little Britain: Twenty-First Century Strategy for a Middling European Power*. 2nd ed. Marston Gate: Amazon, 2015; Tomlinson, Jim. "The Decline of the Empire and the Economic 'Decline' of Britain." *Twentieth Century British History* 14, no. 3 (2003): 203.

2. Ward, Stuart, ed. *British Culture and the End of Empire*. Manchester: Manchester University Press, 2001.

3. The exceptions to this are revisionist accounts that that emphasise that the period after the Second World War saw not just decolonisation but an immense rise in British living standards. See Bernstein, George. *The Myth of Decline: The Rise of Britain Since 1945*. London: Pimlico, 2004.

4. Brendon, Piers. *The Decline and Fall of the British Empire*. London: Vintage, 2008.

5. James, Lawrence. *Rise and Fall of the British Empire*. London: Abacus, 1995; Porter, Bernard. *Britain, Europe and the World, 1850–1982: Delusions of Grandeur*. London: Harper Collins, 1983.

6. Bernstein, *The Myth*.

7. Darwin, John. "Decolonization and the End of Empire." In Robin Winks, ed. *The Oxford History of the British Empire, Volume V: Historiography*. Oxford: Oxford University Press, 2001, 541–57.

8. Reynolds, David. *Britannia Overruled: British Policy and World Power in the Twentieth Century*. 2nd ed. New York: Routledge, 2000.

9. Sampson, Anthony. *Anatomy of Britain*. London: Hodder and Stoughton, 1962; Tomlinson, "The Decline"; Ward, *British Culture*; Winks, *The Oxford History*.

10. See for example Gibbon, Edward. *The History of the Decline and Fall of the Roman Empire*. London: Penguin Classics, 2000; Toynbee, *A Study*.

11. See for example "Scrapping RAF Nimrods 'perverse', Say Military Chiefs", *BBC News*, 27 January 2011, http://www.bbc.co.uk/news/uk-england-12294766, accessed 11 December 2015; Bennett, Asa. "SDSR: What Kit Do Britain's Armed Forces Have, What Do They Want, and What Are They Getting?" *Telegraph*, 23 November 2015. http://www.telegraph.co.uk/news/uknews/defence/12011176/SDSR-What-kit-do-Britains-Armed-Forces-have-what-do-they-want-and-what-are-they-getting.html#disqus_thread, accessed 10 December 2015; Jack, Ian. "A British Fleet with No Aircraft Carrier. Unthinkable!" *Guardian*, 23 October 2010, http://www.theguardian.com/commentisfree/2010/oct/23/ian-jack-british-fleet-no-aircraft-carrier-unthinkable, accessed 10 December 2015.

12. Freedman, *Strategy*.

13. Gaskarth, *British Foreign Policy*.

14. Barnett, Correlli. "Total Strategy and the Collapse of British Power." *The RUSI Journal* 136, no. 4 (1991): 3.

15. Schank, Roger C. *Tell Me a Story: Narrative and Intelligence*. Evanston, IL: Northwestern University Press, 1996.

16. Sanders, *Losing an Empire*.

17. Bernstein, *The Myth*.

18. Freedman, *Strategy*, xi.

19. This closely resembles Dahl's oft-cited definition of power. See Dahl, Robert. "The Concept of Power." *Behavioral Science* 2, no. 3 (1957): 201–15.

20. Ringmar, "On the Ontological".

21. Lakoff, George. "Metaphor and War: The Metaphor System Used to Justify War in the Gulf." *Peace Research* 23, no. 2/3 (1991): 26.

22. For others identifying these as sources of soft power see Hill, Christopher, and Sarah Beadle. "The Art of Attraction: Soft Power and the UK's Role in the World." London: The British Academy, 2014, http://www.britac.ac.uk/intl/softpower.cfm, accessed 17 November 2015; House of Lords, *Persuasion and Power*.

23. Hill and Beadle, "The Art"; Roselle et al., "Strategic Narrative".

24. Wallace, "A Liberal".

25. Barnett, "Total Strategy", 3; MccGwire, Michael. "Comfort Blanket or Weapon of War: What Is Trident For?" *International Affairs* 82, no. 4 (2006): 639–50.

26. Faith, 18–24, Cumbria.

27. Bucholz, Robert, and Newton Key. *Early Modern England 1485–1714: A Narrative History*. Chichester: John Wiley & Sons, 2013.

28. Sanders, *Losing an Empire*, 291.

29. For extremes of this debate see Ferguson, *Empire*; Hannan, *Inventing Freedom*; Grasse, Steve. *Evil Empire: 101 Ways England Ruined the World*. San Francisco: Quirk Books, 2007.

30. Hansen, Lene. *Security as Practice: Discourse Analysis and the Bosnian War*. New York: Routledge, 2006.

31. Wallace, William. "Foreign Policy and National Identity in the United Kingdom." *International Affairs* 67, no. 1 (1991): 65–80.

32. Rennie, David. "American Pullout Leaves Iceland Defenceless", *Telegraph*, 21 July 2006, http://www.telegraph.co.uk/news/1524490/American-pullout-leaves-Iceland-de fenceless.html, accessed 18 August 2016.

33. Hines et al., "Are the Armed Forces".

34. James, *Warrior Race*.

35. See Hernon, Ian. *Fortress Britain: All the Invasions and Incursions since 1066.* Stroud: The History Press, 2013.

36. H.M. Government, *A Strong Britain*.

37. Christopher, 18–24, Dorset.

38. Lily, 18–24, London.

39. "David Cameron Defends Britain in Russia 'small island' Row", *BBC News*, 6 September 2013, http://www.bbc.co.uk/news/uk-politics-23984730, accessed 8 December 2015.

40. Honeyman, Victoria. "Foreign Policy." In Timothy Heppell and David Seawright, eds. *Cameron and the Conservatives: The Transition to Coalition Government*. New York: Palgrave Macmillan, 2012, 121–35.

41. Gaskarth, *British Foreign Policy*; Karvounis, Antonios, Kate Manzo, and Tim Gray. "Playing Mother: Narratives of Britishness in New Labour Attitudes toward Europe." *Journal of Political Ideologies* 8, no. 3 (2003): 311–25.

42. Levine, Philippa. *The British Empire: Sunrise to Sunset*. London: Routledge, 2013.

43. Fry, Robert. "Smart Power and the Strategic Deficit." *The RUSI Journal* 159, no. 6 (2014): 28–30.

44. Barnett, "Total Strategy".

45. Miskimmon et al., "Strategic Narratives".

46. Lindley-French, *Little Britain*, 11.

47. Fry, "Smart Power".

48. According to the 2015 Chatham House-YouGov survey, a plurality (38 percent) of the public saw the military as doing most to serve British interests abroad. See Raines, *Internationalism*, 25.

49. Only 25 percent of the public supported a diminished role in the world, even amid economic 'austerity', according to the 2012 Chatham House-YouGov survey. See Knight et al., *Hard Choices*, 18.

Chapter 4

1. Wallace, "A Liberal".

2. See "UK's World Role: Punching Above Our Weight," *BBC News*. http://news.bbc.co.uk/hi/english/static/in_depth/uk_politics/2001/open_politics/foreign_policy/uks_world_role.stm, accessed 18 December 2015; Cockburn, Patrick. "Why Must Britain

Always Try to 'Punch Above Her Weight'?", *Independent*, 17 July 2011, http://www.inde
pendent.co.uk/voices/commentators/patrick-cockburn-why-must-britain-always-try-
to-punch-above-her-weight-2314908.html, accessed 18 December 2015; "David Cameron: EU Helps Britain Punch Above Its Weight", *Telegraph*, 25 July 2014, http://www.
telegraph.co.uk/news/politics/david-cameron/10987981/David-Cameron-EU-helps-
Britain-punch-above-its-weight.html, accessed 18 December 2015; for academic examples see Cornish, Paul. "United Kingdom." In Heiko Biehl, Bastian Giegerich, and
Alexandra Jonas, eds. *Strategic Cultures in Europe: Security and Defence Policies Across
the Continent*. Dordrecht: Springer, 2013, 371–86; Edgerton, David. "Tony Blair's Warfare State." *New Left Review* 1 (1998): 123–30; Krahmann, "United Kingdom".

3. Frank, *The Wounded Storyteller*, 29 (his emphasis).

4. Jacobs, "Narrative, Civil Society", 26.

5. See "Ipsos MORI September Political Monitor", https://www.ipsos-mori.com/As
sets/Docs/Polls/October_2014_PolMon_Topline_Foreign_policy.pdf, accessed 18 December 2015.

6. Edgerton, "Tony Blair's", 127.

7. Cockburn, "Why Must Britain".

8. See Rogers and Eyal, "Of Tails"; Thompson, Andrew, ed. *Britain's Experience of
Empire in the Twentieth Century*. Oxford: Oxford University Press, 2011, 33.

9. McCourt, *Britain and World Power*, 2.

10. Tan, Andrew. "Punching Above Its Weight: Singapore's Armed Forces and Its
Contribution to Foreign Policy." *Defence Studies* 11, no. 4 (2011): 672–97; Thomson,
Mark. "Punching Above our Weight? Australia as a Middle Power", *Strategic Insights* 18,
Australian Strategic Policy Institute, August 2005, https://www.aspi.org.au/publica
tions/strategic-insights-18-punching-above-our-weight-australia-as-a-middle-power/
SI_Strategic_weight.pdf, accessed 23 December 2015.

11. Galtry, Judith. "Punching Above Its Weight: Does New Zealand's Responsibility
for Protecting, Promoting, and Supporting Breastfeeding Extend beyond Its Own Borders?" *Journal of Human Lactation* 29, no. 2 (2013): 128–31; Huish, Robert. "Punching
above Its Weight: Cuba's Use of Sport for South–South Co-operation." *Third World
Quarterly* 32, no. 3 (2011): 417–33.

12. Edgerton, "Tony Blair's".

13. Cameron, David. "Speech to Lord Mayor's Banquet", 15 November 2010, https://
www.gov.uk/government/speeches/speech-to-lord-mayors-banquet, accessed 9 December 2015.

14. Ibid.

15. Ringmar, "On the Ontological".

16. Lakoff, "Metaphor and War".

17. Miskimmon et al., *Strategic Narratives*.

18. For debate on this issue, see Bennett, Huw. "Minimum Force in British Counterinsurgency." *Small Wars & Insurgencies* 21, no. 3 (2010): 459–75; Ucko, David H., and

Robert Egnell. *Counterinsurgency in Crisis: Britain and the Challenges of Modern Warfare*. New York: Columbia University Press, 2013. See also H.M. Government. *Building Stability Overseas Strategy*. London: The Stationery Office, 2011.

19. Thomson, "Punching Above".

20. Worldometers, "Countries in the World (Ranked by 2014 Population)", http://www.worldometers.info/world-population/population-by-country, accessed 25 September 2015.

21. Baldwin, David. "Power and International Relations." In Walter Carlsnaes, Thomas Risse, and Beth Simmons, eds. *Handbook of International Relations*. London: SAGE, 2002, 177–91.

22. Hill and Beadle, "The Art".

23. Raines, *Internationalism*.

24. "Britain Ousts the U.S. as World's Most Influential Nation: Country Tops Rankings for 'Soft Power'", *Daily Mail*, 18 November 2012, http://www.dailymail.co.uk/news/article-2234726/Britain-tops-global-soft-power-list.html, accessed 6 January 2016.

25. "Britain Wins Esteem at Last as a Global Force in 'Soft Power'", *The Times*, 16 July 2015, http://www.thetimes.co.uk/tto/news/uk/article4499397.ece, accessed 6 January 2016.

26. Edgerton, "Tony Blair's".

27. Mallinson, *The Making*, 4.

28. Gaskarth, Jamie. "Strategizing Britain's Role in the World." *International Affairs* 90, no. 3 (2014): 559–81.

29. See Croft, Stuart. *Securitizing Islam: Identity and the Search for Security*. Cambridge: Cambridge University Press, 2012, 126–27.

30. The exception might be the United States, which might be expected to consult Britain first as one of its primary military allies in recent decades.

31. Edgerton, "Tony Blair's".

32. Bethany, 18–24, London. See also Porter, Patrick. "Why Britain Doesn't Do Grand Strategy." *The RUSI Journal* 155, no. 4 (2010): 6–12.

33. Ward, *British Culture*, 8.

34. Lindley-French, *Little Britain*, 54.

35. Gaskarth, Jamie. "Strategy in a Complex World." *The RUSI Journal* 160, no. 6 (2015): 4–11.

36. Lindley-French, *Little Britain*.

37. According to the 2015 Ipsos MORI Veracity Index, only 16 percent of the population trust politicians to tell the truth, although this has changed little in over 30 years, with the figure being only 18 percent in 1983. See "Ipsos MORI Veracity Index 2015", https://www.ipsos-mori.com/Assets/Docs/Polls/Veracity%20Index%202014%20topline.pdf, accessed 9 January 2016.

38. McCartney, "Hero, Victim"; Strachan, "The Strategic Gap".

39. Bernstein, *The Myth*.

40. Beatrice, 65+, Lancashire.

41. Nathan, 45–54, Dorset.

42. Kenny, *The Politics*.

43. Croft, *Securitizing Islam*, 163.

44. Cited in Dawson, Graham. *Soldier Heroes: British Adventure, Empire and the Imagining of Masculinities*. New York: Routledge, 1994, 11.

45. "David Cameron Defends".

46. Dunne, Tim. "'When the Shooting Starts': Atlanticism in British Security Strategy." *International Affairs* 80, no. 5 (2004): 893–909.

47. Barnett, "Total Strategy", 4.

48. Shaun, 65+, Dorset.

49. Iris, 65+, Oxfordshire.

50. Iris, 65+, Oxfordshire.

51. Croft, *Securitizing Islam*, 198.

52. Leuprecht, "The West's Last War?", 66; Reynolds, *Britannia Overruled*, 2.

Chapter 5

1. Gaskarth, *British Foreign Policy*.

2. Somers, "The Narrative Constitution"; Zerubavel, *Time Maps*.

3. See for example "Threat Level from International Terrorism Raised: PM Press Statement", https://www.gov.uk/government/speeches/threat-level-from-international-terrorism-raised-pm-press-conference, accessed 15 March 2016.

4. Barnett, Michael. *Empire of Humanity: A History of Humanitarianism*. Ithaca, NY: Cornell University Press, 2013; Butterfield, Herbert. *The Whig Interpretation of History*. London: George Bell and Sons, 1931.

5. MacMillan, *The Uses*.

6. Morefield, Jeanne. *Empires Without Imperialism: Anglo-American Decline and the Politics of Deflection*. Oxford: Oxford University Press, 2014.

7. Daddow, Oliver, and Pauline Schnapper. "Liberal Intervention in the Foreign Policy Thinking of Tony Blair and David Cameron." *Cambridge Review of International Affairs* 26, no. 2 (2013): 330–49.

8. Heins, Volker M., Kai Koddenbrock, and Christine Unrau. *Humanitarianism and Challenges of Cooperation*. Abingdon, Oxon: Routledge, 2016.

9. Kenneth, 55–64, Liverpool.

10. Fry, "Smart Power".

11. Perraudin, Frances. "UK Government Defends Role in Ukraine-Russia Crisis", *Guardian*, 10 February 2015, http://www.theguardian.com/politics/2015/feb/10/uk-government-defends-role-in-ukraine-russia-crisis, accessed 15 March 2016; "No 10 Rejects 'bit player' Claim over Ukraine Crisis", *BBC News*. http://www.bbc.co.uk/news/uk-politics-31163190, accessed 15 March 2016.

12. Dunne, "When the Shooting"; Gaskarth, "Strategizing".

13. Olive, 65+, Oxfordshire.

14. Dunne, "When the Shooting"; Edmunds et al., *British Foreign Policy*; Miskimmon, Alister. "Continuity in the Face of Upheaval—British Strategic Culture and the Impact of the Blair Government." *European Security* 13, no. 3 (2004): 273–99.

15. Dunne, "When the Shooting".

16. Gaskarth, "Strategizing".

17. Towle, *Going to War.*

18. Betz, David. "Searching for El Dorado: The Legendary Golden Narrative of the Afghanistan War." In De Graaf et al., *Strategic Narratives*, 37–56; Cawkwell, *UK Communication.*

19. Gaskarth, "Strategizing", 569.

20. For an account that suggests that Trump's approach is more consistent, see Laderman, Charlie, and Brendan Simms. *Donald Trump: The Making of a World View*. London: I. B. Tauris, 2017.

21. Ibid., 13.

22. Lewis, 18–24, London.

23. See Lenin, Vladimir. *Imperialism: The Highest Stage of Capitalism*. Sydney: Resistance Books, 1999; Said, Edward W. *Orientalism*. London: Penguin Books, 2003.

24. Lenin, *Imperialism*, 28.

25. Bricmont, Jean. *Humanitarian Imperialism: Using Human Rights to Sell War.* Translated by Diana Johnstone. New York: NYU Press, 2007.

26. Gott, Richard. "America and Britain: The Dangers of Neo-Imperialism and the Lessons of History." *Global Dialogue* 5, no. 1/2 (2003): 45.

27. Willow, 25–34, London.

28. Oliver, 18–24, London.

29. Lily, 18–24, London.

30. Lebow, Richard Ned. *Why Nations Fight: Past and Future Motives for War*. Cambridge: Cambridge University Press, 2010.

31. Chomsky, Noam. *Hegemony or Survival: America's Quest for Global Dominance.* London: Penguin, 2004.

32. Kümmel and Giegerich, *The Armed Forces.*

33. Freedman, Lawrence. "On War and Choice." *The National Interest*, no. 107 (2010): 9–16.

34. See for example Engdahl, F. William. *Myths, Lies and Oil Wars*. Wiesbaden: Edition.Engdahl, 2012; Fouskas, Vassilis, and Bülent Gökay. *The New American Imperialism: Bush's War on Terror and Blood for Oil*. Westport, CT: Greenwood Publishing Group, 2005; Jones, Toby. "America, Oil, and War in the Middle East." *Journal of American History* 99, no. 1 (2012): 208–18.

35. Lyotard, Jean-Francois. *The Postmodern Condition: A Report on Knowledge*. Manchester: Manchester University Press, 1984, xxiv.

36. Barnett, Michael, and Thomas G. Weiss. *Humanitarianism in Question: Politics, Power, Ethics*. London: Cornell University Press, 2008.

37. Colley, "What's In It", 64.

38. Gribble, Rachael et al. "British Public Opinion after a Decade of War: Attitudes to Iraq and Afghanistan." *Politics* 35, no. 2 (2015): 128–50.

39. Segal, Robert. *Myth: A Very Short Introduction*. New York: Oxford University Press, 2015.

40. O'Shaughnessy, *Politics and Propaganda*; Segal, *Myth*.

41. Gokay, "Oil, War".

42. Central Intelligence Agency. "The World Factbook", https://www.cia.gov/library/publications/the-world-factbook/rankorder/2244rank.html, accessed 14 April 2016.

43. Gribble et al., "British Public Opinion".

44. Gow, James. *Triumph of the Lack of Will: International Diplomacy and the Yugoslav War*. London: Hurst & Co., 1997.

45. Rogers and Eyal, "Of Tails", 166.

46. Butler, Smedley. *War Is a Racket*. New York: Skyhorse Publishing, 2013, 8.

47. The term 'Little Englander' has had numerous meanings. In contemporary popular discourse it is often used to criticise English nationalists. The Cambridge Dictionary describes a 'Little Englander' as 'an English person who thinks England is better than all other countries'. See "Little Englander," http://dictionary.cambridge.org/dictionary/english/little-englander, accessed 21 April 2016.

48. See Caldwell, Dan. *Vortex of Conflict: U.S. Policy Toward Afghanistan, Pakistan, and Iraq*. Stanford, CA: Stanford University Press, 2011; "ISIS Captured 2300 Humvee Armoured Vehicles from Iraqi Forces in Mosul", *Guardian*, 1 June 2015, http://www.theguardian.com/world/2015/jun/01/isis-captured-2300-humvee-armoured-vehicles-from-iraqi-forces-in-mosul, accessed 22 April 2016.

49. Roberts, Andrew. *A History of the English-Speaking Peoples since 1900*. London: Phoenix, 2007, 2.

50. Grasse, *Evil Empire*.

51. Lewis et al. "Generalising from Qualitative Research". In Ritchie et al., *Qualitative Research*, 351.

52. Lincoln, Yvonna, and Egon Guba. *Naturalistic Inquiry*. Beverly Hills, CA: SAGE, 1985, 40.

53. Bruner, "The Narrative Construction".

54. Wintour, Patrick. "Britain Carries Out First Syria Airstrikes after MPs Approve Action against ISIS", *Guardian*, 3 December 2015, https://www.theguardian.com/world/2015/dec/02/syria-airstrikes-mps-approve-uk-action-against-isis-after-marathon-debate, accessed 4 August 2016.

55. "David Cameron's Full Statement Calling for UK Involvement in Syria Air Strikes", *Telegraph*, 26 November 2015, http://www.telegraph.co.uk/news/politics/david-cameron/12018841/David-Camerons-full-statement-calling-for-UK-involvement-in-Syria-air-strikes.html, accessed 4 August 2016.

56. "Prime Minister's Response to the Foreign Affairs Select Committee's Second Re-

port of Session 2015–2016: The Extension of Offensive British Military Operations to Syria", http://www.theguardian.com/politics/2015/nov/26/full-text-of-david-camerons-memorandum-on-syria-airstrikes, accessed 4 August 2016.

57. "Prime Minister's Response".

58. "David Cameron's Full Statement".

59. Gaskarth, "Strategizing".

60. Beale, Jonathan. "Are UK Bombs Making a Difference in Syria?", *BBC News*, 2 January 2016, http://www.bbc.co.uk/news/uk-35166971, accessed 14 January 2016; Gilligan, Andrew. "RAF Bomb Raids in Syria Dismissed as 'non event'", *Telegraph*, 2 January 2016, http://www.telegraph.co.uk/news/worldnews/islamic-state/12078395/RAF-bomb-raids-in-Syria-dismissed-as-non-event.html, accessed 4 August 2016.

61. Stone, Jon. "Britain's 'unique' Brimstone Missiles Still Haven't Killed Any ISIS Fighters in Syria", *Independent*, 18 February 2016, http://www.independent.co.uk/news/uk/politics/britains-unique-brimstone-missiles-still-havent-killed-any-isis-fighters-in-syria-a6881716.html, accessed 16 August 2016.

62. Lindley-French, *Little Britain*, 7.

63. Cruz, "Identity and Persuasion"; Smith, *Why War*; Subotić, "Narrative, Ontological Security".

64. Smith, *Why War*, 62.

65. Ibid.; Subotić, "Narrative, Ontological Security".

66. Ringmar, "Inter-textual Relations", 414.

Chapter 6

1. Much of this chapter is featured in Colley, Thomas. "Is Britain a Force for Good? Investigating British Citizens' Narrative Understanding of War." *Defence Studies* 17, no. 1 (2017): 1–22, reprinted by permission of the publisher (Taylor & Francis Ltd., http://www.tandfonline.com).

2. Spector-Mersel, "Multiplicity and Commonality".

3. Baumeister and Hastings, "Distortions"; MacMillan, *The Uses*.

4. Ministry of Defence. *Defence Plan 2010–2014*. London: The Stationery Office, 2010, https://www.gov.uk/government/uploads/system/uploads/attachment_data/file/27163/Defence_Plan_2010_2014.pdf, accessed 6 October 2016; Strachan, "The Strategic Gap".

5. Spector-Mersel, "Mechanisms of Selection".

6. Spector-Mersel, "Mechanisms of Selection".

7. Pierce, "Research Design".

8. Ministry of Defence, *Defence Plan*; Strachan, "The Strategic Gap".

9. Asari et al., "British National Identity".

10. Dawson, *Soldier Heroes*, 7.

11. Marshall, Alex. "Imperial Nostalgia, the Liberal Lie, and the Perils of Postmodern Counterinsurgency." *Small Wars & Insurgencies* 21, no. 2 (2010): 241.

12. Leichter, David J. "Collective Identity and Collective Memory in the Philosophy of Paul Ricoeur." *Ricoeur Studies* 3, no. 1 (2012): 123.

13. Berlin, Isaiah, cited in Ignatieff, Michael. *Isaiah Berlin: A Life*. London: Random House, 2000, 301.

14. Morefield, *Empires*.

15. Erskine, Andrew. *Roman Imperialism*. Edinburgh: Edinburgh University Press, 2010; Gough, Barry. *Pax Britannica: Ruling the Waves and Keeping the Peace before Armageddon*. Basingstoke: Palgrave Macmillan, 2014.

16. Adler, Eric. "Post-9/11 Views of Rome and the Nature of 'Defensive Imperialism.'" *International Journal of the Classical Tradition* 15, no. 4 (2009): 587–610.

17. Karvounis, "Playing Mother".

18. Henry, 35–44, London.

19. Ferguson, *Empire*.

20. Roberts, *A History*, ix, 2.

21. Dawson, *Soldier Heroes*; Lawrence, T. E. *Seven Pillars of Wisdom*. London: Random House, 2008.

22. Johnson, Rob. *British Imperialism*. New York: Palgrave Macmillan, 2002; Said, *Orientalism*.

23. The book of Genesis, Chapter 1, during God's creation of Heaven and Earth, explains repeatedly that God 'saw that it was good', before proceeding to the next stage of the Creation.

24. MacMillan, *The Uses*.

25. Lyons, Jonathan. *Islam Through Western Eyes: From the Crusades to the War on Terrorism*. New York: Columbia University Press, 2012.

26. Forty-four out of 67 participants named Iraq as their initial response to being asked to recall a war which they opposed (66 percent). The second most frequent was Afghanistan, only named initially by 13 out of 67 respondents (19 percent).

27. Spector-Mersel, "Mechanisms of Selection".

28. Riessman, *Narrative Methods*.

29. Davis, *Stories of Change*.

30. Snyder, "Dueling Security"; Wilkinson, "The Narrative Delusion".

Chapter 7

1. Wertsch, "The Narrative Organization"; Zerubavel, *Time Maps*.

2. Andrews, *Shaping History*; Berenskoetter, "Parameters".

3. Leichter, "Collective Identity"; Baumeister and Hastings, "Distortions".

4. Ricoeur, Paul. *Memory, History, Forgetting*. Translated by Kathleen Blamey and David Pellauer. Chicago: University of Chicago Press, 2004.

5. Birkland, Thomas A. "'The World Changed Today': Agenda-Setting and Policy Change in the Wake of the September 11 Terrorist Attacks." *Review of Policy Research* 21, no. 2 (2004): 179–200; Bolt, Neville. *The Violent Image: Insurgent Propaganda and the*

New Revolutionaries. London: Hurst & Co., 2012; Dudziak, Mary L., ed. *September 11 in History: A Watershed Moment?* Durham: Duke University Press, 2003; Leavy, Patricia. *Iconic Events: Media, Power, and Politics in Retelling History*. Plymouth: Lexington Books, 2007.

6. Al Qaida had also attacked the USS Cole in 2000 and the US embassies in Kenya and Tanzania in 1998.

7. Hodges, *The "War on Terror"*.

8. Roach, Kent. *The 9/11 Effect: Comparative Counter-Terrorism*. Cambridge: Cambridge University Press, 2011.

9. Bluth, Christoph. "The British Road to War: Blair, Bush and the Decision to Invade Iraq." *International Affairs* 80, no. 5 (2004): 871–92.

10. See Croft, *Securitizing Islam*; Tsoukala, "Defining the Terrorist". See also H.M. Government. *Prevent Strategy*. Cm 8092. London: The Stationery Office, 2011.

11. Cawkwell, *UK Communication*, 143. See also Corman et al., *Narrating the Exit*, 122.

12. Finnemore, *The Purpose*; Ruggie, *Constructing the World*.

13. Halas, Matus. "In Error We Trust: An Apology of Abductive Inference." *Cambridge Review of International Affairs* 28, no. 4 (2015): 701–20; Peirce, Charles Sanders. *Collected Papers of Charles Sanders Peirce*. Cambridge, MA: Harvard University Press, 1974.

14. Coman, Alin, David Manier, and William Hirst. "Forgetting the Unforgettable Through Conversation: Socially Shared Retrieval-Induced Forgetting of September 11 Memories." *Psychological Science* 20, no. 5 (2009): 627–33; Fivush, "Speaking Silence".

15. While at the time condemnation of 9/11 was 'nearly universal', in retrospect the legality of the US and British invasion of Afghanistan has become contentious. There was no UN resolution justifying initial intervention but outrage over 9/11 led much of the international community to accept that it was an act of self-defence under Article 51 of the UN Charter, which required no UN resolution. Moreover, UN Security Council Resolution 1386 subsequently mandated the use of force to stabilise the country in December 2001. See Blair, Tony. *A Journey*. London: Random House, 2010, 342; Greenwood, Christopher. "International Law and the Pre-Emptive Use of Force: Afghanistan, Al-Qaida, and Iraq." *San Diego International Law Journal* 4 (2003): 7–37; Smith, Ben, and Arabella Thorp. "The Legal Basis for the Invasion of Afghanistan," House of Commons Library, 26 February 2010, www.parliament.uk/briefing-papers/sn05340.pdf, accessed 25 May 2016.

16. For accounts of the different strategic narratives used to explain Afghanistan, see Cawkwell, *UK Communication*; De Graaf et al., *Strategic Narratives*.

17. Winter, Jay. *Remembering War: The Great War and Historical Memory in the 20th Century*. New Haven: Yale University Press, 2006, 5.

18. Wertsch, "The Narrative Organization", 120.

19. Davis, *Stories of Change*.

20. Zerubavel, *Time Maps*.

21. Fivush, "Speaking Silence".

22. Ibid., 89.

23. Winter, *Remembering War*.

24. Ricoeur, *Memory*, 443.

25. Berenskoetter, "Parameters".

26. Ricoeur, *Memory*, 413; Winter, *Remembering War*, 12.

27. Overy, Richard. *The Morbid Age: Britain and the Crisis of Civilisation, 1919–1939*. London: Penguin, 2010.

28. See for example Ramsden, John. "How Winston Churchill Became 'the Greatest Living Englishman.'" *Contemporary British History* 12, no. 3 (1998): 1–40.

29. Toye, Richard. *The Roar of the Lion: The Untold Story of Churchill's World War II Speeches*. Oxford: Oxford University Press, 2013.

30. Dudziak, *September 11*.

31. Coman et al., "Forgetting the Unforgettable", 627.

32. When considering these statistics it must be remembered that people were only questioned on conflicts they brought up themselves. Far more individuals may be familiar with Afghanistan and 9/11 but chose to discuss other wars instead.

33. Bolt, *The Violent Image*; Hansen, Lene. "How Images Make World Politics: International Icons and the Case of Abu Ghraib." *Review of International Studies* 41, no. 2 (2015): 265; Leavy, *Iconic Events*.

34. Hansen, "How Images".

35. Brown, Roger, and James Kulik. "Flashbulb Memories." *Cognition* 5, no. 1 (1977): 73–99.

36. Kvavilashvili et al. "Comparing Flashbulb Memories of September 11 and the Death of Princess Diana: Effects of Time Delays and Nationality." *Applied Cognitive Psychology* 17, no. 9 (2003): 1017–31.

37. See for example Conway et al. "Flashbulb Memory for 11 September 2001." *Applied Cognitive Psychology* 23, no. 5 (2009): 605–23; Hirst, William, et al. "Long-Term Memory for the Terrorist Attack of September 11: Flashbulb Memories, Event Memories, and the Factors That Influence Their Retention." *Journal of Experimental Psychology: General* 138, no. 2 (2009): 161–76.

38. "9/11 and Death of Diana Top Britain's Most Memorable Events List", *BBC News*, 24 January 2007, http://www.bbc.co.uk/pressoffice/pressreleases/stories/2007/01_janu ary/24/radio4.shtml, accessed 25 May 2016.

39. Scott, Jacqueline, and Lilian Zac. "Collective Memories in Britain and the United States." *Public Opinion Quarterly* 57, no. 3 (1993): 330.

40. Pennebaker et al., *Collective Memory*.

41. Codner, Michael. "The Two Towers, 2001–13." In Johnson, *Wars in Peace*, 49–88.

42. Blair, *A Journey*, 345.

43. "We Are at War", *News of the World*, 15 September 2001.

44. "War on the World", *Daily Mirror*, 12 September 2001.

45. "A Declaration of War", *Guardian*, 12 September 2001.

46. "Blair's Statement in Full", *BBC News*, 11 September 2001, http://news.bbc.co.uk/1/hi/uk_politics/1538551.stm, accessed 30 May 2016; Blair, *A Journey*, 352.

47. "Tony Blair's Statement", *Guardian*, 7 October 2001, http://www.theguardian.com/world/2001/oct/07/afghanistan.terrorism11, accessed 30 May 2016.

48. Ibid.

49. Entman, *Projections of Power*.

50. Jensen, Rikke Bjerg. "Communicating Afghanistan: Strategic Narratives and the Case of UK Public Opinion." In De Graaf et al. *Strategic Narratives*, 300–317; Rogers and Eyal, "Of Tails", 169.

51. Rogers and Eyal, "Of Tails", 163.

52. Kampfner, John. *Blair's Wars*. London: Simon & Schuster, 2004, 133.

53. Ibid., 134.

54. H.M. Government. "2010 to 2015 Government Policy: Afghanistan", 8 May 2015, https://www.gov.uk/government/publications/2010-to-2015-government-policy-afghanistan/2010-to-2015-government-policy-afghanistan, accessed 7 June 2016.

55. Bigo and Tsoukala, *Terror*; Hodges, *The "War on Terror"*.

56. Kettell, Steven. *New Labour and the New World Order: Britain's Role in the War on Terror*. Oxford: Oxford University Press, 2013, 63; "Transcript: President Bush's Speech on the War on Terrorism", *Washington Post*, 30 November 2005, http://www.washingtonpost.com/wpdyn/content/article/2005/11/30/AR2005113000667.html, accessed 30 May 2016. Michaels identifies the Philippines, Pakistan, and Colombia as other named fronts early in the War on Terror in US discourse. An internet search of 'new fronts in the War on Terror' also reveals dozens of supposed examples, be it Britain, Belgium, or Bangladesh, the Sahara, Syria, or the Sinai. See Michaels, Jeffrey. *The Discourse Trap and the US Military: From the War on Terror to the Surge*. New York: Palgrave Macmillan, 2013.

57. Andrews, *Shaping History*; Riessman, *Narrative Methods*.

58. Dudziak, *September 11*, 2.

59. For examples and critics see Neumann, Peter R. *Old and New Terrorism*. Cambridge: Polity Press, 2009; Duyvesteyn, Isabelle. "How New Is the New Terrorism?" *Studies in Conflict & Terrorism* 27, no. 5 (2004): 439–54.

60. Scott and Zac, "Collective Memories", 330; Schuman, Howard, and Cheryl Rieger. "Historical Analogies, Generational Effects, and Attitudes Toward War." *American Sociological Review* 57, no. 3 (1992): 315–26; Schuman, Howard, and Jacqueline Scott. "Generations and Collective Memories." *American Sociological Review* 54, no. 3 (1989): 359–81.

61. Search completed using *AntConc* software (Version 3.4.4.0).

62. Rogers and Eyal, "Of Tails".

63. Miskimmon et al., *Strategic Narratives*.

64. Michaels, *The Discourse Trap*.

65. Goodall, Howard. "Introduction". In Corman et al., *Narrating the Exit*, 2.

66. Kettell, Steven. "Dilemmas of Discourse: Legitimising Britain's War on Terror." *The British Journal of Politics & International Relations* 15, no. 2 (2013): 263–79.

67. Gribble et al. "The UK Armed Forces: Public Support for the Troops but Not for the Missions?" In A. Park et al., eds. *British Social Attitudes: The 29th Report*. London: NatCen, 2012, http://www.bsa.natcen.ac.uk/media/1150/bsa29_armed_forces.pdf, accessed 3 June 2016; Rogers and Eyal, "Of Tails", 169.

68. Dahlgreen, Will. "Memories of Iraq: Did We Ever Support the War?" *YouGov*, 3 June 2015, https://yougov.co.uk/news/2015/06/03/remembering-iraq, accessed 6 June 2016.

69. MacMillan, *The Uses*; Ricoeur, *Memory*.

70. McCartney, "Hero, Victim", 43.

71. Michaels, *The Discourse Trap*, 10.

72. Evidence for this is shown by the deliberate attempts to avoid use of the War on Terror concept in US and British political discourse. Other terms used subsequently included the aptly named 'Long War' and, under the Obama administration, the remarkably vague 'Overseas Contingency Operations'. See Michaels, *The Discourse Trap*, 18; Vlahos, "The Long War".

73. Bluth, "The British"; Kampfner, *Blair's Wars*.

74. Humphreys, James. "The Iraq Dossier and the Meaning of Spin." *Parliamentary Affairs* 58, no. 1 (2005): 156–70; Kettell, "Dilemmas".

75. Gribble et al., "British Public Opinion".

76. Jones, "America, Oil".

77. Clements, Ben. "Examining Public Attitudes towards Recent Foreign Policy Issues: Britain's Involvement in the Iraq and Afghanistan Conflicts." *Politics* 31, no. 2 (2011): 63–71; Wheeler, Nicholas J., and Tim Dunne. *Moral Britannia? Evaluating the Ethical Dimension in Labour's Foreign Policy*. London: Foreign Policy Centre, 2004.

78. See for example Fisk, Robert. "This Looming War Isn't About Chemical Warheads or Human Rights: It's About Oil", *Independent*, 18 January 2003; Jones, Gary, Tom Newton Dunn, and Bob Roberts. "We're Going for Oil: Our Troops Set to Seize Wells", *Daily Mirror*, 21 January 2003.

79. Rogers and Eyal, "Of Tails".

80. Blair, Tony. Hansard HC Debate Vol. 397, Col. 675, 15 January 2003.

81. In the BSA survey, 47 percent named oil as the primary motive for Iraq. Only 32 percent named WMD, the second most common and official government motive. See Gribble et al., "British Public Opinion", 5.

82. See for example Ahmed, Nafeez. "Iraq Invasion was About Oil", *Guardian*, 20 March 2014, http://www.theguardian.com/environment/earth-insight/2014/mar/20/

iraq-war-oil-resources-energy-peak-scarcity-economy, accessed 6 June 2016; Juhasz, Antonia. "Why the War in Iraq Was Fought for Big Oil", *CNN*, 15 April 2013, http://edi tion.cnn.com/2013/03/19/opinion/iraq-war-oil-juhasz/, accessed 7 June 2016.

83. Grace, 55–64, Worcestershire.

84. For an example of media opposition to their attempts, see Cummins, Fiona. "The U.S. Government Has Taken 9/11 and Manipulated My Country's Grief", *Daily Mirror*, February 7, 2003.

85. Milliband, David, cited in Cawkwell, *UK Communication*, 129.

86. Gribble et al., "British Public Opinion". Although the original counterterrorism motives for 9/11 were widely accepted, a few isolated commentators in the British media raised the oil issue early on. See Haslett, Malcolm. "Afghanistan: The Pipeline War?", *BBC News*, 29 October 2001, http://news.bbc.co.uk/1/hi/world/south_asia/1626889. stm, accessed 6 June 2016; Monbiot, George. "America's Pipe Dream", *Guardian*, 23 October 2001, http://www.theguardian.com/world/2001/oct/23/afghanistan.terrorism11, accessed 6 June 2016.

87. Colley, "What's in It".

88. Bolt, Neville. "Strategic Communications in Crisis." *The RUSI Journal* 156, no. 4 (2011): 47.

89. Betz, David. *Carnage and Connectivity: Landmarks in the Decline of Conventional Military Power*. London: Hurst & Co., 2015, 121.

90. Ministry of Defence. *Strategic Communication: The Defence Contribution, Joint Doctrine Note 1/12*, 2012, https://www.gov.uk/government/uploads/system/uploads/at tachment_data/file/33710/20120126jdn112_Strategic_CommsU.pdf, accessed 7 June 2016.

91. Jensen, "Communicating Afghanistan", 310.

92. Fivush, "Speaking Silence"; Schank, *Tell Me a Story*.

93. Cawkwell, *UK Communication*.

94. Blair, Tony. Hansard HC Debate Vol. 372, Col. 673. 4 October 2001.

95. Cawkwell, *UK Communication*, 146.

96. Ibid.

97. Jensen, "Communicating Afghanistan", 310.

98. Betz, "Searching"; Cawkwell, *UK Communication*.

99. Cawkwell, *UK Communication*.

100. Ibid., 110.

101. Ibid. Also see H.M. Government. "The UK's Work in Afghanistan", 14 January 2014, https://www.gov.uk/government/publications/uks-work-in-afghanistan/the-uks-work-in-afghanistan, accessed 7 June 2016.

102. Daddow and Schnapper, "Liberal intervention".

103. Blair, *A Journey*, 343.

104. Leavy, *Iconic Events*.

105. Hodges, *The "War on Terror"*, 160.

Chapter 8

1. "Syria Crisis: Cameron Loses Commons Vote on Syria Action", *BBC News*, http://www.bbc.co.uk/news/uk-politics-23892783, accessed 16 April 2014.

2. House of Lords, *Persuasion and Power*, 129.

3. Black, James, et al. *Defence and Security after Brexit*. Cambridge: RAND Corporation, https://www.rand.org/pubs/research_reports/RR1786.html, accessed 7 December 2017; Clarke, Harold D., Matthew Goodwin, and Paul Whiteley. *Brexit: Why Britain Voted to Leave the European Union*. Cambridge: Cambridge University Press, 2017; Goodwin, Matthew, and Caitlin Milazzo. "Taking Back Control? Investigating the Role of Immigration in the 2016 Vote for Brexit." *British Journal of Politics and International Relations* 19, no. 3 (2017): 450–64; Wincott, Daniel, John Peterson, and Alan Convery. "Introduction: Studying Brexit's Causes and Consequences." *British Journal of Politics and International Relations* 19, no. 3 (2017): 429–33.

4. Brinkley, Douglas. "Dean Acheson and the 'Special Relationship': The West Point Speech of December 1962." *Historical Journal* 33, no. 3 (1990): 599–608.

5. McCormack, "The Emerging".

6. Billig, *Banal Nationalism*.

7. Somers, "The Narrative Constitution"; Subotić, "Narrative, Ontological Security".

8. Krebs, *Narrative*; Subotić, "Narrative, Ontological Security".

9. For an alternative perspective see Koch, Insa. "What's in a Vote? Brexit beyond Culture Wars." *American Ethnologist; Arlington* 44, no. 2 (2017): 225–30.

10. Cable, Vince. "Not Martyrs, Masochists: Lib Dem Leader Sir Vince Cable Launches a Ferocious Attack on Desperate Brexit Fanatics Whose Zealotry Is Igniting a New McCarthyism", *Mail on Sunday*, 6 August 2017, http://www.dailymail.co.uk/debate/article-4764742/Lib-Dem-leader-SIR-VINCE-CABLE-attacks-Brexit-fanatics.html, accessed 19 December 2017.

11. Black, et al., *Defence and Security*; Goodwin and Milazzo, "Taking Back Control?"; Wincott et al., "Introduction".

12. Cruz, "Identity and Persuasion"; Subotić, "Narrative, Ontological Security".

13. Koch, "What's in a Vote?".

14. Marcussen et al, "Constructing Europe?".

15. Ibid.

16. Reynolds, David. "Britain, the Two World Wars, and the Problem of Narrative." *The Historical Journal* 60, no. 1 (2017): 197–231.

17. George, Stephen. *An Awkward Partner: Britain in the European Community*. 3rd ed. Oxford: Oxford University Press, 1998.

18. Reynolds, "Britain", 231.

19. Cocco, Federica. "Brexit, Bent Bananas and Cleavage Regulations: Busting the Euromyths", *Financial Times*, https://www.ft.com/content/d20cabe4-1f16-33d8-8a8e-e9e70c00d4ed, accessed 7 December 2017.

20. See for example Allen and Preiss, "Comparing the Persuasiveness"; Feeley et al., "Reactions to Narrative"; Frey and Eagly, "Vividness Can Undermine".

21. Black et al., *Defence and Security*; Goodwin and Milazzo, "Taking Back Control?.

22. Black et al., *Defence and Security*, 38.

23. See for example Jones, Sam. "Theresa May Uses Defence and Security as Brexit Bargaining Chips", *Financial Times*, 17 January 2017, https://www.ft.com/content/932aef0c-dccc-11e6-86ac-f253db7791c6, accessed 19 December 2017.

24. Holden Reid, Brian. "The British Way in Warfare: Liddell Hart's Idea and Its Legacy." *The RUSI Journal* 156, no. 6 (2011): 70–76.

25. Edgerton, David. "Tony Blair's Warfare State." *New Left Review* 1 (1998): 129.

26. Fraser, Simon. *Can the UK Retain Global Influence after Brexit? Policies and Structures for a New Era.* The Policy Institute at King's College London, January 2017.

27. Subotić, "Narrative, Ontological Security".

28. Fry, "Smart Power".

29. King, Anthony. *Who Governs Britain?* London: Penguin, 2015.

30. Raines, *Internationalism*, 25.

31. As of July 2018, YouGov reported that 77 percent of British citizens hold a negative view of Trump. See Curtis, Chris. "A Plurality of Britons Support Trump Visiting—but They Don't Think He Should Meet the Queen", https://yougov.co.uk/news/2018/07/12/plurality-britons-support-trump-visiting-they-dont/, accessed 7 August 2018.

32. McCourt, *Britain and World Power*, 6.

33. Laycock, Stuart. *All the Countries We've Ever Invaded.* Stroud: The History Press, 2012, 8.

34. Spector-Mersel, "Mechanisms of Selection"; Spector-Mersel, "Multiplicity".

35. Betz, "Searching"; Bolt, "Strategic Communications"; Cawkwell, *UK Communication*.

36. Miskimmon et al., *Strategic Narratives*.

37. Freedman, Lawrence. "The Possibilities and Limits of Strategic Narratives". In De Graaf et al., *Strategic Narratives*, 17–36.

38. Leavy, *Iconic Events*.

39. Hines et al., "Are the Armed Forces"; Towle, *Going to War*.

40. Croft, *Securitizing Islam*.

41. Kriel, Charles. "Fake News, Fake Wars, Fake Worlds". *Defence Strategic Communications* 3 (2017): 171–90.

42. Corner, John. "Fake News, Post-Truth and Media–Political Change." *Media, Culture & Society* 39, no. 7 (2017): 1100–1107.

43. Polletta, Francesca, and Jessica Callahan. "Deep Stories, Nostalgia Narratives, and Fake News: Storytelling in the Trump Era." *American Journal of Cultural Sociology* 5, no. 3 (2017): 392–408.

44. Bennett, W. Lance, and Shanto Iyengar. "A New Era of Minimal Effects? The Changing Foundations of Political Communication." *Journal of Communication* 58, no. 4 (December 1, 2008): 707–31.

45. Taleb, *The Black Swan*; Tilly, *Stories*.

46. Harari, Yuval Noah. *Sapiens: A Brief History of Humankind*. London: Harvill Secker, 2014.

47. The work of Braddock and Dillard is a useful step forward in this regard. See Braddock, Kurt, and James Price Dillard. "Meta-Analytic Evidence for the Persuasive Effect of Narratives on Beliefs, Attitudes, Intentions, and Behaviors." *Communication Monographs* 83, no. 4 (2016): 446–67.

48. Krebs, *Narrative*.

49. Cho, Hyunyi, Lijiang Shen, and Kari Wilson. "Perceived Realism: Dimensions and Roles in Narrative Persuasion." *Communication Research* 41, no. 6 (2014): 828–51.

50. Archetti, *Understanding Terrorism*.

51. Khong, *Analogies at War*; Neustadt and May, *Thinking in Time*.

52. Schuman and Rieger, "Historical Analogies"; Schuman and Scott, "Generations".

References

Abbott, H. Porter. *The Cambridge Introduction to Narrative*. Cambridge: Cambridge University Press, 2008.

Adler, Eric. "Post-9/11 Views of Rome and the Nature of 'Defensive Imperialism.'" *International Journal of the Classical Tradition* 15, no. 4 (2009): 587–610.

Allen, Mike, and Raymond W. Preiss. "Comparing the Persuasiveness of Narrative and Statistical Evidence Using Meta-Analysis." *Communication Research Reports* 14, no. 2 (1997): 125–31.

Almond, Gabriel. *The American People and Foreign Policy*. New York: Praeger, 1950.

Anderson, Benedict. *Imagined Communities: Reflections on the Origin and Spread of Nationalism*. London: Verso Books, 2006.

Andrews, Molly. *Shaping History: Narratives of Political Change*. Cambridge: Cambridge University Press, 2007.

Andrews, Molly, Corinne Squire, and Maria Tamboukou. *Doing Narrative Research*. London: SAGE, 2008.

Archetti, Cristina. *Understanding Terrorism in the Age of Global Media: A Communication Approach*. New York: Palgrave Macmillan, 2013.

Aristotle. *Poetics*. New York: Penguin Classics, 1996.

Asari, Eva-Maria, Daphne Halikiopoulou, and Steven Mock. "British National Identity and the Dilemmas of Multiculturalism." *Nationalism and Ethnic Politics* 14, no. 1 (2008): 1–28.

Baker, David. "Elite Discourse and Popular Opinion on European Union: British Exceptionalism Revisited." *Politique Européenne* 6, no. 2 (2002): 18–35.

Bal, Mieke. *Narratology: Introduction to the Theory of Narrative*. Toronto: University of Toronto Press, 2009.

Baldwin, David. "Power and International Relations." In Walter Carlsnaes, Thomas Risse, and Beth Simmons, eds. *Handbook of International Relations*. London: SAGE, 2002, 177–91.

Bamberg, Michael, and Molly Andrews. *Considering Counter-Narratives: Narrating, Resisting, Making Sense.* Amsterdam: John Benjamins, 2004.

Barber, James. "Britain's Place in the World." *Review of International Studies* 6, no. 2 (1980): 93–110.

Barnett, Correlli. "Total Strategy and the Collapse of British Power." *The RUSI Journal* 136, no. 4 (1991): 1–6.

Barnett, Michael. *Empire of Humanity: A History of Humanitarianism.* Ithaca, NY: Cornell University Press, 2013.

Barnett, Michael, and Thomas G. Weiss. *Humanitarianism in Question: Politics, Power, Ethics.* London: Cornell University Press, 2008.

Barthes, Roland, and Lionel Duisit. "An Introduction to the Structural Analysis of Narrative." *New Literary History* 6, no. 2 (1975): 237–72.

Baumeister, R., and S. Hastings. "Distortions of Collective Memory: How Groups Flatter and Deceive Themselves." In J. Pennebaker, D. Paez, and B. Rime, eds. *Collective Memory of Political Events: Social Psychological Perspectives.* Hoboken: Taylor and Francis, 2013, 277–94.

Baynham, Mike. "Narratives in Space and Time: Beyond 'Backdrop' Accounts of Narrative Orientation." *Narrative Inquiry* 13, no. 2 (2003): 347–66.

Benford, Robert D., and David A. Snow. "Framing Processes and Social Movements: An Overview and Assessment." *Annual Review of Sociology* 26 (2000): 611–39.

Bennett, Huw. "Minimum Force in British Counterinsurgency." *Small Wars & Insurgencies* 21, no. 3 (2010): 459–75.

Bennett, W. Lance, and Shanto Iyengar. "A New Era of Minimal Effects? The Changing Foundations of Political Communication." *Journal of Communication* 58, no. 4 (2008): 707–31.

Berenskoetter, Felix. "Parameters of a National Biography." *European Journal of International Relations* 20, no. 1 (2014): 262–88.

Bernardi, Daniel Leonard, Pauline Hope Cheong, Chris Lundry, and Scott W. Ruston. *Narrative Landmines: Rumors, Islamist Extremism, and the Struggle for Strategic Influence.* New Brunswick, NJ: Rutgers University Press, 2012.

Bernays, Edward. *Propaganda.* New York: Ig Publishing, 1928.

Bernstein, George. *The Myth of Decline: The Rise of Britain Since 1945.* London: Pimlico, 2004.

Betz, David. *Carnage and Connectivity: Landmarks in the Decline of Conventional Military Power.* London: Hurst & Co., 2015.

Betz, David. "Searching for El Dorado: The Legendary Golden Narrative of the Afghanistan War." In Beatrice De Graaf, George Dimitriu, and Jens Ringsmose, eds. *Strategic Narratives, Public Opinion and War: Winning Domestic Support for the Afghan War.* New York: Routledge, 2015, 37–56.

Bevir, Mark, Oliver Daddow, and Ian Hall. "Introduction: Interpreting British Foreign Policy." *The British Journal of Politics & International Relations* 15, no. 2 (2013): 163–74.

Bigo, Didier, and Anastassia Tsoukala, eds. *Terror, Insecurity and Liberty: Illiberal Practices of Liberal Regimes after 9/11*. London: Routledge, 2008.

Billig, Michael. *Banal Nationalism*. London: SAGE, 1995.

Birkland, Thomas A. "'The World Changed Today': Agenda-Setting and Policy Change in the Wake of the September 11 Terrorist Attacks." *Review of Policy Research* 21, no. 2 (2004): 179–200.

Black, James, Alex Hall, Kate Cox, Martha Kepe, and Erik Silfversten. *Defence and Security after Brexit: Understanding the Possible Implications of the UK's Decision to Leave the EU*. Cambridge: RAND Europe, 2017, https://www.rand.org/pubs/research_reports/RR1786.html, accessed 7 December 2017.

Blair, Tony. Hansard HC Debate Vol. 372, Col. 673, 4 October 2001.

Blair, Tony. Hansard HC Debate Vol. 397, Col. 675, 15 January 2003.

Blair, Tony. *A Journey*. London: Random House, 2010.

Bluth, Christoph. "The British Road to War: Blair, Bush and the Decision to Invade Iraq." *International Affairs* 80, no. 5 (2004): 871–92.

Bolt, Neville. "Strategic Communications in Crisis." *The RUSI Journal* 156, no. 4 (2011): 44–53.

Bolt, Neville. *The Violent Image: Insurgent Propaganda and the New Revolutionaries*. London: Hurst & Co., 2012.

Booker, Christopher. *The Seven Basic Plots: Why We Tell Stories*. London: Continuum, 2004.

Braddock, Kurt, and James Price Dillard. "Meta-Analytic Evidence for the Persuasive Effect of Narratives on Beliefs, Attitudes, Intentions, and Behaviors." *Communication Monographs* 83, no. 4 (2016): 446–67.

Brendon, Piers. *The Decline and Fall of the British Empire*. London: Vintage, 2008.

Bricmont, Jean. *Humanitarian Imperialism: Using Human Rights to Sell War*. Translated by Diana Johnstone. New York: NYU Press, 2007.

Brinkley, Douglas. "Dean Acheson and the 'Special Relationship': The West Point Speech of December 1962." *The Historical Journal* 33, no. 3 (1990): 599–608.

Brown, Andrew D. "A Narrative Approach to Collective Identities." *Journal of Management Studies* 43, no. 4 (2006): 731–53.

Brown, Roger, and James Kulik. "Flashbulb Memories." *Cognition* 5, no. 1 (1977): 73–99.

Bruner, Jerome. *Actual Minds, Possible Worlds*. Cambridge, MA: Harvard University Press, 1986.

Bruner, Jerome. "Life as Narrative." *Social Research* 54, no. 1 (1987): 11–32.

Bruner, Jerome. "The Narrative Construction of Reality." *Critical Inquiry* 18, no. 1 (1991): 1–21.

Bryman, Alan. *Social Research Methods*. 4th ed. New York: Oxford University Press, 2012.

Bubandt, Nils. "Vernacular Security: The Politics of Feeling Safe in Global, National and Local Worlds." *Security Dialogue* 36, no. 3 (2005): 275–96.

Bucholz, Robert, and Newton Key. *Early Modern England 1485–1714: A Narrative History*. Chichester: John Wiley & Sons, 2013.

Burke, Kenneth. *A Grammar of Motives*. Berkeley: University of California Press, 1969.

Butler, Smedley. *War Is a Racket*. New York: Skyhorse Publishing, 2013.

Butterfield, Herbert. *The Whig Interpretation of History*. London: George Bell and Sons, 1931.

Caldwell, Dan. *Vortex of Conflict: U.S. Policy Toward Afghanistan, Pakistan, and Iraq*. Stanford, CA: Stanford University Press, 2011.

Carranza, Isolda. "Low-Narrativity Narratives and Argumentation." *Narrative Inquiry* 8, no. 2 (1998): 287–317.

Casebeer, William, and James Russell. "Storytelling and Terrorism: Towards a Comprehensive 'Counter-Narrative Strategy.'" *Strategic Insights* 4, no. 3 (2005): 1–16.

Cavanaugh, William T. *The Myth of Religious Violence: Secular Ideology and the Roots of Modern Conflict*. Oxford: Oxford University Press, 2009.

Cawkwell, Thomas. *UK Communication Strategies for Afghanistan, 2001–2014*. Farnham: Ashgate Publishing, 2015.

Chaiken, S. "Attitude Formation: Function and Structure." In Neil Smeler and Paul Baltes, eds. *International Encyclopedia of the Social & Behavioral Sciences*. Oxford: Pergamon, 2001, 899–905.

Charmaz, Kathy. *Constructing Grounded Theory: A Practical Guide through Qualitative Analysis*. London: SAGE, 2006.

Cho, Hyunyi, Lijiang Shen, and Kari Wilson. "Perceived Realism: Dimensions and Roles in Narrative Persuasion." *Communication Research* 41, no. 6 (2014): 828–51.

Chomsky, Noam. *Hegemony or Survival: America's Quest for Global Dominance*. London: Penguin, 2004.

Clarke, Harold D., Matthew Goodwin, and Paul Whiteley. *Brexit: Why Britain Voted to Leave the European Union*. Cambridge: Cambridge University Press, 2017.

Clements, Ben. "Examining Public Attitudes towards Recent Foreign Policy Issues: Britain's Involvement in the Iraq and Afghanistan Conflicts." *Politics* 31, no. 2 (2011): 63–71.

Codner, Michael. "The Two Towers, 2001–13." In Adrian Johnson, ed. *Wars in Peace: British Military Operations since 1991*. London: Royal United Services Institute for Defence Studies, 2014, 49–88.

Cohen, Robin. "Fuzzy Frontiers of Identity: The British Case." *Social Identities* 1, no. 1 (1995): 35–62.

Colley, Linda. *Britons: Forging the Nation, 1707–1837*. New Haven, CT: Yale University Press, 2009.

Colley, Thomas. "Is Britain a Force for Good? Investigating British Citizens' Narrative Understanding of War." *Defence Studies* 17, no. 1 (2017): 1–22.

Colley, Thomas. "What's in It for Us." *The RUSI Journal* 160, no. 4 (2015): 60–69.

Coman, Alin, David Manier, and William Hirst. "Forgetting the Unforgettable Through

Conversation Socially Shared Retrieval-Induced Forgetting of September 11 Memories." *Psychological Science* 20, no. 5 (2009): 627–33.

Conway, Andrew R. A., Linda J. Skitka, Joshua A. Hemmerich, and Trina C. Kershaw. "Flashbulb Memory for 11 September 2001." *Applied Cognitive Psychology* 23, no. 5 (2009): 605–23.

Corman, Steven, et al., eds. *Narrating the Exit from Afghanistan.* Tempe, AZ: Center for Strategic Communication, 2013.

Corner, John. "Fake News, Post-Truth and Media–political Change." *Media, Culture & Society* 39, no. 7 (2017): 1100–1107.

Cornish, Paul. "United Kingdom." In Heiko Biehl, Bastian Giegerich, and Alexandra Jonas, eds. *Strategic Cultures in Europe: Security and Defence Policies Across the Continent.* Dordrecht: Springer, 2013, 371–86.

Croft, Stuart. *Securitizing Islam: Identity and the Search for Security.* Cambridge: Cambridge University Press, 2012.

Croft, Stuart, and Nick Vaughan-Williams. "Fit for Purpose? Fitting Ontological Security Studies 'into' the Discipline of International Relations: Towards a Vernacular Turn." *Cooperation and Conflict* 52, no. 1 (2017): 12–30.

Cronon, William. "A Place for Stories: Nature, History, and Narrative." *The Journal of American History* 78, no. 4 (1992): 1347–76.

Cruz, Consuelo. "Identity and Persuasion: How Nations Remember Their Pasts and Make Their Futures." *World Politics* 52, no. 3 (2000): 275–312.

Curtis, Chris. "A Plurality of Britons Support Trump Visiting—but They Don't Think He Should Meet the Queen." YouGov, 12 July 2018, https://yougov.co.uk/news/2018/07/12/plurality-britons-support-trump-visiting-they-dont, accessed 7 August 2018.

Czarniawska, Barbara. *Narratives in Social Science Research.* London: SAGE, 2004.

Daddow, Oliver, and Pauline Schnapper. "Liberal Intervention in the Foreign Policy Thinking of Tony Blair and David Cameron." *Cambridge Review of International Affairs* 26, no. 2 (2013): 330–49.

Dahl, Robert. "The Concept of Power." *Behavioral Science* 2, no. 3 (1957): 201–15.

Darwin, John. "Decolonization and the End of Empire." In Robin Winks, ed. *The Oxford History of the British Empire, Volume V: Historiography.* Oxford: Oxford University Press, 2001, 541–57.

Davies, Graeme, and Robert Johns. "British Public Attitudes about International Affairs." Economic and Social Research Council, The Role of the FCO in UK Government Inquiry, http://www.esrc.ac.uk/my-esrc/grants/RES-062-23-1952/outputs/Read/4a8a5ef5-16ca-40ba-8b1b-0983464a6365, accessed April 29, 2013.

Davis, Joseph, ed. *Stories of Change: Narrative and Social Movements.* Albany: State University of New York Press, 2002.

Dawson, Graham. *Soldier Heroes: British Adventure, Empire and the Imagining of Masculinities.* New York: Routledge, 1994.

De Fina, Anna. "Crossing Borders: Time, Space, and Disorientation in Narrative." *Narrative Inquiry* 13, no. 2 (2003): 367–91.

De Fina, Anna. "Narratives in Interview—The Case of Accounts: For an Interactional Approach to Narrative Genres." *Narrative Inquiry* 19, no. 2 (2009): 233–58.

De Fina, Anna, and Alexandra Georgakopoulou. *Analyzing Narrative: Discourse and Sociolinguistic Perspectives*. Cambridge: Cambridge University Press, 2012.

De Graaf, Anneke, Hans Hoeken, José Sanders, and Johannes W. J. Beentjes. "Identification as a Mechanism of Narrative Persuasion." *Communication Research* 39, no. 6 (2012): 802–23.

De Graaf, Beatrice, George Dimitriu, and Jens Ringsmose, eds. *Strategic Narratives, Public Opinion and War: Winning Domestic Support for the Afghan War*. New York: Routledge, 2015.

Delehanty, Will, and Brent Steele. "Engaging the Narrative in Ontological (in)Security Theory: Insights from Feminist IR." *Cambridge Review of International Affairs* 22, no. 3 (2009): 523–40.

De Waal, James. "Is the UK's Expeditionary Posture Both Necessary and Sustainable?" *The RUSI Journal* 159, no. 6 (2014): 20–26.

Drury, A. Cooper, L. Marvin Overby, Adrian Ang, and Yitan Li. "'Pretty Prudent' or Rhetorically Responsive? The American Public's Support for Military Action." *Political Research Quarterly* 63, no. 1 (2010): 83–96.

Dudziak, Mary L., ed. *September 11 in History: A Watershed Moment?* Durham: Duke University Press, 2003.

Dudziak, Mary L. *War Time: An Idea, Its History, Its Consequences*. Oxford: Oxford University Press, 2013.

Dunne, Tim. "'When the Shooting Starts': Atlanticism in British Security Strategy." *International Affairs* 80, no. 5 (2004): 893–909.

Duyvesteyn, Isabelle. "How New Is the New Terrorism?" *Studies in Conflict & Terrorism* 27, no. 5 (2004): 439–54.

Edgerton, David. "Tony Blair's Warfare State." *New Left Review* 1 (1998): 123–30.

Edmunds, Timothy. "Complexity, Strategy and the National Interest." *International Affairs* 90, no. 3 (2014): 525–39.

Edmunds, Timothy. "The Defence Dilemma in Britain." *International Affairs* 86, no. 2 (2010): 377–94.

Edmunds, Timothy, Jamie Gaskarth, and Robin Porter. *British Foreign Policy and the National Interest: Identity, Strategy and Security*. Basingstoke: Palgrave Macmillan, 2014.

Elliott, Jane. *Using Narrative in Social Research: Qualitative and Quantitative Approaches*. London: SAGE, 2005.

Engdahl, F. William. *Myths, Lies and Oil Wars*. Wiesbaden: Edition.Engdahl, 2012.

Entman, Robert. *Projections of Power: Framing News, Public Opinion, and US Foreign Policy*. Chicago: University of Chicago Press, 2004.

Epstein, Charlotte. "Who Speaks? Discourse, the Subject and the Study of Identity in International Politics." *European Journal of International Relations* 17, no. 2 (2011): 327–50.

Erskine, Andrew. *Roman Imperialism*. Edinburgh: Edinburgh University Press, 2010.

Evans, Michael. "From Kadesh to Kandahar: Military Theory and the Future of War." *Naval War College Review* 56, no. 3 (2003): 132–50.

Feeley, Thomas, Heather M. Marshall, and Amber M. Reinhart. "Reactions to Narrative and Statistical Written Messages Promoting Organ Donation." *Communication Reports* 19, no. 2 (2006): 89–100.

Feldman, Martha S., Kaj Sköldberg, Ruth Nicole Brown, and Debra Horner. "Making Sense of Stories: A Rhetorical Approach to Narrative Analysis." *Journal of Public Administration Research and Theory* 14, no. 2 (2004): 147–70.

Ferguson, Niall. *Empire: How Britain Made the Modern World*. London: Penguin, 2004.

Finnemore, Martha. *The Purpose of Intervention: Changing Beliefs about the Use of Force*. Ithaca, NY: Cornell University Press, 2004.

Fisher, Walter. "Narration as a Human Communication Paradigm: The Case of Public Moral Argument." *Communication Monographs* 51, no. 1 (1984): 1–22.

Fiske, Susan, and Shelley Taylor. *Social Cognition*. 2nd ed. New York: Mcgraw-Hill, 1991.

Fivush, Robyn. "Speaking Silence: The Social Construction of Silence in Autobiographical and Cultural Narratives." *Memory* 18, no. 2 (2010): 88–98.

Forster, Anthony. *Armed Forces and Society in Europe*. New York: Palgrave Macmillan, 2005.

Foucault, Michel. "Orders of Discourse." *Social Science Information* 10, no. 2 (1971): 7–30.

Fouskas, Vassilis, and Bülent Gökay. *The New American Imperialism: Bush's War on Terror and Blood for Oil*. Westport, CT: Greenwood Publishing Group, 2005.

Frank, Arthur. *The Wounded Storyteller: Body, Illness, and Ethics*. Chicago: University of Chicago Press, 2013.

Fraser, Simon. *Can the UK Retain Global Influence after Brexit? Policies and Structures for a New Era*. London: The Policy Institute at King's College London, January 2017.

Freedman, Lawrence. "Introduction: Strategies, Stories and Scripts." In Lawrence Freedman and Jeffrey Michaels, eds. *Scripting Middle East Leaders: The Impact of Leadership Perceptions on US and UK Foreign Policy*. New York: Bloomsbury, 2012, 1–14.

Freedman, Lawrence. "On War and Choice." *The National Interest*, no. 107 (2010): 9–16.

Freedman, Lawrence. "The Possibilities and Limits of Strategic Narratives." In Beatrice De Graaf, George Dimitriu, and Jens Ringsmose, eds. *Strategic Narratives, Public Opinion and War: Winning Domestic Support for the Afghan War*. New York: Routledge, 2015, 17–36.

Freedman, Lawrence. *Strategy: A History*. New York: Oxford University Press, 2013.

Freedman, Lawrence. "The Transformation of Strategic Affairs." *Adelphi Papers*, No. 379. International Institute for Strategic Studies, 2006.

Frey, Kurt P., and Alice H. Eagly. "Vividness Can Undermine the Persuasiveness of Messages." *Journal of Personality and Social Psychology* 65, no. 1 (1993): 32–44.

Fry, Robert. "Smart Power and the Strategic Deficit." *The RUSI Journal* 159, no. 6 (2014): 28–32.

Frye, Northrup. *Anatomy of Criticism: Four Essays.* Princeton: Princeton University Press, 2000.

Galtry, Judith. "Punching Above Its Weight: Does New Zealand's Responsibility for Protecting, Promoting, and Supporting Breastfeeding Extend beyond Its Own Borders?" *Journal of Human Lactation* 29, no. 2 (2013): 128–31.

Gamson, William A., David Croteau, William Hoynes, and Theodore Sasson. "Media Images and the Social Construction of Reality." *Annual Review of Sociology* 18 (1992): 373–93.

Gaskarth, Jamie. *British Foreign Policy: Crises, Conflicts and Future Challenges.* Cambridge: Polity Press, 2013.

Gaskarth, Jamie. "Strategizing Britain's Role in the World." *International Affairs* 90, no. 3 (2014): 559–81.

Gaskarth, Jamie. "Strategy in a Complex World." *The RUSI Journal* 160, no. 6 (2015): 4–11.

Georgakopoulou, Alexandra, and Dionysis Goutsos. "Revisiting Discourse Boundaries: The Narrative and Non-Narrative Modes." *Text-Interdisciplinary Journal for the Study of Discourse* 20, no. 1 (2000): 63–82.

George, Stephen. *An Awkward Partner: Britain in the European Community.* 3rd ed. Oxford: Oxford University Press, 1998.

Gergen, Kenneth, and Mary Gergen. "Narratives of the Self." In Theodore Sarbin and Karl Scheibe, eds. *Studies in Social Identity.* New York: Praeger, 1983, 254–73.

Ghoshal, Raj. "Argument Forms, Frames, and Value Conflict: Persuasion in the Case of Same-Sex Marriage." *Cultural Sociology* 3, no. 1 (2009): 76–101.

Gibbon, Edward. *The History of the Decline and Fall of the Roman Empire.* London: Penguin Classics, 2000.

Giddens, Anthony. *Modernity and Self-Identity: Self and Society in the Late Modern Age.* Cambridge: Polity Press, 1991.

Glaser, Barney, and Anselm Strauss. *The Discovery of Grounded Theory: Strategies for Qualitative Research.* New Brunswick, NJ: Transaction, 1967.

Gokay, Bulent. "Oil, War and Geopolitics from Kosovo to Afghanistan." *Journal of Southern Europe and the Balkans Online* 4, no. 1 (2002): 5–13.

Goodall, Howard. "Introduction." In Steven Corman et al., eds. *Narrating the Exit from Afghanistan.* Tempe, AZ: Center for Strategic Communication, 2013, 1–10.

Goodwin, Matthew, and Caitlin Milazzo. "Taking Back Control? Investigating the Role of Immigration in the 2016 Vote for Brexit." *British Journal of Politics and International Relations* 19, no. 3 (2017): 450–64.

Gott, Richard. "America and Britain: The Dangers of Neo-Imperialism and the Lessons of History." *Global Dialogue* 5, no. 1/2 (2003): 42–51.

Gough, B. *Pax Britannica: Ruling the Waves and Keeping the Peace before Armageddon.* Basingstoke: Palgrave Macmillan, 2014.

Gow, James. *Triumph of the Lack of Will: International Diplomacy and the Yugoslav War*. London: Hurst & Co., 1997.

Grasse, Steve. *Evil Empire: 101 Ways Britain Ruined the World*. San Francisco: Quirk Books, 2007.

Gray, Garry, and Michael D. Jones. "A Qualitative Narrative Policy Framework? Examining the Policy Narratives of US Campaign Finance Regulatory Reform." *Public Policy and Administration* 31, no. 3 (2016): 193–220.

Green, Melanie C., and Timothy C. Brock. "The Role of Transportation in the Persuasiveness of Public Narratives." *Journal of Personality and Social Psychology* 79, no. 5 (2000): 701–21.

Greenwood, Christopher. "International Law and the Pre-Emptive Use of Force: Afghanistan, Al-Qaida, and Iraq." *San Diego International Law Journal* 4 (2003): 7–37.

Gregory, Derek. *The Colonial Present: Afghanistan, Palestine, Iraq*. Oxford: Blackwell, 2004.

Gribble, Rachael, Simon Wessley, Susan Klein, David A. Alexander, Christopher Dandeker, and Nicola T. Fear. "British Public Opinion after a Decade of War: Attitudes to Iraq and Afghanistan." *Politics* 35, no. 2 (2015): 128–50.

Gribble, Rachael, Simon Wessley, Susan Klein, David A. Alexander, Christopher Dandeker, and Nicola T. Fear. "The UK Armed Forces: Public Support for the Troops but Not for the Missions?" In A. Park, E. Clery, J. Curtice, M. Phillips, and D. Utting, eds. *British Social Attitudes: The 29th Report*. London: NatCen, 2012, http://www.bsa.natcen.ac.uk/media/1150/bsa29_armed_forces.pdf, accessed 3 June 2016.

H.M. Government. *Building Stability Overseas Strategy*. London: The Stationery Office, 2011.

H.M. Government. *The National Security Strategy of the United Kingdom; Security in an Interdependent World*. Cm 7291. London: The Stationery Office, 2008.

H.M. Government. *Prevent Strategy*. Cm 8092. London: The Stationery Office, 2011.

H.M. Government. *A Strong Britain in an Age of Uncertainty: The National Security Strategy*. Cm 7953. London: The Stationery Office, 2010.

H.M. Government. "2010 to 2015 Government Policy: Afghanistan", 8 May 2015, https://www.gov.uk/government/publications/2010-to-2015-government-policy-afghanistan/2010-to-2015-government-policy-afghanistan, accessed 7 June 2016.

H.M. Government. "The UK's Work in Afghanistan", 14 January 2014, https://www.gov.uk/government/publications/uks-work-in-afghanistan/the-uks-work-in-afghanistan, accessed 7 June 2016.

Halas, Matus. "In Error We Trust: An Apology of Abductive Inference." *Cambridge Review of International Affairs* 28, no. 4 (2015): 701–20.

Halbwachs, Maurice. *On Collective Memory*. Chicago: University of Chicago Press, 1992.

Halverson, Jeffry R., Steven R. Corman, and H. L. Goodall. *Master Narratives of Islamist Extremism*. New York: Palgrave Macmillan, 2011.

Hannan, Daniel. *Inventing Freedom: How the English-Speaking Peoples Made the Modern World*. New York: Harper Collins, 2014.

Hansen, Lene. "How Images Make World Politics: International Icons and the Case of Abu Ghraib." *Review of International Studies* 41, no. 2 (2015): 263–88.

Hansen, Lene. *Security as Practice: Discourse Analysis and the Bosnian War*. New York: Routledge, 2006.

Harari, Yuval Noah. *Sapiens: A Brief History of Humankind*. London: Harvill Secker, 2014.

Hart, Liddell. *Strategy: The Indirect Approach*. London: Faber and Faber, 1967.

Haven, Kendall. *Story Proof: The Science Behind The Startling Power Of Story*. Westport, CT: Libraries Unlimited, 2007.

Heins, Volker M., Kai Koddenbrock, and Christine Unrau. *Humanitarianism and Challenges of Cooperation*. Abingdon: Routledge, 2016.

Herbst, Susan. *Reading Public Opinion: How Political Actors View the Democratic Process*. Chicago: University of Chicago Press, 1998.

Hernon, Ian. *Fortress Britain: All the Invasions and Incursions since 1066*. Stroud: The History Press, 2013.

Hill, Christopher, and Sarah Beadle. "The Art of Attraction: Soft Power and the UK's Role in the World." London: The British Academy, 2014, http://www.britac.ac.uk/intl/softpower.cfm, accessed 17 November 2015.

Hines, Lindsey, Rachael Gribble, Simon Wessely, Christopher Dandeker, and Nicola Fear. "Are the Armed Forces Understood and Supported by the Public? A View from the United Kingdom." *Armed Forces & Society* 41, no. 4 (2014): 688–713.

Hirst, William, Elizabeth A. Phelps, Randy L. Buckner, et al. "Long-Term Memory for the Terrorist Attack of September 11: Flashbulb Memories, Event Memories, and the Factors That Influence Their Retention." *Journal of Experimental Psychology: General* 138, no. 2 (2009): 161–76.

Hodges, Adam. *The "War on Terror" Narrative: Discourse and Intertextuality in the Construction and Contestation of Sociopolitical Reality*. New York: Oxford University Press, 2011.

Hoggart, Richard. *The Uses of Literacy: Aspects of Working-Class Life*. London: Penguin Classics, 2009.

Holden Reid, Brian. "The British Way in Warfare: Liddell Hart's Idea and Its Legacy." *The RUSI Journal* 156, no. 6 (2011): 70–76.

Honeyman, Victoria. "Foreign Policy." In Timothy Heppell and David Seawright, eds. *Cameron and the Conservatives: The Transition to Coalition Government*. New York: Palgrave Macmillan, 2012, 121–35.

House of Lords Select Committee on Soft Power and the UK's Influence. *Persuasion and Power in the Modern World*. London: The Stationery Office, 2014.

Huish, Robert. "Punching above Its Weight: Cuba's Use of Sport for South–South Cooperation." *Third World Quarterly* 32, no. 3 (2011): 417–33.

Humphreys, James. "The Iraq Dossier and the Meaning of Spin." *Parliamentary Affairs* 58, no. 1 (2005): 156–70.

Huntington, Samuel P. *The Clash of Civilizations and the Remaking of World Order.* New York: Simon & Schuster, 1996.

Hyvärinen, Matti. "Towards a Conceptual History of Narrative." *Studies across Disciplines in the Humanities and Social Sciences* 1 (2006): 20–41.

Ignatieff, Michael. *Isaiah Berlin: A Life.* London: Random House, 2000.

Jacobs, Ronald. "Narrative, Civil Society and Public Culture." In Molly Andrews, S. D. Sclater, Corinne Squire, and Amal Treacher, eds. *Lines of Narrative.* London: Routledge, 2000, 18–35.

Jacobs, Ronald, and Sarah Sobieraj. "Narrative and Legitimacy: U.S. Congressional Debates about the Nonprofit Sector." *Sociological Theory* 25, no. 1 (2007): 1–25.

James, Lawrence. *Rise and Fall of the British Empire.* London: Abacus, 1995.

James, Lawrence. *Warrior Race: A History of the British at War.* London: Abacus, 2010.

Jensen, Rikke Bjerg. "Communicating Afghanistan: Strategic Narratives and the Case of UK Public Opinion." In Beatrice De Graaf, George Dimitriu, and Jens Ringsmose, eds. *Strategic Narratives, Public Opinion and War: Winning Domestic Support for the Afghan War.* New York: Routledge, 2015, 300–317.

Jentleson, Bruce. "The Pretty Prudent Public: Post-Vietnam American Opinion on the Use of Military Force." *International Studies Quarterly* 36, no. 1 (1992): 49–73.

Johns, Robert, et al. *Foreign Policy Attitudes and Support for War among the British Public ESRC End of Award Report.* RES-062-23-1952-A. Swindon: ESRC, 2012.

Johnson, Adrian, ed. *Wars in Peace: British Military Operations since 1991.* London: Royal United Services Institute for Defence Studies, 2014.

Johnson, Rob. *British Imperialism.* New York: Palgrave Macmillan, 2002.

Jones, Michael D., Elizabeth A. Shanahan, and Mark K. McBeth, eds. *The Science of Stories: Applications of the Narrative Policy Framework in Public Policy Analysis.* New York: Palgrave Macmillan, 2014.

Jones, Michael D., and Mark K. McBeth. "A Narrative Policy Framework: Clear Enough to Be Wrong?" *Policy Studies Journal* 38, no. 2 (2010): 329–53.

Jones, Toby. "America, Oil, and War in the Middle East." *Journal of American History* 99, no. 1 (2012): 208–18.

Kampfner, John. *Blair's Wars.* London: Simon & Schuster, 2004.

Karvounis, Antonios, Kate Manzo, and Tim Gray. "Playing Mother: Narratives of Britishness in New Labour Attitudes toward Europe." *Journal of Political Ideologies* 8, no. 3 (2003): 311–25.

Kenny, Michael. *The Politics of English Nationhood.* Oxford: Oxford University Press, 2014.

Kertzer, Joshua D., and Kathleen M. McGraw. "Folk Realism: Testing the Microfoundations of Realism in Ordinary Citizens." *International Studies Quarterly* 56, no. 2 (2012): 245–58.

Kettell, Steven. "Dilemmas of Discourse: Legitimising Britain's War on Terror." *The British Journal of Politics & International Relations* 15, no. 2 (2013): 263–79.

Kettell, Steven. *New Labour and the New World Order: Britain's Role in the War on Terror.* Oxford: Oxford University Press, 2013.

Khong, Yuen Foong. *Analogies at War: Korea, Munich, Dien Bien Phu, and the Vietnam Decisions of 1965.* Princeton, NJ: Princeton University Press, 1992.

King, Anthony. *Who Governs Britain?* London: Penguin, 2015.

Kinnvall, Catarina. "Globalization and Religious Nationalism: Self, Identity, and the Search for Ontological Security." *Political Psychology* 25, no. 5 (2004): 741–67.

Knight, Jonathan, Robin Niblett, and Thomas Raines. *Hard Choices Ahead: The Chatham House–YouGov Survey 2012: British Attitudes Towards the UK's International Priorities.* London: Chatham House, July 2012.

Knight, Lynn, and Kieran Sweeney. "Revealing Implicit Understanding through Enthymemes: A Rhetorical Method for the Analysis of Talk." *Medical Education* 41, no. 3 (2007): 226–33.

Koch, Insa. "What's in a Vote? Brexit beyond Culture Wars." *American Ethnologist; Arlington* 44, no. 2 (2017): 225–30.

Krahmann, Elke. "United Kingdom: Punching Above Its Weight." In Emil Kirchner and James Sperling, eds. *Global Security Governance: Competing Perceptions of Security in the Twenty-First Century.* New York: Routledge, 2007, 93–112.

Krebs, Ronald R. *Narrative and the Making of US National Security.* Cambridge: Cambridge University Press, 2015.

Kriel, Charles. "Fake News, Fake Wars, Fake Worlds." *Defence Strategic Communications* 3 (2017): 171–90.

Kull, Steven, and Irving Destler. *Misreading the Public: The Myth of a New Isolationism.* Washington, DC: Brookings Institution Press, 1999.

Kümmel, Gerhard, and Bastian Giegerich. *The Armed Forces: Towards a Post-Interventionist Era?* Dordrecht: Springer, 2013.

Kvavilashvili, Lia, Jennifer Mirani, Simone Schlagman, and Diana E. Kornbrot. "Comparing Flashbulb Memories of September 11 and the Death of Princess Diana: Effects of Time Delays and Nationality." *Applied Cognitive Psychology* 17, no. 9 (2003): 1017–31.

Laderman, Charlie, and Brendan Simms. *Donald Trump: The Making of a World View.* London: I. B.Tauris, 2017.

Lakoff, George. "Metaphor and War: The Metaphor System Used to Justify War in the Gulf." *Peace Research* 23, no. 2/3 (1991): 25–32.

Lawrence, T. E. *Seven Pillars of Wisdom.* London: Random House, 2008.

Laycock, Stuart. *All the Countries We've Ever Invaded.* Stroud: The History Press, 2012.

Leavy, Patricia. *Iconic Events: Media, Power, and Politics in Retelling History.* Plymouth: Lexington Books, 2007.

Lebow, Richard Ned. *Why Nations Fight: Past and Future Motives for War.* Cambridge: Cambridge University Press, 2010.

Leichter, David J. "Collective Identity and Collective Memory in the Philosophy of Paul Ricoeur." *Ricoeur Studies* 3, no. 1 (2012): 114–31.

Lenin, Vladimir. *Imperialism: The Highest Stage of Capitalism.* Sydney: Resistance Books, 1999.

Leuprecht, Christian. "The West's Last War? Neo-interventionism, Strategic Surprise, and the Waning Appetite for Playing the Away Game." In Gerhard Kümmel and Bastian Giegerich, eds. *The Armed Forces: Towards a Post-Interventionist Era?* Dordrecht: Springer, 2013, 63–72.

Levine, Philippa. *The British Empire: Sunrise to Sunset.* London: Routledge, 2013.

Lewis, Jane, Jane Ritchie, Rachel Ormston, and Gareth Morrell. "Generalising from Qualitative Research." In Jane Ritchie, Jane Lewis, Carol McNaughton Nicholls, and Rachel Ormston, eds. *Qualitative Research Practice: A Guide for Social Science Students and Researchers.* 2nd ed. Thousand Oaks, CA: SAGE, 2013, 347–66.

Lincoln, Yvonna, and Egon Guba. *Naturalistic Inquiry.* Beverly Hills, CA: SAGE, 1985.

Linde, Charlotte. "Private Stories in Public Discourse: Narrative Analysis in the Social Sciences." *Poetics* 15, no. 1–2 (1986): 183–202.

Lindley-French, Julian. *Little Britain? Twenty-First Century Strategy for a Middling European Power.* 2nd ed. Marston Gate: Amazon, 2015.

Los, Bart, Philip McCann, John Springford, and Mark Thissen. "The Mismatch between Local Voting and the Local Economic Consequences of Brexit." *Regional Studies* 51, no. 5 (2017): 786–99.

Lyons, Jonathan. *Islam Through Western Eyes: From the Crusades to the War on Terrorism.* New York: Columbia University Press, 2012.

Lyotard, Jean-Francois. *The Postmodern Condition: A Report on Knowledge.* Manchester: Manchester University Press, 1984.

Macmillan, Alan. "Strategic Culture and National Ways in Warfare: The British Case." *The RUSI Journal* 140, no. 5 (1995): 33–38.

MacMillan, Margaret. *The Uses and Abuses of History.* London: Profile Books, 2009.

Mallinson, Allan. *The Making of the British Army.* London: Transworld Publishers, 2011.

Marcussen, Martin, Thomas Risse, Daniela Engelmann-Martin, Hans Joachim Knopf, and Klaus Roscher. "Constructing Europe? The Evolution of French, British and German Nation State Identities." *Journal of European Public Policy* 6, no. 4 (1999): 614–33.

Marks, Michael. *Metaphors in International Relations Theory.* New York: Palgrave Macmillan, 2011.

Marshall, Alex. "Imperial Nostalgia, the Liberal Lie, and the Perils of Postmodern Counterinsurgency." *Small Wars & Insurgencies* 21, no. 2 (2010): 233–58.

Maxwell, Joseph. *Qualitative Research Design: An Interactive Approach.* 3rd ed. Thousand Oaks, CA: SAGE, 2012.

Mazzocco, Philip J., Melanie C. Green, Jo A. Sasota, and Norman W. Jones. "This Story Is Not for Everyone: Transportability and Narrative Persuasion." *Social Psychological and Personality Science* 1, no. 4 (2010): 361–68.

McCartney, Helen. "Hero, Victim or Villain? The Public Image of the British Soldier and

Its Implications for Defense Policy." *Defense & Security Analysis* 27, no. 1 (2011): 43–54.

MccGwire, Michael. "Comfort Blanket or Weapon of War: What Is Trident For?" *International Affairs* 82, no. 4 (2006): 639–50.

McCormack, Tara. "The Emerging Parliamentary Convention on British Military Action and Warfare by Remote Control." *The RUSI Journal* 161, no. 2 (2016): 22–29.

McCourt, David M. *Britain and World Power since 1945: Constructing a Nation's Role in International Politics*. Ann Arbor: University of Michigan Press, 2014.

Meister, Jan Christoph, Tom Kindt, and Wilhelm Schernus, eds. *Narratology Beyond Literary Criticism: Mediality, Disciplinarity*. Berlin: Walter de Gruyter, 2005.

Michaels, Jeffrey. *The Discourse Trap and the US Military: From the War on Terror to the Surge*. New York: Palgrave Macmillan, 2013.

Miles, Matthew, and Michael Huberman. *Qualitative Data Analysis: An Expanded Sourcebook*. 2nd ed. Thousand Oaks, CA: SAGE, 1994.

Ministry of Defence. *Defence Plan 2010–2014*. London: The Stationery Office, 2010, https://www.gov.uk/government/uploads/system/uploads/attachment_data/file/27163/Defence_Plan_2010_2014.pdf, accessed 6 October 2016.

Ministry of Defence. *Strategic Communication: The Defence Contribution, Joint Doctrine Note 1/12*, 2012, https://www.gov.uk/government/uploads/system/uploads/attachment_data/file/33710/20120126jdn112_Strategic_CommsU.pdf, accessed 7 June 2016.

Mishler, Elliot. *Research Interviewing: Context and Narrative*. Cambridge, MA: Harvard University Press, 1986.

Miskimmon, Alister. "Continuity in the Face of Upheaval—British Strategic Culture and the Impact of the Blair Government." *European Security* 13, no. 3 (2004): 273–99.

Miskimmon, Alister, Ben O'Loughlin, and Laura Roselle. *Forging the World: Strategic Narratives and International Relations*, 2012, http://newpolcom.rhul.ac.uk/storage/Forging%20the%20World%20Working%20Paper%202012.pdf, accessed 19 June 2013.

Miskimmon, Alister, Ben O'Loughlin, and Laura Roselle. *Strategic Narratives: Communication Power and the New World Order*. New York: Routledge, 2013.

Mitzen, Jennifer. "Ontological Security in World Politics: State Identity and the Security Dilemma." *European Journal of International Relations* 12, no. 3 (2006): 341–70.

Mludzinski, Tom. "The Brits Aren't Coming: Syria and the Legacy of Iraq." *The Ipsos MORI Almanac*. London: Ipsos MORI, 2013, 96–101.

Morefield, Jeanne. *Empires Without Imperialism: Anglo-American Decline and the Politics of Deflection*. Oxford: Oxford University Press, 2014.

Neumann, Peter R. *Old and New Terrorism*. Cambridge: Polity Press, 2009.

Neustadt, Richard E., and Ernest R. May. *Thinking in Time: The Uses of History for Decision-Makers*. New York: Free Press, 1988.

Nincic, Miroslav. "A Sensible Public: New Perspectives on Popular Opinion and Foreign Policy." *Journal of Conflict Resolution* 36, no. 4 (1992): 772–89.

Nye, Joseph, Jr. "Soft Power and the UK's Influence Committee: Oral and Written Evidence—Volume 2." House of Lords Select Committee on Soft Power and the UK's Influence, 2014, http://www.parliament.uk/documents/lords-committees/soft-power-ukinfluence/SoftPowerEvVol2.pdf, accessed 2 May 2014.

Nye, Joseph, Jr. Soft Power: The Means to Success in World Politics. New York: Public Affairs, 2005.

O'Shaughnessy, Nicholas. Politics and Propaganda: Weapons of Mass Seduction. Manchester: Manchester University Press, 2000.

Ó'Tuathail, Gearóid. "Theorizing Practical Geopolitical Reasoning: The Case of the United States' Response to the War in Bosnia." Political Geography 21, no. 5 (2002): 601–28.

Overy, Richard. The Morbid Age: Britain and the Crisis of Civilisation, 1919—1939. London: Penguin, 2010.

Page, Benjamin, and Robert Shapiro. The Rational Public: Fifty Years of Trends in Americans' Policy Preferences. Chicago: University of Chicago Press, 2010.

Paris, Michael. Warrior Nation: Images of War in British Popular Culture, 1850–2000. London: Reaktion Books, 2002.

Patterson, Molly, and Kristen Monroe. "Narrative in Political Science." Annual Review of Political Science 1, no. 1 (1998): 315–31.

Patterson, Wendy, ed. Strategic Narrative: New Perspectives on the Power of Personal and Cultural Stories. Lanham, MD: Lexington Books, 2002.

Peirce, Charles Sanders. Collected Papers of Charles Sanders Peirce. Cambridge, MA: Harvard University Press, 1974.

Pennebaker, J., D. Paez, and B. Rime, eds. Collective Memory of Political Events: Social Psychological Perspectives. Hoboken: Taylor and Francis, 2013.

Petty, Richard, and John T. Cacioppo. Communication and Persuasion: Central and Peripheral Routes to Attitude Change. New York: Springer, 2011.

Pierce, Jonathan, Aaron Smith-Walter, and Holly Peterson. "Research Design and the Narrative Policy Framework." In Michael D. Jones, Elizabeth A. Shanahan, and Mark K. McBeth, eds. The Science of Stories: Applications of the Narrative Policy Framework in Public Policy Analysis. New York: Palgrave Macmillan, 2014, 27–44.

Polkinghorne, Donald. Narrative Knowing and the Human Sciences. Albany: State University of New York Press, 1988.

Polletta, Francesca, and Jessica Callahan. "Deep Stories, Nostalgia Narratives, and Fake News: Storytelling in the Trump Era." American Journal of Cultural Sociology 5, no. 3 (2017): 392–408.

Porter, Bernard. Britain, Europe and the World, 1850–1982: Delusions of Grandeur. London: Harper Collins, 1983.

Porter, Patrick. "Why Britain Doesn't Do Grand Strategy." The RUSI Journal 155, no. 4 (2010): 6–12.

Potter, Jonathan, and Margaret Wetherell. Discourse and Social Psychology: Beyond Attitudes and Behaviour. London: SAGE, 1987.

Propp, Vladimir. *Morphology of the Folktale*. 2nd ed. Austin: University of Texas Press, 2010.

Raines, Thomas. *Internationalism or Isolationism? The Chatham House-YouGov Survey: British Attitudes Towards the UK's International Priorities*. London: Chatham House, 2015.

Ramsden, John. "How Winston Churchill Became 'the Greatest Living Englishman.'" *Contemporary British History* 12, no. 3 (1998): 1–40.

Reynolds, David. "Britain, the Two World Wars, and the Problem of Narrative." *The Historical Journal* 60, no. 1 (2017): 197–231.

Reynolds, David. *Britannia Overruled: British Policy and World Power in the Twentieth Century*. 2nd ed. New York: Routledge, 2000.

Richardson, Laurel. *Writing Strategies: Reaching Diverse Audiences*. Newbury Park, CA: SAGE, 1990.

Ricoeur, Paul. *Memory, History, Forgetting*. Translated by Kathleen Blamey and David Pellauer. Chicago: University of Chicago Press, 2004.

Ricoeur, Paul. *Time and Narrative, Volume 1*. Translated by Kathleen McLaughlin and David Pellauer. Chicago: University of Chicago Press, 1990.

Riessman, Catherine Kohler. *Narrative Methods for the Human Sciences*. London: SAGE, 2008.

Riessman, Catherine Kohler. "Strategic Uses of Narrative in the Presentation of Self and Illness: A Research Note." *Social Science & Medicine* 30, no. 11 (1990): 1195–1200.

Ringmar, Erik. "Inter-Textual Relations: The Quarrel Over the Iraq War as a Conflict between Narrative Types." *Cooperation and Conflict* 41, no. 4 (2006): 403–21.

Ringmar, Erik. "On the Ontological Status of the State." *European Journal of International Relations* 2, no. 4 (1996): 439–66.

Ringsmose, Jens, and Berit Kaja Børgesen. "Shaping Public Attitudes towards the Deployment of Military Power: NATO, Afghanistan and the Use of Strategic Narratives." *European Security* 20, no. 4 (2011): 505–28.

Ritchie, Jane, Jane Lewis, Carol McNaughton Nicholls, and Rachel Ormston, eds. *Qualitative Research Practice: A Guide for Social Science Students and Researchers*. 2nd ed. Thousand Oaks, CA: SAGE, 2013.

Ritchie, Nick. "A Citizen's View of 'National Interest.'" In Timothy Edmunds, Jamie Gaskarth, and Robin Porter, eds. *British Foreign Policy and the National Interest: Identity, Strategy and Security*. Basingstoke: Palgrave Macmillan, 2014, 85–101.

Ritchie, Nick. "Trident and British Identity: Letting Go of Nuclear Weapons." *Bradford Disarmament Research Centre*, September 2008.

Roach, Kent. *The 9/11 Effect: Comparative Counter-Terrorism*. Cambridge: Cambridge University Press, 2011.

Roberts, Andrew. *A History of the English-Speaking Peoples since 1900*. London: Phoenix, 2007.

Rogers, Joel, and Jonathan Eyal. "Of Tails and Dogs: Public Support and Elite Opinion."

In Adrian Johnson, ed. *Wars in Peace: British Military Operations since 1991*. London: Royal United Services Institute for Defence Studies, 2014, 161–90.

Roselle, Laura, Alister Miskimmon, and Ben O'Loughlin. "Strategic Narrative: A New Means to Understand Soft Power." *Media, War and Conflict* 7, no. 1 (2014): 70–84.

Rosenau, James. *Public Opinion and Foreign Policy: An Operational Formulation*. New York: Random House, 1961.

Rosenthal, Gabriele. "Reconstruction of Life Stories: Principles of Selection in Generating Stories for Narrative Biographical Interviews." *The Narrative Study of Lives* 1 (1993): 59–91.

Ruggie, John. *Constructing the World Polity: Essays on International Institutionalisation*. London: Routledge, 1998.

Ryan, Marie-Laure, ed. *Narrative Across Media: The Languages of Storytelling*. Lincoln: University of Nebraska Press, 2004.

Ryan, Marie-Laure. "On the Theoretical Foundations of Transmedial Narratology." In Jan Christoph Meister, Tom Kindt, and Wilhelm Schernus, eds. *Narratology Beyond Literary Criticism: Mediality, Disciplinarity*. Berlin: Walter de Gruyter, 2005, 1–24.

Said, Edward W. *Orientalism*. London: Penguin Books, 2003.

Salmon, Christian. *Storytelling: Bewitching the Modern Mind*. Translated by David Macey. Brooklyn, NY: Verso, 2010.

Sampson, Anthony. *Anatomy of Britain*. London: Hodder and Stoughton, 1962.

Sanders, David. *Losing an Empire, Finding a Role: British Foreign Policy since 1945*. Basingstoke: Palgrave Macmillan, 1990.

Sangar, Eric. "'Regimes of Historicity' in Media Discourses on Wars and Interventions: The Missing Link between Collective Memory and Foreign Policy Identity?" Paper presented at 57th Annual Convention of the International Studies Association, Atlanta, 16–19 March 2016.

Sarbin, Theodore, and Karl Scheibe, eds. *Studies in Social Identity*. New York: Praeger, 1983.

Schank, Roger C. *Tell Me a Story: Narrative and Intelligence*. Evanston, IL: Northwestern University Press, 1996.

Schuman, Howard, and Cheryl Rieger. "Historical Analogies, Generational Effects, and Attitudes Toward War." *American Sociological Review* 57, no. 3 (1992): 315–26.

Schuman, Howard, and Jacqueline Scott. "Generations and Collective Memories." *American Sociological Review* 54, no. 3 (1989): 359–81.

Scott, Jacqueline, and Lilian Zac. "Collective Memories in Britain and the United States." *Public Opinion Quarterly* 57, no. 3 (1993): 315–31.

Segal, Robert. *Myth: A Very Short Introduction*. New York: Oxford University Press, 2015.

Selbin, Eric. *Revolution, Rebellion, Resistance: The Power of Story*. New York: Zed Books, 2010.

Simpson, Emile. *War from the Ground Up: Twenty-First Century Combat as Politics*. London: Hurst & Co., 2012.

Slater, Michael D., and Donna Rouner. "Entertainment—Education and Elaboration Likelihood: Understanding the Processing of Narrative Persuasion." *Communication Theory* 12, no. 2 (2002): 173–91.

Smith, Ben, and Arabella Thorp. "The Legal Basis for the Invasion of Afghanistan", House of Commons Library, 26 February 2010, www.parliament.uk/briefing-papers/sn05340.pdf, accessed 25 May 2016.

Smith, Philip. *Why War? The Cultural Logic of Iraq, the Gulf War, and Suez.* Cambridge: Cambridge University Press, 2012.

Snyder, Jack. "Dueling Security Stories: Wilson and Lodge Talk Strategy." *Security Studies* 24, no. 1 (2015): 171–97.

Somers, Margaret. "The Narrative Constitution of Identity: A Relational and Network Approach." *Theory and Society* 23, no. 5 (1994): 605–49.

Spector-Mersel, Gabriela. "'I Was . . . Until . . . Since Then . . .': Exploring the Mechanisms of Selection in a Tragic Narrative." *Narrative Works* 4, no. 1 (2014): 19–48.

Spector-Mersel, Gabriela. "Mechanisms of Selection in Claiming Narrative Identities: A Model for Interpreting Narratives." *Qualitative Inquiry* 17, no. 2 (2011): 172–85.

Spector-Mersel, Gabriela. "Multiplicity and Commonality in Narrative Interpretation." *Narrative Works* 4, no. 1 (2014): 1–18.

Steele, Brent J. "Ontological Security and the Power of Self-Identity: British Neutrality and the American Civil War." *Review of International Studies* 31, no. 3 (2005): 519–40.

Steele, Brent J. *Ontological Security in International Relations: Self-Identity and the IR State.* New York: Routledge, 2007.

Stone, Deborah. "Causal Stories and the Formation of Policy Agendas." *Political Science Quarterly* 104, no. 2 (1989): 281–300.

Stone, Deborah. *Policy Paradox: The Art of Political Decision Making.* New York: W. W. Norton & Co., 2001.

Strachan, Hew. "The Strategic Gap in British Defence Policy." *Survival* 51, no. 4 (2009): 49–70.

Subotić, Jelena. "Narrative, Ontological Security, and Foreign Policy Change." *Foreign Policy Analysis* 12, no. 4 (2015): 610–27.

Swidler, Ann. "Culture in Action: Symbols and Strategies." *American Sociological Review* 51, no. 2 (1986): 273–86.

Taleb, Nassim Nicholas. *The Black Swan: The Impact of the Highly Improbable.* London: Penguin, 2008.

Tan, Andrew. "Punching Above Its Weight: Singapore's Armed Forces and Its Contribution to Foreign Policy." *Defence Studies* 11, no. 4 (2011): 672–97.

Teddlie, Charles, and Fen Yu. "Mixed Methods Sampling a Typology with Examples." *Journal of Mixed Methods Research* 1, no. 1 (2007): 77–100.

Thompson, Andrew, ed. *Britain's Experience of Empire in the Twentieth Century.* Oxford: Oxford University Press, 2011.

Thomson, Mark. "Punching Above Its Weight? Australia as a Middle Power." *Strategic Insights* 18, Australian Strategic Policy Institute, August 2005, https://www.aspi.org. au/publications/strategic-insights-18-punching-above-our-weight-australia-as-a-middle-power/SI_Strategic_weight.pdf, accessed 23 December 2015.

Tilly, Charles. *Stories, Identities, and Political Change.* Oxford: Rowman & Littlefield, 2002.

Tobias, Ronald B. *20 Master Plots: And How to Build Them.* Cincinnati: Writer's Digest Books, 2012.

Todorov, Tzvetan. *The Poetics of Prose.* Paris: Ithaca, 1977.

Tomlinson, Jim. "The Decline of the Empire and the Economic 'Decline' of Britain." *Twentieth Century British History* 14, no. 3 (2003): 201–21.

Towle, Philip. *Going to War: British Debates from Wilberforce to Blair.* Basingstoke: Palgrave Macmillan, 2010.

Toye, Richard. *The Roar of the Lion: The Untold Story of Churchill's World War II Speeches.* Oxford: Oxford University Press, 2013.

Toynbee, Arnold. *A Study of History.* New York: Oxford University Press, 1972.

Tsoukala, Anastassia. "Defining the Terrorist Threat in the Post-September 11 Era." In Didier Bigo and Anastassia Tsoukala, eds. *Terror, Insecurity and Liberty: Illiberal Practices of Liberal Regimes after 9/11.* London: Routledge, 2008, 49–99.

Ucko, David H., and Robert Egnell. *Counterinsurgency in Crisis: Britain and the Challenges of Modern Warfare.* New York: Columbia University Press, 2013.

Venn, C. "Narrative Identity, Subject Formation and the Transfiguration of Subjects." In Wendy Patterson, ed. *Strategic Narrative: New Perspectives on the Power of Personal and Cultural Stories.* Lanham, MD: Lexington Books, 2002, 29–50.

Vlahos, Michael. "The Long War: A Self-Fulfilling Prophecy of Protracted Conflict-and Defeat", http://nationalinterest.org/commentary/the-long-war-a-self-fulfilling-prophecy-of-protractedconflict-and-defeat-1061, accessed 20 June 2013.

Wallace, William. "Foreign Policy and National Identity in the United Kingdom." *International Affairs* 67, no. 1 (1991): 65–80.

Wallace, William. "A Liberal Democrat View of UK Defence Policy." Royal United Services Institute, London, April 20, 2015.

Ward, Stuart, ed. *British Culture and the End of Empire.* Manchester: Manchester University Press, 2001.

Wertsch, James. "The Narrative Organization of Collective Memory." *Ethos* 36, no. 1 (2008): 120–35.

Wheeler, Nicholas J., and Tim Dunne. *Moral Britannia? Evaluating the Ethical Dimension in Labour's Foreign Policy.* London: Foreign Policy Centre, 2004.

White, Hayden. *Metahistory: The Historical Imagination in Nineteenth-Century Europe.* London: JHU Press, 1975.

Wilkinson, Benedict. "The Narrative Delusion: Strategic Scripts and Violent Islamism in Egypt, Saudi Arabia and Yemen." PhD diss., King's College London, 2013.

Wincott, Daniel, John Peterson, and Alan Convery. "Introduction: Studying Brexit's Causes and Consequences." *The British Journal of Politics and International Relations* 19, no. 3 (2017): 429–33.

Winks, Robin, ed. *The Oxford History of the British Empire, Volume V: Historiography*. Oxford: Oxford University Press, 2001.

Winter, Jay. *Remembering War: The Great War and Historical Memory in the 20th Century*. New Haven, CT: Yale University Press, 2006.

Zerubavel, Eviatar. "Historical Narratives and Collective Memory". In Steven Corman et al., eds. *Narrating the Exit from Afghanistan*. Tempe, AZ: Center for Strategic Communication, 2013, 99–116.

Zerubavel, Eviatar. "Social Memories: Steps to a Sociology of the Past." *Qualitative Sociology* 19, no. 3 (1996): 283–99.

Zerubavel, Eviatar. *Time Maps: Collective Memory and the Social Shape of the Past*. Chicago: University of Chicago Press, 2012.

Media Articles and Internet Sources

Ahmed, Nafeez. "Iraq Invasion Was About Oil", *Guardian*, 20 March 2014, http://www.theguardian.com/environment/earth-insight/2014/mar/20/iraq-war-oil-resources-energy-peak-scarcity-economy, accessed 6 June 2016.

Beale, Jonathan. "Are UK Bombs Making a Difference in Syria?", *BBC News*, 2 January 2016, http://www.bbc.co.uk/news/uk-35166971, accessed 14 January 2016.

Bennett, Asa. "SDSR: What Kit Do Britain's Armed Forces Have, What Do They Want, and What Are They Getting?", *Telegraph*, 23 November 2015, http://www.telegraph.co.uk/news/uknews/defence/12011176/SDSR-What-kit-do-Britains-Armed-Forces-have-what-do-they-want-and-what-are-they-getting.html#disqus_thread, accessed 10 December 2015.

"The Blair Doctrine", http://www.pbs.org/newshour/bb/international-jan-june99-blair_doctrine4-23/, accessed 9 November 2016.

"Blair's Statement in Full", *BBC News*, 11 September 2001, http://news.bbc.co.uk/1/hi/uk_politics/1538551.stm, accessed 30 May 2016.

"Britain Ousts the U.S. as World's Most Influential Nation: Country Tops Rankings for 'Soft Power'", *Daily Mail*, 18 November 2012, http://www.dailymail.co.uk/news/article-2234726/Britain-tops-global-soft-power-list.html, accessed 6 January 2016.

"Britain Wins Esteem at Last as a Global Force in 'Soft Power'", *The Times*, 16 July 2015, http://www.thetimes.co.uk/tto/news/uk/article4499397.ece, accessed 6 January 2016.

"Britain's 100 Years of Conflict", *Guardian*, 11 February 2014, http://www.theguardian.com/uk-news/ng-interactive/2014/feb/11/britain-100-years-of-conflict, accessed 8 September 2015.

Cable, Vince. "Not Martyrs, Masochists: Lib Dem Leader Sir Vince Cable Launches a Ferocious Attack on Desperate Brexit Fanatics Whose Zealotry Is Igniting a New

McCarthyism", *Mail on Sunday*, 6 August 2017, http://www.dailymail.co.uk/debate/article-4764742/Lib-Dem-leader-SIR-VINCE-CABLE-attacks-Brexit-fanatics.html, accessed 19 December 2017.

Cameron, David. "Speech to Lord Mayor's Banquet", 15 November 2010, https://www.gov.uk/government/speeches/speech-to-lord-mayors-banquet, accessed 9 December 2015.

Central Intelligence Agency. "The World Factbook", https://www.cia.gov/library/publications/the-world-factbook/rankorder/2244rank.html, accessed 14 April 2016.

Cocco, Federica. "Brexit, Bent Bananas and Cleavage Regulations: Busting the Euromyths", https://www.ft.com/content/d20cabe4-1f16-33d8-8a8e-e9e70c00d4ed, accessed 7 December 2017.

Cockburn, Patrick. "Why Must Britain Always Try to 'Punch Above Her Weight'?", *Independent*, 17 July 2011, http://www.independent.co.uk/voices/commentators/patrick-cockburn-why-must-britain-always-try-to-punch-above-her-weight-2314908.html, accessed 18 December 2015.

Cummins, Fiona. "The U.S. Government Has Taken 9/11 and Manipulated My Country's Grief", *Daily Mirror*, February 7, 2003.

Dahlgreen, Will. "Memories of Iraq: Did We Ever Support the War?", YouGov, 3 June 2015, https://yougov.co.uk/news/2015/06/03/remembering-iraq/, accessed 6 June 2016.

"David Cameron Defends Britain in Russia 'Small Island' Row", *BBC News*, 6 September 2013, http://www.bbc.co.uk/news/uk-politics-23984730, accessed 8 December 2015.

"David Cameron: EU Helps Britain Punch Above Its Weight", *Telegraph*, 25 July 2014, http://www.telegraph.co.uk/news/politics/david-cameron/10987981/David-Cameron-EU-helps-Britain-punch-above-its-weight.html, accessed 18 December 2015.

"David Cameron's Full Statement Calling for UK Involvement in Syria Air Strikes", *Telegraph*, 26 November 2015, http://www.telegraph.co.uk/news/politics/david-cameron/12018841/David-Camerons-full-statement-calling-for-UK-involvement-in-Syria-air-strikes.html, accessed 4 August 2016.

"A Declaration of War", *Guardian*, 12 September 2001.

"Department of Defense Dictionary of Military and Associated Terms", Department of Defense, 2010, http://www.dtic.mil/doctrine/new_pubs/jp1_02.pdf, accessed 30 September 2016.

Fisk, Robert. "This Looming War Isn't About Chemical Warheads or Human Rights: It's About Oil", *Independent*, 18 January 2003.

Foster, Peter. "Bluff, Fold, Check, or Raise? Britain's Brexit Options Explained", *Telegraph*, 18 October 2017, http://www.telegraph.co.uk/news/2017/10/18/bluff-fold-check-raise-britains-brexit-options-explained/, accessed 31 October 2017.

Gilligan, Andrew. "RAF Bomb Raids in Syria Dismissed as 'Non-event'", *Telegraph*, 2 January 2016, http://www.telegraph.co.uk/news/worldnews/islamic-state/12078395/RAF-bomb-raids-in-Syria-dismissed-as-non-event.html, accessed 4 August 2016.

Haslett, Malcolm. "Afghanistan: The Pipeline War?", *BBC News*, 29 October 2001, http://news.bbc.co.uk/1/hi/world/south_asia/1626889.stm, accessed 6 June 2016.

Henley, Jon. "Why Vote Leave's £350m Weekly EU Cost Claim Is Wrong", *Guardian*, 10 June 2016, https://www.theguardian.com/politics/reality-check/2016/may/23/does-the-eu-really-cost-the-uk-350m-a-week", accessed 31 October 2017.

"Ipsos MORI September Political Monitor", https://www.ipsos-mori.com/Assets/Docs/Polls/October_2014_PolMon_Topline_Foreign_policy.pdf, accessed 18 December 2015.

"Ipsos MORI Veracity Index 2015", https://www.ipsos-mori.com/Assets/Docs/Polls/Veracity%20Index%202014%20topline.pdf, accessed 9 January 2016.

"ISIS Captured 2300 Humvee Armoured Vehicles from Iraqi Forces in Mosul", *Guardian*, 1 June 2015, http://www.theguardian.com/world/2015/jun/01/isis-captured-2300-humvee-armoured-vehicles-from-iraqi-forces-in-mosul, accessed 22 April 2016.

Jack, Ian. "A British Fleet with No Aircraft Carrier. Unthinkable!", *Guardian*, 23 October 2010, http://www.theguardian.com/commentisfree/2010/oct/23/ian-jack-british-fleet-no-aircraft-carrier-unthinkable, accessed 10 December 2015.

Jones, Gary, Tom Newton Dunn, and Bob Roberts. "We're Going for Oil: Our Troops Set to Seize Wells", *Daily Mirror*, 21 January 2003.

Jones, Sam. "Theresa May Uses Defence and Security as Brexit Bargaining Chips", *Financial Times*, 17 January 2017, https://www.ft.com/content/932aef0c-dccc-11e6-86ac-f253db7791c6, accessed 19 December 2017.

Juhasz, Antonia. "Why the War in Iraq Was Fought for Big Oil", *CNN*, 15 April 2013, http://edition.cnn.com/2013/03/19/opinion/iraq-war-oil-juhasz/, accessed 7 June 2016.

"Little Englander", http://dictionary.cambridge.org/dictionary/english/little-englander, accessed 21 April 2016.

McDonald, Karl. "David Davis: We Coped with World War Two, We Can Cope with Brexit." *Independent*, 18 January 2017, https://inews.co.uk/essentials/news/politics/david-davis-we-coped-with-world-war-two-we-can-cope-with-brexit, accessed 31 October 2017.

Monbiot, George. "America's Pipe Dream", *Guardian*, 23 October 2001, http://www.theguardian.com/world/2001/oct/23/afghanistan.terrorism11, accessed 6 June 2016.

"National Readership Survey", http://www.nrs.co.uk/nrs-print/lifestyle-and-classification-data/social-grade/, accessed 12 August 2015.

"9/11 and Death of Diana Top Britain's Most Memorable Events List", *BBC News*, 24 January 2007, http://www.bbc.co.uk/pressoffice/pressreleases/stories/2007/01_january/24/radio4.shtml, accessed 25 May 2016.

"No 10 Rejects 'Bit Player' Claim over Ukraine Crisis", *BBC News*, http://www.bbc.co.uk/news/uk-politics-31163190, accessed 15 March 2016.

Perraudin, Frances. "UK Government Defends Role in Ukraine-Russia Crisis", *Guard-

ian, 10 February 2015, http://www.theguardian.com/politics/2015/feb/10/uk-gov ernment-defends-role-in-ukraine-russia-crisis, accessed 15 March 2016.

"Prime Minister's Response to the Foreign Affairs Select Committee's Second Report of Session 2015–2016: The Extension of Offensive British Military Operations to Syria", http://www.theguardian.com/politics/2015/nov/26/full-text-of-david-camerons-memorandum-on-syria-airstrikes, accessed 4 August 2016.

Reiermann, Christian. "Fighting Words: Schäuble Says Putin's Crimea Plans Reminiscent of Hitler", *Der Spiegel*, 31 March 2014.

Rennie, David. "American Pullout Leaves Iceland Defenceless", *Telegraph*, 21 June 2006, http://www.telegraph.co.uk/news/1524490/American-pullout-leaves-Iceland-de fenceless.html, accessed 18 August 2016.

Rucker, Philip. "Hillary Clinton Says Putin's Actions Are Like 'What Hitler Did Back in the '30s'", *Washington Post*, 5 March 2014.

Ryan, Missy, and Karen DeYoung. "Obama Alters Afghanistan Exit Plan Once More, Will Leave 8,400 Troops", *Washington Post*, 6 July 2016, https://www.washington post.com/world/national-security/obama-alters-afghanistan-exit-plan-once-more/ 2016/07/06/466c54f2-4380-11e6-88d0-6adee48be8bc_story.html, accessed 20 September 2016.

"Scrapping RAF Nimrods 'Perverse', Say Military Chiefs", *BBC News*, 27 January 2011, http://www.bbc.co.uk/news/uk-england-12294766, accessed 11 December 2015.

Stone, Jon. "Britain's 'Unique' Brimstone Missiles Still Haven't Killed Any ISIS Fighters in Syria", *Independent*, 18 February 2016, http://www.independent.co.uk/news/uk/ politics/britains-unique-brimstone-missiles-still-havent-killed-any-isis-fighters-in-syria-a6881716.html, accessed 16 August 2016.

Sylvester, Rachel. "No Appeasement—This Is All-Out War on Isis", *The Times*, 21 July 2015.

"Threat Level from International Terrorism Raised: PM Press Statement", https://www. gov.uk/government/speeches/threat-level-from-international-terrorism-raised-pm-press-conference, accessed 15 March 2016.

"Tony Blair's Statement", *Guardian*, 7 October 2001, http://www.theguardian.com/ world/2001/oct/07/afghanistan.terrorism11, accessed 30 May 2016.

"Transcript: President Bush's Speech on the War on Terrorism", *Washington Post*, 30 November 2005, http://www.washingtonpost.com/wpdyn/content/article/2005/11/30/ AR2005113000667.html, accessed 30 May 2016.

"The UK and United Nations Peace Operations", United Nations Association, March 2016, https://www.una.org.uk/sites/default/files/UNA-UK%20briefing%20on%20 the%20UK%20and%20UN%20peace%20operations%2016%20March%202016. pdf, accessed 20 September 2016.

"UK's World Role: Punching Above Our Weight", *BBC News*, http://news.bbc.co.uk/hi/ english/static/in_depth/uk_politics/2001/open_politics/foreign_policy/uks_ world_role.stm, accessed 18 December 2015.

"War on the World", *Daily Mirror*, 12 September 2001.

"We Are at War", *News of the World*, 15 September 2001.

Wintour, Patrick. "Britain Carries Out First Syria Airstrikes after MPs Approve Action Against ISIS", *Guardian*, 3 December 2015, https://www.theguardian.com/world/2015/dec/02/syria-airstrikes-mps-approve-uk-action-against-isis-after-marathon-debate, accessed 4 August 2016.

Worldometers, "Countries in the World (Ranked by 2014 Population)", http://www.worldometers.info/world-population/population-by-country/, accessed 25 September 2015.

Index

7/7 terrorist attack, 169, 173, 183
9/11: as act of war, 172; as beginning of War
  on Terror, 44, 163, 172, 200; flashbulb
  memories of, 169; forgetting of, vii, 13, 17,
  161–85 *passim*, 198–99, 201; iconicity of,
  169, 173, 199; narration over time, 173–77,
  179–85, 198–99; significance to British
  people, 168–71; as turning point in history,
  172–73, 200

abductive reasoning, 15, 163
Acheson, Dean, 187
Afghanistan war, vii, 44, 97, 111, 122, 134, 142,
  153–55; 9/11 as cause of, vii, 13, 17, 163–85
  passim, 198–99; conflation with Iraq, 164,
  173–76, 179–81, 198–99; as counternarcotics mission, 182–83; as counterterrorism mission, 170–71, 182–83; for female
  education, 182–83; ineffectiveness of intervention, 4, 68–69, 84, 96, 115–17; ISAF mission, 55, 182; justification for intervention,
  9; lessons learned, 57–58; natural resource
  motive, 46, 131; as stabilisation mission, 182;
  strategic communication about, 7, 181–85;
  withdrawal from, 54
Al Qaida, 163, 170–71, 179
alliances, British: International Security Assistance Force in Afghanistan, 55, 182; in international system, 37, 48, 50, 135–36; reliance on in war, 62, 118–24; in Second World
  War, 34, 91; with United States, 102–3, 118–
  24. *See also* special relationship with US

allusion, in narrative, 9–10, 14, 50, 90, 146, 202
American Revolutionary War, 61, 118
analogy, 2, 7, 30–32, 49–50, 191, 204
Anglo-Saxons, exceptionalism of, 94, 98, 104
Anglosphere, 53
argument: conflation with narrative, 3, 6–8,
  31; definition of, 9, 24–25; distinction to
  narrative, 6–9, 24–27, 32, 41–42, 50, 160,
  194, 203; persuasion through, 24–27, 160,
  203; relationship to analogy, 32
Armistice Day, 164
arms trade, as motive for war, 85, 119, 128, 132–
  34, 137, 155
Atlanticism, 22, 118–20
attitudes: of British public to immigration,
  187, 192; of British public to war, 4–5, 11–12,
  177, 180, 200–201; relationship with narrative, 33–35, 187, 199–201
Australia, 53, 86

banal nationalism, 59, 189
banality of war, 36–38, 40, 59, 189
barbarism to civilisation meta-narrative, 20–
  21, 109, 150
Barnett, Corelli, 63, 70, 78
Battle of Britain, 75
Battle of Hastings (1066), 45, 192
BBC, 12, 66, 86, 130, 169, 178
Belgium, 120, 136, 194
Berlin, Isaiah, 145
Billig, Michael, 59
Bin Laden, Osama, 58, 170

265